SAVING GRACE

SAVING GRACE – RISE ABOVE DOMESTIC VIOLENCE. ISBN Published in 2025 in Australia by (PUBLISIING COMPANY). ©Copyright 2025 Grace Amore. **To contact the author, visit** https://www.graceamore.com. No part of this book may be reproduced or transmitted in whole or part by any person or entity (including Google, Amazon or similar organisations), in any form or by any means, electronic or mechanical, including photocopying, recording, scanning or by any information storage or retrieval system, and it is not to be used as educational or teaching material without the written permission of the author, except by a reviewer, who may quote brief passages in a review. All trademarks, service marks, and company names are the property of their respective owners.

Reproduction and Communications for educational purposes

The Australian Copyright Act 1968 (the Act) allows a maximum of one chapter or 10 percent of the pages of this work, whichever is greater, to be reproduced and/or communicated by any educational institution for its educational purposes provided that the educational institution (or the body that administers it) has given a remuneration notice to Copyright Agency Limits (CAL) under the Act. For details of the CAL license for educational institutions contact: info@copyright.com.au.

The information provided in this book is designed to provide helpful information on the subjects discussed. This book is not meant to be used, nor should it be used, to diagnose or treat any medical condition. For diagnosis or treatment of any medical problem, consult your own physician. The publisher and author are not responsible for any specific health or allergy needs that may require medical supervision and are not liable for any damages or negative consequences from any treatment, action, application or preparation, to any person reading or following the information in this book. References are provided for informational purposes only and do not constitute endorsement of any websites or other sources. Readers should be aware that the websites listed in this book may change.

There is a thin line between stupidity and courage. That thin line will be determined by time and hindsight. The truth is we never know whether an action is courage or stupidity until we've enjoyed a breakthrough or fallen on our backsides. Therefore, be sure to keep your head about what you do and use your common sense.

Chapters

Chapters 1
Dedication 3
Forward by R!k Schnabel 4
Preface 6
Trigger Warning 8
Introduction 13
Prologue: The Day I Tasted the Blood of Loyalty ... 14
PART I **18**
1: Emergency 18
2: A Prison Without Bars 31
3: Wounds No One Could See 48
4: Sea of Betrayal 52
5: Beginning of the End 58
6: A Legacy of Strength 62
7: Descent into the Maelstrom 74
8: Weight of Silence 85
9: Caught in the Crossfire 91
10: The Torture Chamber 100
11: The Longest Night 107
12: Chains of Control 114
13: Through Death's Door a New Beginning 124
14: Sanctuary in the Storm 136
15: The Reckoning 142
16: Pixie And The Ascension 2020 157
17: Reclaiming Rights to My Body 177
18: Echoes of Silence 194
19: Rebuilding My Sanctuary 204
20: A Reluctant Decision 216

21: Baptism of Cleansing.. 229
PART II **255**
22: How Animals Absorb Trauma.. 255
23: Note to Younger Self: The Child 257
24: Faith, Angels and God 264
25: Escape and Freedom.. 268
PART III - RESOURCES..**270**
26: Act When You Sense Danger 270
27: The Effects of Prayer on the Brain and Body 273
28: Coercion and Sexual Control... 276
29: Recognise Coercion For What It Is................................... 294
30: Impact of Violence on Brain and Body 298
31: Saving Grace: My Recovery and Healing........................ 309
What Others Say About Grace 314
Book Grace as a Speaker 316
Domestic and Family Violence Services................................ 317
Acknowledgements 323
About The Author 333
Selected Bibliography... 335
Closing Prayer 344

Dedication

To my three darling babies, Violet (November 2009), James (April 2012), and Christy (September 2015). And to my cherished fur babies, Matisse and Frida. And to Buddy, our beloved Labrador pup, who left at just two years old during the time of separation, a parting made in mutual agreement, at a time when I was too unwell to hold on.

To Violet, James, and Christy, of all the things I lost, the one thing he could never take from me was the sacred honour of carrying your lives within me. Our time together, just us, was sacred and private, and remains one of the most intimate and holy gifts I've ever known. I love you dearly.

Forever your mamma.

I dedicate this book to all those that are living in family violence, that have lost their lives due to family violence, childhood sexual abuse and medical gaslighting. In closing I dedicate this book to all those that are not able to speak up for themselves that have been shut down and silenced through oppression. It is time to set the captives free. May the next generation rise into new heights, to start from our ceiling, to be given the armour needed to live a life free of generational abuse. I dedicate my story to my best friend Jesus.

Forward by R!k Schnabel

A wedding day is meant to be the beginning of a beautiful journey, a promise of love, trust, and partnership. When a woman stands before her loved ones and says, "I do," she envisions a future built on devotion and mutual respect. But for Grace Amore those words started a chilling descent into a world of control, fear, and suffering.

Grace's story is not just a personal account; it is a wake-up call for every parent and every bride-to-be. It exposes the dark reality that lurks behind some closed doors. The unfortunate truth is not every groom is kind, nor is every love story one of safety and care. Beneath the charm, the vows, and the promises, some women unknowingly step into a life of manipulation and abuse.

As a man, it pains me to see that there are those within my own gender who exploit marriage as a means of domination rather than devotion. The statistics are horrifying: In 2022 alone, 48,800 women and girls lost their lives at the hands of an intimate partner or family member that's more than five lives stolen every hour. Behind each number is a woman who deserved love, a daughter whose dreams were cut short, a mother whose children now grieve. These are not just figures; they are shattered lives, voices silenced by violence that thrives in the places meant to offer protection.

Grace's book is more than a cautionary tale; it is a lifeline. A raw, unfiltered testament to survival and resilience. Grace shines a light on the silent epidemic of abuse, urging women to see beyond romantic ideals and assess their partners through the lens of truth, not fantasy. Her experiences serve as a stark warning that love should never come at the cost of one's freedom, dignity, or soul. But the issue runs even deeper. At its core, the acceptance of suffering within marriage normalises a culture of control, one that, at a larger scale, fuels global atrocities such as human trafficking. Today, more than 21 million people are trapped in this modern-day form of slavery, exploited for forced labour and sexual abuse. While the focus is often on women and girls, boys, too, are ensnared in this hidden horror. Abuse does not discriminate, and neither should our fight against it.

As a father of two daughters, Grace's story is one I cannot ignore. No daughter, mine or anyone's should ever endure the torment she faced. Her decade-long marriage was not a union; it was a prison, one that sought to suffocate her spirit and faith. But through sheer determination, courage, and an unyielding will, she fought her way back to freedom.

I'm privileged by witnessing Grace's transformation firsthand, not just as her coach but as someone who deeply admires her strength. Every word in this book was forged from pain and perseverance, written with the hope of protecting others from suffering the same fate.

Grace Amore is more than a survivor; she is a beacon for those still trapped in the darkness. Though she is a woman who defied the odds. Grace is uniquely equipped to guide us through the harrowing realities of abuse and, more importantly, the path to reclaiming one's life. This book is a call to action, a plea to break the cycle, to stand up against abuse, and to build a world where love is not synonymous with pain, but with kindness, respect, and safety.

Let us step into the light together. Change begins with awareness, and awareness begins with this book. R!k Schnabel, Brain Untrainer and Founder of Life Beyond Limits Pty Ltd. https://lifebeyondlimits.com.au/

Preface

What should you expect from **SAVING GRACE – Rise Above Domestic Violence**? This book is to help give voice to all those that need a voice but can't speak up for themselves. With this book you may go through some dark corridors, but they hold a promise of learning.

1. Learning to trust your own body.
2. Learning to Listen to your body.
3. It's a journey not into darkness but into the light of love.

Writing this book was raw and real and it hurt. It was taxing, reliving the sordid underbelly world of Melbourne. So, I started to write the truth in third person but with support and encouragement I went back to writing in first person. Frankly, it felt unreal as I read my own voice in it. You could be forgiven for thinking that you are reading a Hollywood script but it's not. As they say, there is more truth in fiction. It is for this reason that I have changed some of the real names of the people in this book, other than mine, to turn them into fictional characters with a nom-de-plume. This allowed me to tell the truth and nothing but the truth. Otherwise, some people would be embarrassed, and some could go to jail. To maintain their anonymity, I have changed the names of individuals and places, I too have changed some identifying characteristics and details such as physical properties, occupations and residences.

This book also speaks up about the silence surrounding medical gaslighting, when people, especially women, are dismissed, disbelieved, or misdiagnosed in the systems meant to care for them. It is a call to reclaim the right to be heard, to make informed decisions, and to trust the wisdom of our own bodies. Because true healing begins when we're empowered to speak up, not just in relationships, but in the consulting rooms. To also highlight that our bodies possess an innate wisdom. As health educator, nutritionist, author and naturopath, Barbara O'Neill teaches, giving our bodies the right conditions allow them to heal and guide us toward well-being. By attuning ourselves to our body's signals, we can foster holistic health and make empowered choices.

I am Grace Amore and welcome to the craziest time of my life. I wrote this book to raise awareness that we all have an inner guidance and to take heed of that inner guidance. To help women to understand where they have come from to bring to conscious awareness to generational patterns. To never fall for a narcissist and compromise their life or safety.

Ultimately the intent of the book is to bring the message of freedom for all, women, men and children. My message is to speak agency into the reader's life. **Saving Grace: Rise above domestic violence** is giving a voice to those that don't feel heard, seen or validated.

I am going to talk about faith. You can call it whatever you like. For me I call my faith, Jesus Christ, God and the Holy Spirit. You can replace those with your own belief of course.

This book is about my personal relationship with Jesus Christ and how that small quiet voice has whispered its intuitive wisdom into my soul but the noise of the world was louder and instead of listening to the voice of love, I listened to others and this is the story of navigating through the sometimes deep jungle of life and through the wilderness into the promised land of coming back to my body, my voice, my truth. This book has been a series of contractions in physically birthing this memoir.

Trigger Warning

Dear reader,

Before you begin this book, I invite you to gently check in with your own body. Some of what you're about to read may stir memories or emotions from your own lived experience.

These pages hold stories that are raw, real, and at times difficult, because what is hard to speak about is often what most needs to be brought into the light.

As much as there are triggers in these chapters, there are also glimmers, moments of hope, healing, and light in the darkness. Please remember to look after yourself as you read. Take breaks when you need to. Breathe. Pause. Reflect. You are not alone.

This book is here to break silence, raise awareness and consciousness, and offer a way forward, not just individually, but collectively, as we learn how to support one another with more compassion, understanding, kindness and care. Thank you for being here, for turning these pages, and for allowing this story to meet you wherever you are on your own journey.

Content Warning

This book contains references to childhood sexual abuse, medical gaslighting, family violence, emotional and spiritual abuse, and traumatic loss. Some of the content may be distressing for readers who have experienced similar harm. Please take care of your well-being as you read. If at any point you need to pause or seek support, I encourage you to do so. You are not alone.

Understanding Trauma and Abuse

Trauma is not just the event; it's the impact it leaves behind. It's how the body remembers what the mind tries to forget.

As Dr. Bessel van der Kolk writes in *The Body Keeps the Score* (2014):

"Trauma is not the story of something that happened back then. It's the current imprint of that pain, horror, and fear living inside people."

Abuse can be physical, emotional, psychological, financial, sexual, or spiritual. It often hides behind smiles, polite words, or systems that appear trustworthy. Abuse is when your boundaries are ignored, and your soul is silenced.

Trauma bonding and coercive control are complex dynamics that often occur in abusive relationships, especially those involving narcissistic personalities.

These patterns can create confusion, self-blame, and a deep sense of entrapment. The abused person may feel emotionally attached to someone who is harming them, especially when that harm is interwoven with moments of affection, manipulation, or dependence.

Trauma and abuse aren't always visible. They may show up as chronic pain, fatigue, anxiety, hypervigilance, people-pleasing, or the inability to trust. The body often carries what the heart never got to speak.

I use these words, *trauma* and *abuse*, throughout my book because they shaped my world. This is not a clinical book, it is a lived one. My aim is not to define everything perfectly, but to give voice to what was once voiceless.

References

Van der Kolk, B. A. (2014). The Body Keeps the Score: Brain, Mind, and Body in the Healing of Trauma. Penguin Books.

Herman, J. L. (1992). Trauma and Recovery: The Aftermath of Violence, From Domestic Abuse to Political Terror. Basic Books.

National Child Traumatic Stress Network. (n.d.). "What is Child Trauma?" https://www.nctsn.org Blue Knot Foundation (Australia's national centre for complex trauma), https://www.blueknot.org.au

Understanding Family Violence and Domestic Violence

Family violence is any behaviour within a family or close relationship that causes fear, harm, or control. It includes not just physical violence, but also emotional abuse, financial control, threats, sexual coercion, and spiritual manipulation.

Domestic violence is a form of family violence that happens between people in an intimate or romantic relationship, such as partners or spouses.

Both family violence and domestic violence can look like:

- A partner controlling who you can see or what you can do.
- A family member using finances to trap or punish you.
- Humiliation, threats, silent treatment, or constant criticism.
- Physical harm, or the threat of it.
- Pressuring someone sexually without consent.
- Mocking, belittling, or restricting someone's faith or spirituality.

Example: A woman may be financially dependent on her husband, who controls all the money and refuses to let her work. He may criticise her constantly, isolate her from her family, and use threats of harm if she tries to leave. Even if he rarely uses physical violence, this is still domestic and family violence.

Important: Family violence is not always loud or visible. It often hides behind closed doors, polite smiles, and social appearances. It is always serious, and it is never the victim's fault.

Helpful Resources:
1800RESPECT (Australia's national domestic, family and sexual violence support service),https://www.1800respect.org.au
Blue Knot Foundation (for survivors of complex trauma), https://www.blueknot.org.au

A Note Before We Begin

If at any point you need extra support as you read, please know help is available. You can contact 1800RESPECT (Australia's national domestic, family, and sexual violence support service) at 1800 737 732 or visit www.1800respect.org.au.

You don't have to walk this journey alone. If you recognise pieces of your own story here, I pray these pages bring you comfort, courage, and the quiet reminder that your story is not over.

This story is for the ones who have felt invisible, voiceless, or broken. You are seen. You are heard. You are deeply loved.

If you have lived through pain, silence, or fear, may these words offer a soft place for your heart to rest, and a strong place for your spirit to rise.

Before we begin, please know: Healing is possible. Freedom is possible. And you are already worthy of both, exactly as you are, right here and now.

Take a slow breath. Feel your body.

Notice where you are, the chair beneath you, the ground supporting you, the space around you.

As you read, I invite you to stay close to yourself:

Notice what stirs in your body.

Notice what feels tight, what feels soft, what feels tender.

There is no rush.

There is no pressure to do anything but observe, breathe, and be.

You are safe here.

You are welcome here.

You are enough.

Introduction

My intention for this book is to break the cycle of generational abuse by using my story. To speak up about what happened in my life and use it to educate and inform others of what I went through, highlighting what I learned along the way. This is my story of coming back to my body with God's love, the small quiet voice that has always been there when I was despairing in the darkness of pain and questioning whether to live or die. The gentleness of the holy spirit kindly let me know there is a plan and a purpose, even if I can't see it.

I was told that my story would be someone else's story that needs to be heard. Deep inside, I knew there was a way out of the shit. I knew forgiveness was key. That forgiveness is not for the perpetrator. It's to release me from the chains of being tied to that person that did harm. Not saying it's easy. It's been a bloody mess of an emotional rollercoaster. In and out of the depths of the ocean, where at times I felt like I was drowning in shame. Forgiving myself was the first step.

As Desmond Tutu and Mpho Tutu highlights in *The Book of Forgiving- The fourfold path for healing ourselves in the world shares,* "Telling our stories helps us integrate our implicit memories and begin to heal from our traumas." (2015, Pg. 72).

This is a true story about finding my voice in the dark of Melbourne's Lockdown 2020: From entrapment in domestic violence, medical gaslighting and childhood sexual abuse to finding freedom and speaking up.

Prologue: The Day I Tasted the Blood of Loyalty

It was a cold and windy July afternoon, in 2019. I had just finished work, and the air seemed very unsettled with leaves starting to blow into a fury. I remember coming home and pulling up into the driveway. Approaching the front door, I never knew what to expect. When my husband opened the door, my senses were filled with the aroma of chicken soup. This was unusual. What was going on for him to make chicken soup? Something was up. I just didn't know it yet.

Instead of coming in for dinner, I picked up our six-month-old Labrador, Buddy, fetching his leash, and off we went on our regular walk. It was brisk as the weather seemed to become increasingly wild with a storm approaching. It was brewing with intensity as we trotted back home on our regular path. But something was different.

> *"Faith is the strength by which a shattered world shall emerge into the light."* – Helen Keller

There we were, Buddy and I, about to cross the road, getting closer to home. We were just one street away. It happened in an instant. As we attempted to cross the road onto the footpath, we didn't make it because two aggressive dogs from down the street came charging at us with gnarling teeth. We were like a target to kill. The deathly growls went through my body. I remember the feeling of the leash in my hand and sensing Buddy shifting into protector mode. I murmured to Buddy, our six-month-old Labrador, "It's on, Buddy, here we go."

The attack was brutal. One dog lunged for Buddy's jugular, while the other went for my cheek. Their ferocity was unrelenting, their intent clear: to kill.

I screamed for help, my voice ripping through the storm like a siren. The sound startled even me. My shriek was primal and raw, as if dredged it up from the depths of my being.

We both went into battle with these two raging beasts, a Staffy and a Pitbull, off leash, clearly trained to kill. One dog went for Buddy's jugular and the other for my cheek. It was the neighbour on the corner who heard my cries for help. He had just come home from work and was still in his steel-capped work boots. One dog had Buddy by the jugular, and the other had torn a bite into my cheek. Warm blood streamed down my neck.

My neighbour vaulted his fence and ran to our aid, his boots connecting with the dogs in powerful kicks. One of them was seconds away from going for my throat when his boot struck, sending it reeling. The other dog clung to Buddy's neck; its jaws locked. My neighbour kicked it again and again until it finally let go. The dogs retreated, but not before leaving behind a scene of chaos and blood.

It is hard to describe an experience where time stopped or paused, as though the frame froze with Buddy and me in a battle for our lives. One dog had Buddy by the neck, and I was intertwined amongst the animals, screaming for help from the depths of my being. I had not heard myself scream like that before.

My screams pierced my soul deeply, harrowing like a horror movie. These dogs were nothing like I had come across before. They were not family pets by any means; they were dogs trained to destroy. In that battle of trying to set Buddy free from the grip of gnashing teeth, an awareness surfaced, amid this bloody chaos on the street corner, just one street away from home. In that space of fighting for our lives, my body felt a sensation that had been absent since meeting my husband: loyalty.

Buddy was fighting for my life and I for his. I had not felt this within my marriage. This fight to the death woke something in me that had been dormant. Buddy showed me, in the battle for our lives, that my life was worth fighting for. Buddy alerted me to what it meant to have loyalty in my life. Someone that truly cares, by my side. Buddy was on my team, and I was on his. It was in that window of clarity, frozen in time, that I felt the spirit of loyalty. I had a crystal-clear moment of what it looks and feels like to have a loved one in my corner. Buddy made me realise what loyalty is.

As I reflected after the attack, on that stormy day, behind the aroma of chicken soup, that something stirred in my broken spirit, alerting me to wake up to the madness. The lunacy I was living in each day. This event happened outside of the home, but really, this was my day-to-day life in an abusive marriage.

I realised that I regularly gnashed my teeth when I was in the house with my husband. I never knew how much he had drunk or smoked and what I was coming home to.

My home life was just as unpredictable and dangerous as these two killer-trained dogs. At least with animals there are no mind games. I knew where I stood in that dog attack. There were no blurred boundaries or confusion. It was the clarity I needed to wake up to the chaos I endured in my daily life. That day, I drank my own blood, not knowing how much of my cheek was hanging onto my face.

I could feel a deep hole in my left cheek, close to my eye. It was an odd sensation having a hole in my face and swallowing blood. There was so much blood, warm, gluggy blood pouring down my throat. I was in shock, but Buddy's loyalty sobered me up somewhat to something I couldn't put my finger on just yet.

The hospital wasn't sure whether the bite had penetrated my gums; there was a risk of infection, but surgery showed that the bite was deep but not into the gums.

It was gruesome. I looked like a horror movie in action. I had stitches to my fingers, thigh, and cheek, and Buddy suffered with two deep puncture wounds in the nape of his neck.

"Buddy, you are a true warrior," I thought. At just six months old, Buddy had fought for our lives. Victorious, amazing, brilliant Buddy Boy. Loving, loyal Buddy stood up for my life twice in the two years we were together. We weren't together long in the natural world, but in the supernatural world, our bond felt like a lifetime. In that battle, I heard a small, quiet voice. It was subtle yet unshakable, urging me to see the truth: "This is not where you belong." That voice carried strength and clarity, like a faint light piercing through a storm.

In the days that followed, I carried the storm inside me. My wounds began to heal, but the shock of the attack lingered. The hospital's chaos faded into silence, but my thoughts were louder than ever. I returned home to a reality that was brutal as the dogs' teeth, a marriage that gnawed away at my soul.

It spoke not only to the battle outside but to the war I faced every day in my home. That day brought on a new sense of clarity, stirring something in my broken spirit about the dangerous, abusive marriage I was living in. That day in July 2019 was my first hard wake-up call to the horror I was enduring. This dog attack represented my marriage. I found out later in emergency that two other people had died from brutal dog attacks that day during the stormy weather. This was a prelude to the COVID-19 lockdowns in 2020.

PART I

1: Emergency

The metallic taste of blood filled my mouth as I clutched a rag to my face. My hands trembled, sticky with crimson streaks. The cloth too soaked to contain it. Around me, the emergency room pulsed with chaos, moans, shouted names, and the sharp smell of disinfectant. Outside, the storm raged as wildly as my thoughts. I felt like a freak, holding the piece of my cheek that the dog had torn loose. I was stunned to hear a song echoing in my mind: Kasey Chambers' "Am I Not Pretty Enough?" Why now? Why *this* song? Would my husband mock my scars, the way he mocked so many other things?

Everything about my life felt fractured. My face, my body, my soul. Lying in that emergency bed, I had no energy left to hide the truth. Not even from myself.

I was broken in ways that couldn't be stitched up like these wounds. As the nurse examined my injuries, I realised that this was the first time in years someone had treated my pain as real. The thought struck me like a jolt, when was the last time my husband showed true concern for me, beyond appearances?

There was a silent pressure to look a certain way, to always present well. He frequently commented on my body, my weight, my clothes, just as he did about other women. It was relentless. I was under a constant lens of comparison and sexual scrutiny, and it chipped away at my sense of self.

Over time, it became more unnerving.

The husband would compare me to the women he saw on porn sites. or make casual comments about the bodies of women on sex sites or in public, as if they were up for discussion. I felt like I was always being measured against an endless stream of sexualised imagery, images I never consented to compete with. It was dehumanising. His gaze wasn't protective, it was critical, objectifying, and rooted in a world I never wanted to be part of.

The dog attack had shaken me awake to a deeper reality: my marriage was its own kind of mauling, leaving scars no one could see.

Buddy, my Labrador pup, had fought for me with the courage of a warrior. I longed to be by his side to tell him I loved him. To thank him for his bravery. He was my protector, my loyal companion. My husband, on the other hand, was the opposite. When he was in a good mood, it felt uneasy, like he knew something I didn't, like he was hiding something just out of reach.

He'd tell me to always trust him, that he knew better than me. And so, my gut lived with this tension I didn't have a name for. I couldn't explain it, but something in me never settled. Even in the so-called calm moments, there was an undercurrent of confusion. Like I was missing a piece of the puzzle. I tried to silence it, and trust that his intentions were good. I pushed the doubt down, but it sat in my body like a warning light flickering quietly on the dashboard of my car.

I know now that this was my intuition speaking, that quiet voice that warns you before your mind can make sense of what's wrong. It wasn't just anxiety. It was my body's alarm system. At the time, I kept silencing it, reasoning it away, convincing myself that I was just overreacting. But I wasn't. That first whisper of danger is the truth trying to break through. You don't need bruises to know you're not safe. Sometimes, it's a whisper in your gut, a feeling you can't explain, and that's enough.

Later, I'd realise it was emotional manipulation, but back then, all I had was a sense that something wasn't right.

My body often alerting me, giving signals of his secrets: nausea, dread, a sense of unease that clung to me like a second skin.

And yet, here he was, playing the role of the caring husband. He rushed to the triage window, pointing at me, speaking with urgency. Was it genuine concern or just a performance for the strangers watching? I couldn't tell anymore. His actions had become a series of masks, each one more suffocating than the last.

The nurse waved me through to bypass the queue. She expressed concern about the depth of the bite, explaining that bacteria from the dog's mouth could pose a serious risk. Gently but firmly, she said, "You'll need surgery."

My face, my hand, my thigh, all needed stitching. Blood loss, she assured me, was normal for facial wounds. "It's a lot of blood," I told her, choking back tears. "I can taste it." The metallic fluid trickled down my throat, a bitter reminder of how raw and exposed I felt.

My older sister and parents arrived later through the storm. Their love broke me open. I had missed them so much. Family gatherings had become battlegrounds of jealousy and accusations. My husband often accused me of being 'married' to my family, despite how infrequently I saw them. I knew I wasn't 'married' to my family; I was married to him. The truth was, I barely saw my family anymore. I'd already pulled away from them, often without even realising I had, just to avoid the backlash that came after every visit. He'd sulk, rage, or belittle me after every visit. But here, in the emergency room, their presence brought a flicker of warmth to an otherwise cold and chaotic night.

Buddy's injuries were treated, and he was back home with antibiotics. My husband returned briefly with Buddy for a quick visit, letting me hug my warrior pup before leaving again. Alone in the hospital for three days, I underwent surgery, stitching, and bandaging. If my face were a piece of artwork, it would depict the messy reality of living in domestic terrorism, a splattered canvas of pain, fear, and survival.

Buddy didn't hesitate to put himself in danger for me. He bared his teeth, fought with everything he had, and never let go. That's what love looks like, I thought. Fierce, protective, selfless. And for the first time, I wondered why I had settled for anything less.

The emergency department held its own threats that night. Police questioned a shooting victim in the bed next to mine, asking if someone might "finish the job." The surreal scene mirrored the violence I lived with at home. My husband never struck me, but his threats hung in the air like a clenched fist. "You're lucky I'm not like those guys who hit women," he'd say, his voice low and menacing. The absence of physical blows didn't make his violence less real. Coercive control isn't worn like a broken arm; it's invisible, hidden in the shadows of closed doors and whispered threats.

And yes, it absolutely made it harder to recognise, and even harder to justify leaving. There were no bruises to point to, no clear evidence. Just a constant chipping away at my confidence, my choices, my connections. He blurred the lines so much that I began questioning my own reality. I told myself, "He hasn't hit me, so maybe it's not that bad," even though my spirit felt bruised daily. When you're surviving on scraps of approval and walking on eggshells, it doesn't feel like abuse, it feels like *your fault*. That confusion kept me there far longer than I ever imagined.

That night, amidst the chaos, the small, quiet voice spoke to me. It wasn't audible, but I heard it clearly in my spirit just as I did in the peak of the dog attack.

The voice said, "See this, Grace. This is what it means to have someone fight for you. This is loyalty. Buddy fought for your life because he loves you. He is your protector. Your husband is a predator and perpetrator. You're living in a marriage with gnashing teeth. You need to get out."

The voice was firm yet gentle, a light into the darkness.

The voice continued, "I am with you. I will never leave you nor forsake you. You are worthy of love. Your life has value. One step at a time, you will be free. Breathe, Grace. There are no mind games here. Buddy is loyal. Loyalty is love in action. It is a sacred bond. Your husband's world is destruction. It is time to escape the death trap. Breathe."

What stopped me from leaving after hearing that voice? Shame. Fear. Shock. And the weight of years spent second-guessing myself.

That voice pierced through the fog, I knew it was God, and I knew it was truth. But hearing the truth and having the strength to act on it are two very different things when you've been living under coercion and confusion for so long. I was traumatised, depleted, and emotionally tangled in a web of control.

Shame was a heavy burden. I was caught in the underbelly of Melbourne's sex scene; a world laced with secrecy and humiliation. I couldn't see a way out; it felt like doom cloaked in silence. Add to that the trauma of the dog attack, the period pain that had overtaken my body, and medications that dulled my clarity, I was barely functioning. My thinking was hazy. My body was in survival mode. And on top of it all, his voice loomed over every part of my life, convincing me he knew better, about my health, my finances, my work, my friendships, even my own body.

Although I heard the still, small voice calling me to leave, it felt like I was buried under a mound of shit. Spiritually, emotionally, physically, it was suffocating.

The pain was unbearable, searing through every nerve in my body. I lay there in that hospital bed, rattled beyond words, shaken to my core. Tears spilled over bloody face wounds, streaking my cheeks as I sobbed silently. My mouth throbbed; mangled and swollen, my gums inflamed. The thought of how close the dog's teeth had come to my own sent a shiver down my spine. The bite was also terrifyingly close to my left eye, with stitches just underneath it. How freaky it was to have a bite to the face. If my gums had been punctured, dental treatment would have piled onto the surgery I was already enduring. I didn't know how much more my body could take.

The shame in my marriage pressed on me like a weight I couldn't lift, suffocating and relentless. I had sunk so deep into this life of coercion and control that rising above it seemed impossible. The Grace I once knew, vibrant, hopeful, full of life, was buried beneath layers of fear and exhaustion. I felt like a ghost of myself, just barely surviving.

Confusion had become the air I breathed. At home, there was no space to think, no privacy to reflect. My husband was always there, demanding something, needing something, accusing me of something. He mocked everything I found solace in, my love for learning, my faith in God, church, family, and even my dedication to work, which he resented for how much I gave to it. He questioned why I gave so much to the people I worked with, trying to explain, clients have needs and that is my work, to help people in need. His expression and arguments were not worth my energy in explaining why I love working with people, to serve those in need. What made that life seem *better* than being alone?

It wasn't better. It was survival. I was living in a body that had adapted to an oppressive environment, and that adaptation came at the cost of clarity, identity, and peace.

I felt so confused all the time. It was hard to make even the smallest decision without him meddling. It was like he had set up camp in my head. I couldn't hear my own thoughts over his constant noise, his opinions, his corrections, his needs. There was no clarity with him, only chaos.

I was buried under shame and pain, literal pain. The pelvic pain from my period left me collapsing at work, and the medications I was on only added to the fog. I was walking around half-dazed, unsure of what was real anymore. Meanwhile, he was everywhere, in my health decisions, my finances, my work. He had an opinion about everything, and I slowly disappeared under it all. I didn't know who I was anymore.

The shame was suffocating. I was entangled in a world that felt dark and hidden, the underbelly of a sex scene filled with secrets and humiliation, and I couldn't see a way out. On top of that, he constantly blamed me for his own pain. Every day was a barrage of how I needed to change, how *I* was the problem, how *if I just got it right,* everything would be better.

But the truth is, my brain and body had adapted to survive it. When you live under chronic emotional oppression, your nervous system gets wired for survival. I was constantly in fight, flight, freeze, or fawn. My body was on high alert, always bracing for the next blow, whether it came through silence, sarcasm, rage, or rejection.

And shame? Shame changes everything. It distorts your self-perception, shuts down your voice, and collapses your sense of worth. The damage shame does to the brain and body is beyond words. It keeps you trapped, not just physically, but mentally, emotionally, and spiritually. I was living in the mud and mire of the husband's constant need for admiration, forever writing a letter on his behalf for some argument he had had at work. With no family around, there was no one to consult with, no one to turn to plus the shame had silenced me so much I didn't know where to even start what was going on internally. I was a mess. I lived in his world of partying and debauchery where he supported passions that suited his lifestyle, like DJ'ing, because that fitted into events, festivals, the party lifestyle.

In our dating phase which wasn't very long, he patiently taught me how to use his DJ equipment, teaching me techniques of how to mix music. It was so much fun to learn, and he had patience which seemed to dry up as time went on. I remember him explaining the mixer and how to cue tracks, and tweak music in ways I hadn't experienced before. It opened a new world to music. This passion he supported.

Though when it came to other passions I had, that were not in the party world, he would attack them and publicly humiliate me.

He turned everything sacred to me into something to be mocked or twisted. If it wasn't connected to *his* world, parties, sex, status, then he couldn't tolerate it. He sexualised my love for learning, made it something shameful instead of something beautiful. I felt like I had to hide my faith around him, or at least water it down just to avoid his ridicule.

Any time I found joy or meaning outside of him, it threatened his control. And so, he crushed it, with sarcasm, shame, and public humiliation. He couldn't stand that I had a mind, a heart, or a spirit that reached for more than what he could offer.

His presence was suffocating, his constant criticisms and manipulations leaving no room for clarity. Adding to the stress, he would publicly air complaints about our sex life, humiliating me with intimate details in front of others. Reducing my sense of worth and safety even further.

The thought of returning home filled me with dread, I knew there would be no rest, no reprieve, only more demands. My survival mode would kick in again, pushing me through the motions, but I would remain trapped in a cycle that drained the life from me.

What was it going to take to get out of this mess I was living in? I knew this dog attack had awakened something deep in my bones. It forced me to see the truth about my husband, his shifting faces, the nice guy one minute and the nasty guy the next. There was no loyalty, no stability. He wasn't someone I could count on, and his constant demands and volatile moods had eroded my sense of self so completely that I hardly recognised who I had become. Grace had faded into the background, her voice silenced by years of walking on eggshells. I was alive, but just, hanging on.

In that moment of raw clarity, I realised something I could no longer deny. Buddy had fought for me with a loyalty that showed me what I was missing. If he could fight with all his strength to protect me, then maybe it was time for me to fight for myself, to break free from the relentless grip of this marriage. I just didn't know how as the exhaustion was overwhelming making it hard to think, plus the medications for period pain were now more frequent and stronger in dose. I was on the brink.

The weight of everything crashing down on me felt unbearable. The dog attack had shattered the lies I had told myself, exposing truths I had long avoided, but now I was drowning in the aftermath. The endless search for answers for my excruciating period pain felt like a battle I was fighting alone, with no one truly listening. At home, the demands piled up, coping with my husband's constant needs, feeling voiceless in my own life, and trapped in a cycle of coercion that left me traumatised and drained. The sexual pressures from him loomed over me like a shadow I couldn't escape, and I had no idea how to deal with the intensity of it all.

Lying there in the emergency department, I was having a meltdown. I was having the kind of meltdown that people don't always see, not yelling or flailing, but the kind where your whole internal world collapses under the weight of everything you've been holding in. I was already worn down by the unexplained period pain, which had left me bent over at work and doubled up in tears at home. But this was more than pain, it was everything crashing in at once.

I couldn't stop crying. The kind of crying that comes from somewhere deep, where there are no words left, just gasps of breath between sobs. I felt like I was disappearing. I couldn't think clearly, I wanted to curl into myself and vanish. I was shaking. My body felt unsafe. I felt like I was drowning in something I couldn't name, grief, shame, exhaustion, spiritual distress.

Everything felt too loud, voices, lights, even my own thoughts. I felt raw, like my nervous system had no filter left. The nurses were kind, but I remember thinking, *they don't know I'm falling apart on the inside.* I was polite on the outside, but inside, I was breaking.

It wasn't just the pain. It was the years of holding it all together finally giving way.

The pain from my wounds collided with the pain of my life, an overwhelming wave of helplessness that I couldn't suppress. Returning to work, my one safe space, now felt like another looming pressure. While I loved the connection and sense of purpose it gave me, I didn't know how I would manage everything when my body and mind were already at their breaking point. For the first time in years, I felt something stir within me.

It wasn't just fear or pain; it was the faint, fragile whisper of hope, reminding me that, despite how deeply exhausting the battle had been, I had survived this night. The sheer effort of fighting for my life and Buddy's against the dogs had left me physically shattered and emotionally raw, yet it also revealed a truth I couldn't ignore I was still here.

That same night, two others in Melbourne had tragically lost their lives to brutal dog attacks. The weight of that reality pressed heavily on me, amplifying how close I had come to losing everything. The thought of it was overwhelming, and yet, I had survived. Step by step, I would learn to fly.

> *"The caged bird sings with a fearful trill of things unknown but longed for still, and his tune is heard, for the caged bird sings of freedom."*
> *- Maya Angelou, Caged Bird*

Maya Angelou speaks of the caged bird that sings not because it is free, but because it has hope. That night, lying in the emergency bed, I felt like a wounded bird in a cage, my wings broken, unable to escape. The pain in my body was unbearable, and the emotional weight of the marriage felt just as crushing. My husband's relentless daily demands had stripped me of my strength, leaving me trapped in a cycle of despair. I felt so alone in the madness of it all, drowning in pain and isolation.

I was like a mirror permanently fogged over, unable to see who I was, what I loved, what I deserved. His voice became my own inner critic. Over time, I stopped trusting my reflection. I stopped believing I could ever live a life that wasn't defined by his moods, his needs, his power.

In so many words, he told me I was obligated to him, that I belonged to him, body, mind, and soul. He didn't need to shout it. It was in his tone, his expectations, the way he sulked when

I pulled away, the way he raged when I dared to say "No." My autonomy wasn't just ignored, it was *erased*.

I lived in a psychological contract that had no expiry date. One that said: You owe me your silence. You owe me your body. You owe me your life.

Yet, somewhere deep inside, there was a flicker of hope, God's voice reminding me that I was not alone. But at that moment, I didn't know how I would ever get out. It all felt too hard, too overwhelming, too much to bear. The storm of my life had not passed, and I wasn't sure if I could survive it. Still, the faint whisper of hope lingered, promising that freedom was possible, even if I couldn't see the way yet.

When I was finally discharged, I stepped into a different kind of storm, one that brewed quietly within the walls of my home. My stitches pulled with every movement, a physical reminder of the attack, but the real pain was walking back into the suffocating chaos that awaited me. The emergency room had been frantic, but at least there, someone cared about my wounds. Home, however, offered no such solace.

Reflection

Although I felt trapped in an invisible cage within a dark force that lay heavy over my life, I knew God's light was what I held onto. I knew I was living in an oppressive environment, that whatever idea I had he seemed to squash instantly. I knew my body had taken a king hit with that battle on that street corner and I still didn't have answers for the period pain that had no name. I was tired of fighting to be heard by doctors to be taken seriously and by the husband that added to medical gaslighting. I didn't know how I was going to break free from the systemic challenges that didn't recognise women's health, I was at wits end. Trapped within the marriage and trapped within a healthcare system that had no heart. A healthcare system that was sucking me dry of finances and energy. It was as though I was in a daily battle to be taken seriously for period pain, that was impacting every area of life with a husband that called me a hypochondriac. There was no breathing space. I was in a cage but could still see the sky through the bars. Was there anyone that would hear my cry for help. I didn't want to die in this cage. The dog attack had taken so much out of me. I was barely hanging on.

2: A Prison Without Bars

Like the caged bird, I felt my spirit, bruised and battered, my cries for freedom muffled by invisible bars. Each prayer I whispered was not a carol of joy but a plea for deliverance. My wings were clipped, my heart heavy with sorrow. Yet even in my darkest moments, I clung to the hope that one day, I would be free.

"I know why the caged bird sings, ah me, when his wing is bruised and his bosom sore, when he beats his bars and he would be free; it is not a carol of joy or glee, but a prayer that he sends from his heart's deep core."
- Paul Laurence Dunbar

Before Him

Before the husband, my life was filled with possibility. I thrived in Melbourne's inner suburbs, Moonee Ponds, Fitzroy, Brunswick, where community and creativity surrounded me.

I worked in the family business; it was the manufacturing and distribution of edible nuts. Like many family-run operations, we all pitched in wherever we were needed.

There were no set roles, we did everything. From sweeping the floors and packing orders, to serving customers, managing accounts, and processing truck deliveries with pallets of nuts. It was hard work, but it was what we knew. We managed a team of staff, helping keep the day-to-day operations running smoothly. We ran the business as a family, with Mum and Dad at the head. It was a shared responsibility, and there was a sense of pride in keeping it going together, even when it was exhausting.

In my spare time after work, I taught English to migrants. I danced in Flamenco classes. I smiled, laughed and cried in Melbourne's theatre performances, and immersed myself in yoga, Aussie netball, Sicilian theatre and netball groups, women's workshops, and the gym. I loved deeply, explored widely, and lived boldly.

But beneath that vibrant life, I carried a pain I didn't understand. My period pain was relentless, an ever-present shadow that worsened over time. At first, I managed with *Panadol*, Nurofen, and Ponstan but when they lost their effectiveness, I sought stronger relief in my 30s.

The suffering had started long before then. My childhood and teenage years had been marked by layers of pain, sexual abuse from my paternal grandfather from 3 years old to my teens. Then there was the spiritual oppression from a fanatical cult I had been introduced to at 12 years old, with an ongoing internal battle I didn't know how to express. The cult, which my older sister had been introduced to by a friend, consumed our lives with rigid control, using the name of God to oppress and dictate every aspect of our existence.

Even then, I didn't realise how early trauma rewires the brain. I now understand that childhood sexual abuse wires the nervous system for survival, fight, flight, freeze, or fawn. My body was always bracing for something, always in a subtle state of danger, even when I was smiling. That early imprint stayed with me, shaping my relationships, my boundaries, my sense of safety. I didn't have words for it then. But my body remembered everything.

Though my trauma started from an incident of sexual abuse from my paternal grandfather when I was very young and silenced me into my teens. I wasn't the only one, others were hurt too in the family and outside of the family, including a cousin.

Around the age of twelve, we made a quiet pact to protect each other, to make sure we were never left alone with him again. It was the era of silence. We saw abuse, but no one did anything about it. I remember another cousin growing up with red welts on his legs, and no one ever asked why. Some may have known or suspected, but nothing was ever said that I know of, and no one stepped in. That silence became its own form of trauma. The abuse stopped when I was old enough to pull away, but the emotional toll lasted much longer. There were no consequences for him.

My healing began when I started to speak up, to trust my memories, and to understand that what happened to me was never my fault. My life became filled with possibility when I realised that breaking the silence was a form of freedom, not just for me, but for others who couldn't yet speak.

At 13, I walked two paths, one in my Catholic school uniform, blending into a world of textbooks, doctrine, and structure. The other was dictated by the cult. Where faith wasn't gentle or freeing but an iron grip, tightening around my throat.

They pressured me to convert the school, to bring them under their control. And slowly, my world darkened, the light of childhood swallowed by fear, duty and loss of identity.

I was monitored, every book I read, everything I did, every thought I dared to question. I learned quickly that stepping out of line meant punishment, if not physical, then the kind that lingered in the silence. The disapproving stares, the shame that weighed heavily like a death trap.

By 17, when I switched to a technical school in Essendon, the weight of my reality had become unbearable. I went from not drinking to suddenly using alcohol as an escape, getting wasted to numb the suffering inside. The darkness was manifesting in ways I couldn't control, and I spiralled further into self-destruction. Parties, drunken nights, copious amounts of cheap wine to drown out the pain that had been accumulating for years.

By my early 30s, I was given MDMA's known as Mollys or officially, methylenedioxymethamphetamine. Their euphoric high blurred the lines between pain and pleasure, making me feel weightless, if only for a moment. I would dance for hours, momentarily weightless, free from the suffering that bound me. The bass pulsed through my body, a heartbeat outside of my own.

Neon lights flickered across the crowd, casting shadows on swaying bodies lost in the music. My skin buzzed, whether from the cold night air or the ecstasy rushing through my bloodstream, I wasn't sure.

I moved in rhythm, my feet light, my body no longer tethered to pain. For hours, I was free. No period pain, no memories clawing at the edges of my mind. Just the music, the euphoria, the moment.

But too soon, the high faded. Then pain crept back in, slow at first, then sharp, gnawing at my lower back and pelvic region like a dull knife twisting. I pressed a hand to my stomach, trying to will it away, trying to hold on to the illusion of freedom just a little longer.

My friends somewhere in the crowd, dancing. I turned toward the dark field behind the tents, the reality of my body crashing down on me. The night that had felt so alive now seemed empty, like a song ending too soon.

But the highs never lasted, and the debilitating period pain always came back, stronger, deeper, relentless. I needed more than an escape. I needed a way out. And so, I searched elsewhere, diets, programs, meditation retreats like Vipassana, health retreats, anywhere that offered even the smallest light of hope. But no doctor took my suffering seriously.

The relentless, unexplained period pain I endured left me incapacitated for half of every month, with debilitating contractions that drained my energy and will. Intimate relationships felt unattainable, out of reach and impossible to maintain. Menstruation wasn't openly discussed; it was cloaked in taboo, something women were expected to endure in silence.

The medical system dismissed my pain, implying it was all in my head. This dismissal left me adrift, struggling to navigate a condition without a name. If doctors couldn't validate or treat my pain, how could I expect an intimate partner to understand?

Looking back now, I see how many professionals missed the signs. They didn't ask the right questions, didn't recognise the trauma behind my symptoms. Today, in Victoria, the MARAM framework, Multi-Agency Risk Assessment and Management, legally requires doctors, psychologists, and support workers to recognise and respond to family violence. It was created after the Royal Commission into Family Violence in 2016.

But back then, I was just a 'difficult patient'. A woman in pain with no name for it. A woman they dismissed, when what I needed was for someone, anyone, to see through the fog and ask what was really going on.

The First Cage

Long before my marriage became a prison, I had already tried to escape once before. Not in a way that could be undone. Not in a way that left room for second chances.

I was 21, studying fine art photography, capturing beauty while feeling numb. I moved through the world like a ghost, taking pictures of light and shadow, longing to feel something real. I was in a relationship with a man who was coming out. I was trying to break free myself, from what, I wasn't sure. But I felt trapped, my existence pressing in on me like a room with no air.

The pressure built in silence, unnoticed. So, one Saturday morning, while working in my family's business, I made a decision. I was alone, stocking shelves, serving customers, going through the motions. I swallowed a concoction of 84 tablets that I found in the medicine cabinet. I slipped them down my throat between transactions unnoticed. No one was around.

The store felt like it always did, but the air was heavier. That day was different. The demons were more relentless than usual, whispering, pressing in, making it hard to breathe. It felt like they had been waiting for this moment, pushing me toward a choice I had no strength left to fight. The store felt like it always did, but I wasn't there anymore. I was slipping away.

I carried on as usual, speaking to customers, processing their orders, but inside, I was fading. By 12:30, I finished my shift. I was supposed to go to the gym with a friend, and when she arrived to pick me up, I told her, mechanically, that I wasn't going. I remember that, how mechanical I was. Like no one was home. She left, upset that I hadn't told her earlier, but I wasn't thinking straight. The pressure from the cult had taken its toll. On top of that, I had been surrounded by death, working with two women whose partners had passed away. Conversations about grief and dying filled my days, and I absorbed every word, carrying it inside me. It built up like a weight I could no longer hold.

After my friend left, I lay down, ready to die. I wrote a goodbye letter, closed my eyes, to sleep.

But something stirred in the room.

A presence stood at the end of my bed. Not darkness, not fear, but light.

Jesus. His voice was clear, unmistakable. "Get up. Go to the bathroom and vomit."

So, I did. I stumbled to the sink, my body trembling, and threw up the pills. The moment I did, something shifted. My mind cleared. I felt like I had returned to myself, like I had been pulled back from the edge. And then Jesus spoke again.

"Now call your sister. Tell her you need help."

I picked up the phone, my hands unsteady. My sister answered.

"I've taken too many tablets," I told her. "I need to go to the hospital."

Sandra replied, "I'm coming now." And dropped the phone.

At the hospital, they made me drink charcoal to protect my stomach from ulcerating. The nurses moved efficiently. Their voices were calm, but I could see the concern in their eyes. A psychiatrist came to assess me.

"What made you take the tablets?" he asked.

"I split up with my boyfriend." I lied.

He nodded, as if that answer made sense. He understood that pain.

But I knew the truth was bigger than that. I knew if I told him I had seen demons, that I had been suffocating under the weight of a cult's control, he would label me schizophrenic. They would medicate me but it wouldn't heal the wound of my paternal grandfather's abuse, along with period pain, and the pain of the cult stripping away my identity. I was drowning in a deep, dark ocean of confusion and sadness.

Later, a nurse told my parents and older sister that if I had gone to sleep without vomiting, they would have found me dead in the morning.

I had cried out to God so many times in that cult. "God, if You are a God of love, why am I in so much pain?" I knew it wasn't God who caused the pain. It was man. A man who led a church that was more interested in control than love. A system that used God's name to justify harm. I never blamed God. I knew it was man who had free will. And it was man who had done the damage.

Surviving that night didn't mean the pain disappeared. It would take years to unravel the weight of my past, to piece together who I was outside of trauma. But through it all, Jesus remained, guiding me, pulling me back when I drifted too far.

The road to healing wasn't linear. There were moments of progress, setbacks that left me breathless, and a grief that reshaped me in ways I never expected. Education was often a pleasant distraction. Learning something new was like a birth, I guess.

By 2012, I was studying at the *Australian Catholic University* (ACU), pursuing a *Bachelor of Arts* degree. It was a step toward rebuilding my career, reclaiming control over my life after a cold hardship and mess. But that year, my second miscarriage in April shattered me in ways I couldn't have imagined, and I withdrew from the degree, resuming it in 2014 at Berwick, where I completed a Bachelor of Community Mental Health & Alcohol and Other Drugs.

Though I was still carrying the weight of my past, I was determined to move forward. Step by step, I tried to build a life that resembled something whole. Education felt like a way to reclaim control, to rewrite the narrative of loss and pain into one of purpose. But grief has a way of finding cracks, slipping through when you least expect it.

Loss and Isolation

I had entered 2012 with a quiet determination to rebuild my life, to create something meaningful after all the hardship. But grief has a way of unravelling even the best-laid plans. My second miscarriage in April shattered me in ways I couldn't have imagined.

Of course, I haven't as yet shared how I had my first miscarriage or even how I came to be married to a narcissist. I'll get to that later.

Losing James, my second baby, consumed me. I had barely recovered from my first miscarriage with Violet in November 2009, and now, another loss. I remember sitting in class, my mind miles away, unable to focus on anything but the hollow ache in my body and heart. I was part of a health program at the time, trying to address my worsening period pain, but grief made everything unbearable.

Instead of holding space for my sorrow, my husband dismissed it. I sat in silence, unable to speak, my body still aching from the loss. He scrolled through his phone. "You need to move on," he said without looking up with an air of finality.

"You just need to move on," he repeated, never seeing me, never connecting, still scrolling through his phone. His voice as casual as if we were discussing what to eat for dinner. The husband spoke as if James had never existed. As if I hadn't bled for him. His words cut deeper than the grief itself, like a door slamming shut between us, sealing me inside my sorrow alone.

My world caved in on itself. It became a black hole in space, and I felt utterly alone. I tried desperately to cling to the memory of the independent woman I had been before him. But I was slipping. The hopeful, vibrant version of myself was fading, consumed by grief and his indifference.

A Life That Wasn't My Own

After my first miscarriage, we had returned from a road trip and settled into his house in Cranbourne, Gippsland in 2011.

His house had been rented out since our marriage in 2009. But 'settling' was a generous word for how I felt in Cranbourne. It was foreign to me, nothing like the Melbourne I had grown up in. It never felt like home.

Cranbourne felt like a cage, each day pressing in on me, reminding me of all I had left behind. In the city, I had been alive. I was surrounded by people, by purpose, by a sense of belonging that now felt like a distant memory.

I longed for the life I had built for myself, a life filled with movement, connection, and freedom, everything Cranbourne seemed to strip away.

In the city, I had built a thriving community. I travelled freely, my days filled with purpose and connection. At 25, I had even defied tradition, leaving home against my parents' wishes to move into a share house in Fitzroy.

In Sicilian culture, family was everything, and a daughter leaving before marriage was unthinkable. Years later, when I visited Sicily, a relative looked at me with disappointment and said, "Graziella, you've dishonoured your father." To them, my independence wasn't strength, it was betrayal.

Growing up, we didn't talk about our bodies. We talked about food, family, work, and survival, never about pain. Even in a house full of women, we didn't talk about period pain. There was an expectation to push through, and so I did. I worked, studied, travelled, and played sports, forcing myself to function through pain that should have stopped me.

At Sunday lunches, my father's stories painted a picture of resilience forged through hardship. "I was a shepherd boy at ten, gone for months at a time," he'd say. His voice tinged with both pride and sorrow. Harder still were the stories spoken through tears, like when his father broke his arm in the street for a mistake. He had accidentally thrown a rock at a man passing by instead of the boy that threw the rock at him first.

"He grabbed me so violently, my arm just snapped," Dad had said, his voice catching. For a moment, I saw him not as my father, but as a small, defenceless boy.

The stories taught me endurance. My father's pain taught me resilience, not just through what he endured, but through the way my father spoke of it. He carried his suffering in stories, turning hardship into lessons of strength.

The Turning Point

In my 20s after attempting suicide, I travelled the world. Travel was a way of healing, it took me away from the cult, from my darkness, I stood in awe before the pyramids of Egypt, roamed the landscapes of Sicily, soaked in the art and history of Europe. I had travelled across almost every state in America and taught photography to children at Camp Nashoba in Maine as a camp counsellor for two months.

I went onto explore America with another Aussie counsellor, parting ways in California before I took the train back to New York, passing through Texas and New Orleans, where I experienced the warmth of Southern laughter. Each journey shaped me, reminding me of the fearless woman I once was.

But no amount of resilience, no lesson in endurance, could have prepared me for what came next. I didn't see it coming, how could I? How could I have known that the violence I had endured in silence for years would finally take form, would finally leave scars I could no longer ignore?

Pain. Trauma. A desperate fight to survive.

And like the caged bird, I still longed for the open skies.

The first time I understood that my body was both a gift and a prison, I was three years old.

I didn't have the words for it yet, but I knew.

I knew when my grandfather's hands stole the sense of safety I didn't even know I had.

I knew when I looked down at my small frame and felt trapped, locked inside flesh that would never truly be mine again.

I remember looking down at my small frame and feeling trapped, as though I had been caged in a suit of flesh that brought pain instead of protection. Even then, I felt my spirit was bigger than this body, a spirit yearning to expand beyond the confines of a form that had already been scarred.

> *"Shame hates it when we reach out and tell our story. It hates having words wrapped around it, it can't survive being shared. Shame loves secrecy." - Brene Brown*

At three, I didn't have the words for what had happened, but I understood something deeply, instinctually, my body was not safe. It was a thing that could be taken, used, hurt. A thing that existed in the world not for me, but for others. That understanding never left me.

Not when I bled for the first time at twelve. Overwhelmed by a pain I had no language for.

Not when doctors dismissed me, telling me that all women suffered, that my body wasn't different, that pain was just my lot in life.

Not when I was told, over and over again, that my body's suffering was all in my head. That I was 'too sensitive,' 'too much,' 'too dramatic.'

Living in a female body has never been just about existence. It has been about survival.

Shame buried itself in my skin, my bones, my blood.

Shame from my grandfather's hands, from doctors who dismissed my pain, from a world that told me over and over again:

Your body is not yours to own.

Your suffering is not yours to name.

Your voice is not yours to use.

Shame wrapped around my pelvis, my womb, my blood.

And yet, shame hates speaking. It hates light. It hates being exposed.

Naming my pain, naming what had been done to me, was the only way to free my body from the silence it had been forced to live in.

"Shame is the intensely painful feeling or experience of believing that we are flawed and therefore unworthy of love and belonging" Brené Brown.

Brown explains it clearly:

"Guilt says, 'I did something bad.' Shame says, 'I *am* bad.'"

And the most liberating truth of all:

"Shame cannot survive being spoken. It cannot survive empathy."

As Brene Brown articulates "shame loves secrecy"–Speaking up for my body lets it know that it is worth speaking up for and that my body deserves to be respected and to take up space in this world with safety.

For so long, my body felt like a prison.

A thing that had been taken from me. A thing I had to endure.

But now, I am beginning to see it differently.

Not as something broken. Not as something to apologise for.

But as something that has carried me through hell and still stands.

My body is not a burden.

It is a survivor.

It is mine.

Our body is so remarkable. It is a self-healing system that breathes life into life itself.

And so, I began.

At twelve, my body changed again.

The first blood came suddenly, a silent warning of what was to come.

I was on holiday with my family in Surfers Paradise, Queensland but there was nothing paradise-like about what was happening inside me.

The cramps hit like a dull, unrelenting blade, carving pain into my abdomen with every wave.

I didn't know then that this was only the beginning. That my body would become a battlefield.

The first bleed brought with it unimaginable pain, something that I was not expecting. When this event happened in my body, I was overwhelmed with these sensations I hadn't experienced before. The feeling was heavy with discomfort that I had no language for. I remember how my life changed from that moment. I knew something would never be the same again.

This body event changed life in ways I didn't see coming. I didn't know it at the time that I was carrying a whole lot of unworthiness in my body from a grandfather that treated my body like it had no worth or value. That my body was brought into this world to be desecrated and abused by a grandfather that felt entitled to control the trajectory of my life by doing things to my body that brought on a lifetime of unrest and unease.

A female without rights. A female without a voice. A body that was tainted from the beginning.

Every doctor's office became another courtroom where I was put on trial for my own pain.

They looked at my body, then at their charts, and ruled the same verdict every time:

'It's normal.'

'You're exaggerating,'

'Take a *Panadol* and go home.' Or 'Just have a baby'

Their indifference cut deeper than the pain itself.

Because if they wouldn't believe me, if they wouldn't name it, then did it even exist?

Every time I sat in a doctor's office, explaining how each month felt like my insides were being torn apart, I was met with the same blank stare, the same dismissive script.

'You're not the only woman with period pain.'

It was as if my body wasn't my own. As if it existed for someone else's convenience.

First my grandfather. Then my ex-husband. Then the doctors, who refused to see me beyond their textbooks. But this time, I was done being silent.

The pain of the paternal grandfather's poisonous actions twisted my insides into a messy contortion of pelvic pain, infiltrating monthly bleeds with contorted pain, twisted with unspoken emotions and mental torment that had no voice or name for the internal anguish.

Giving voice to all that has been suppressed and shut down, is a way of releasing the body from all the shame and bondage it has endured starting with the paternal grandfather.

Reflection

I can see now how much I self-medicated through the unrelenting period pain that left me incapacitated for weeks each month. Drinking, drugs, and partying weren't just about having fun, they were my only escape from pain I couldn't name, from suffering those doctors refused to acknowledge.

I begged for help. I cried in clinics, desperate for answers. But the medical system dismissed me, as they always had. My pain was minimised, brushed aside as something women simply endured. And so, I turned elsewhere.

At outdoor festivals, I found better pain relief than I ever had in a clinic. Among the music, the fire twirlers, and the sea of moving bodies, the medical staff weren't off in some tent, they were among us, blending into the crowd with everything they needed on hand. They shared what they had, and it worked. It eased pain, loosened muscles, made dancing effortless.

Then there was the dentist with a nitrous oxide tank, casually handing out balloons for $5 a hit. I took one deep inhale, and in seconds, the pain that had ruled my body for years vanished. I kept moving, weightless, free. It was absurd, there, under the stars, surrounded by music and strangers, I finally felt relief. The irony wasn't lost on me. A dentist at a festival had done more for my pain than any doctor ever had.

Yet at home, I needed even more relief. The pain of regular, unwanted sex from the husband compounded my suffering. My body, already wracked with agony, became a battleground I had no power over.

If doctors had believed me. If I had been diagnosed with adenomyosis and endometriosis sooner, perhaps I would have had words to explain my pain. Perhaps knowing the truth would have repelled my husband. Perhaps it would have saved me. But I wasn't believed.

So, I did what I had always done, I endured. And the alcohol and drugs that I used to cope as a single woman became a lifeline in marriage. The pain intensified, and so did my need for escape. Something was clearly wrong, but I trusted him. I trusted the doctors. I kept searching for answers that no one seemed to care about finding. And all the while, I remained trapped in a prison without bars. I was barely hanging on. But something had shifted. The cage door had opened, just a crack. And for the first time, I saw the sky.

By the way, if you're wondering what adenomyosis and endometriosis is, let me share. Endometriosis is a chronic condition where tissue similar to the lining of the uterus (the endometrium) grows outside the uterus. This misplaced tissue can cause severe pain, inflammation, scar tissue, and even infertility. The most common symptoms include intense pelvic pain, painful periods, pain during intercourse, heavy bleeding, fatigue, and digestive issues. Despite being a common condition affecting 1 in 10 women, it is often misdiagnosed or dismissed, a reality I lived through for years.

Adenomyosis is a condition where the endometrial tissue grows into the muscle wall of the uterus, causing the uterus to become enlarged and inflamed. This leads to severe cramping, heavy or prolonged bleeding, and chronic pelvic pain. Unlike endometriosis, which occurs outside the uterus, adenomyosis is contained within the uterine walls but can be just as debilitating.

Both conditions deeply affected my health, relationships, and mental well-being. They were dismissed by doctors for years, leading to unnecessary suffering. My pain was not "normal period pain." It was a battle against a system that refused to believe me.

3: Wounds No One Could See

After the dog attack, hope felt distant, buried beneath terror, exhaustion, and the weight of what had just happened. My body bore stitches and bruises, but the deeper wounds, the ones no one could see, were harder to carry. And yet, even then, something stirred. A faint light broke through the bars, flickering like a distant star. It wasn't bright, but it was there, a whisper of freedom, reminding me it still existed.

"Abuse is the very opposite of love. Abuse is the betrayal of the heart, the violation of trust, and the destruction of the soul."- Beverly Engel

That light dimmed after the dog attack. My body bore the stitches and bruises of that terrifying day, but it was the invisible wounds that lingered, the creeping dread, the constant replay of teeth and claws in my mind. Every step I took felt heavier, every shadow sharper, as if the world itself had become a threat.

When I finally walked through the front door, it wasn't just my body that felt fragile. My home, the place that should have been my refuge, felt like a second battleground. The quiet didn't soothe; it suffocated. And he was there, waiting, not with comfort or concern, but with his usual barrage of demands.

The hospital stitched me up, but no one could see the invisible wounds, the terror that lingered in my body or the dread of returning to my home. Three days later, when I walked through the door, it felt like stepping back into another kind of attack.

The house was quiet, but not the comforting kind of quiet. It was oppressive, like a storm brewing just beneath the surface. He greeted me the way he always did, as if nothing had happened, as if I hadn't just narrowly escaped death. His words were routine, a stream of demands that felt like weights tied to my already fragile body. "You've been home for three days, Grace," he said, his tone sharp with impatience. "We need to get out of the house. You've been resting long enough."

My stomach tightened as he continued, oblivious to the pain I was in. I heard his voice, saw his lips moving, but all I could process was his self-entitled tone. "Grace, now that you're back, there's something I need you to do online. It's for an event coming up. Oh, and don't forget about the birthday party, they really want us there."

He didn't ask how I was feeling. He didn't acknowledge the deep gashes on my thigh or the stitches pulling with every movement. To him, I was just a cog in the machine of his life. My needs, my pain, my trauma, it didn't matter.

Walking back into that house felt like entering a dungeon, the air thick with the oppression of his expectations. There was no space for recovery, no time to process what had happened. My body and spirit were both battered, but I was expected to move on, to meet his demands as though I hadn't just survived one of the most terrifying moments of my life.

I wanted to cry out, to scream for help like I had during the dog attack, but I knew no one would come. This was a different kind of cage, one where the bars were made of manipulation, control, and indifference. Yet, even in this darkness, a part of me refused to give up. The caged bird within me still sang, whispering prayers of hope, clinging to the faint light breaking through the bars. One day, I thought, I will be free.

Reflection

I can see how confusion and the constant barrage of intruding demands left my head reeling with my husband's incessant demands on daily life. I knew I was drowning, but I wasn't sure how to escape it, except to pray. There was something about prayer that seemed to quiet the internal storm, even if it was for a few minutes. Years later, I would learn what my body already knew, that prayer doesn't just feel comforting; it literally changes your brain. It engages the parasympathetic nervous system, lowering the heart rate and calming the flood of stress hormones. I wasn't just imagining the relief. Prayer was physically helping me survive. It was one of the only times my body and mind felt quiet, even if just for a few moments.

I remember having arguments with him and going out for a walk, doing 4 x 4 breathing to calm myself down. I'd breathe in for four steps, hold for four, exhale for four, and repeat, tears flowing as I walked the streets, wondering: *Is this normal in marriage?*

Was it normal for a husband to demand sex constantly, then deny it had ever happened? He didn't just argue, he rewrote reality. He made me question my own memory so often that, one day, I started marking a calendar.

I didn't know it then, but what I was experiencing had a name: 'gaslighting'. It's when someone manipulates you into doubting your memory, your perception, even your sanity. It's not just confusion; it's a calculated erosion of your reality. Survivors of gaslighting often start documenting things, not because they're obsessive, but because they've been made to feel crazy. That calendar became my sanity. Proof that what I was experiencing was real. I needed proof. Proof that I wasn't crazy. Proof that it wasn't just in my head. It was real.

I remember one incident where he had spent an entire weekend indulging in debauchery, and come Monday, he still had the audacity to complain. "I'm missing out because of you, Grace. You're not like one of those wives who helps her husband get sex, you get in the way."

I stared at him in disbelief. *Hadn't he just slept with multiple men and women over the weekend? Was that nothing?* But he would go on complaining like it never happened. I felt like I was going mad, unsure how to get out of this cycle of insanity. My trust was continually violated, as was my body, and my soul felt the betrayal so deeply that it was drowning in an ocean of destruction.

By 2012, I had come to know the bong in a new way. After losing James, our second baby, the grief consumed me. I remember staring at that stupid piece of glass, the very thing I had wanted to destroy, and instead, I picked it up. I drew a long breath in and lost myself in the clouds of smoke. For a brief moment, it offered relief, false and fleeting, but relief, nonetheless.

It's strange how grief works. The more I smoked, the more lost I became. It felt as though each inhalation was a farewell to a part of myself. A piece of me had died when Violet passed through my womb in November 2009, followed by James in April 2012. I didn't know it yet, but a third loss, Christy, would meet me in 2015.

Each child's passing took something from me, leaving empty spaces that I tried to fill with smoke and silence. The bong became a crutch, but it also became a reminder of how far I had fallen from who I once was. I hated it, yet I reached for it, over and over, as though I could escape the unbearable weight of my grief.

I wasn't free yet, but for the first time, I could see the bars of my cage clearly. The loyalty I saw in Buddy gave me hope, a glimmer of belief that freedom was possible. And like the caged bird, I sang, not because I was free, but because, for the first time, I could imagine the sky.

4: Sea of Betrayal

At the start, he was kind. He was patient. He was interested in my life. He listened intently. He wanted a life together.

We dreamed the same dream, a country home, children, chickens, a dog, a cat, a veggie patch, fruit trees.

In my dream, it was an idyllic setting, A place of health and family. A place where family and friends visited, stayed, felt at home. Not far, but close enough to connection.

I wanted space for animals. I wanted a stream of running water. I wanted to see the sunrise and sunset while sitting under the stars, feeling the country air.

I wanted peace.

But he never wanted that, even though he said he did.

He wanted:

✓ Sex parties.

✓ Getting wasted.

✓ Pornography.

✓ A life of debauchery.

A life without boundaries, where alcohol, endless bong hits, and degrading porn were his reality.

I was hopeful.

I thought we could work through both our limitations together, as a team. I thought we could help each other heal and grow. But the cycle of entrapment doesn't allow for healing.

One day, he was relentless, nagging, pushing, justifying, making me feel like I was the problem. The next, he was loving. Gentle. Apologetic.

Then, just as quickly, another storm rolled in.

This is how entrapment works.

It's not just the bad days that keep you trapped; it's the hope that the good days mean something.

And when the good is woven so tightly with the bad, it's easy to lose your way.

Somewhere in the mayhem of 2019, I stopped at the store after work, my body screaming for rest. My period pain that day was relentless. A constant throb left me drained. But the fridge was empty, and the shopping needed to be done.

The Toilet Paper Incident

When done, I carried the heavy, cumbersome bags and set them down in the kitchen. All I wanted was to put them away, grab a moment to sit down, and breathe.

Instead, I heard the husband's footsteps storm into the room. He tore into the shopping bags; his face twisted with anger.

"This isn't the right toilet paper," he spat! Shaking the package at me like it was some unforgivable crime.

I froze, staring at him in disbelief. "What do you mean?" I asked, my voice steady but edged with exhaustion.

"It's not the brand I wanted," he snapped, his voice rising. "I've told you this before!"

His anger filled the room. He towered over me like a dark shadow, the sheer force of his rage making him feel even larger, more threatening.

> *"You may not control all the events that happen to you, but you can decide not to be reduced by them."*
> *- Maya Angelou*

I stood there, lost for words. I was exhausted from a long day at work, working with the NDIS, aching from the relentless pain in my body, and I had done the shopping for us both while he stayed home all day. And yet, this was the thanks I got, a torrent of rage over toilet paper. No gratitude. No acknowledgment of my efforts. Just anger.

What I wanted most was care. To feel safe. To be met with kindness instead of this storm of anger. But instead, I stood silently, his words echoing in my ears, while my exhaustion pressed down on me like a lead blanket. I didn't argue. What was the point? The anger would only escalate, and I didn't have the energy to fight.

As I stood there, I never imagined how this moment would later resurface in the strangest way during Melbourne's 2020 lockdown. Toilet paper had become a scarce commodity. People hoarded it, fought over it in supermarkets, and shelves were stripped bare. It was bizarre, almost comical in its absurdity. 'Crap' jokes became the norm and delivered social relief. One day, out of sheer desperation, we ended up paying $60 for toilet paper.

There we were, in the car park of Cranbourne's homemaker centre, handing over cash to a stranger for a large pack of unbranded, scratchy rolls. No complaints from him this time. The irony struck me like a blow, this toilet paper, a far cry from the specific brand he had once raged about, was now acceptable. He didn't bat an eye at the price or the lack of quality.

His sudden adaptability wasn't born of practicality or perspective; it was about convenience for him. When the scarcity of lockdown affected him personally, his fury disappeared. It was proof, yet again, that his anger had never been about the things he claimed, it was always about control. That day, I saw the pattern for what it was, control disguised as dissatisfaction, exhaustion disguised as love. But control didn't just exist in the small moments. It ran deeper, darker, pulling me under in ways I had yet to fully understand. And soon, it would show itself again, in the quiet glow of his laptop screen.

A Sea of Betrayal

It was late, and the house was cloaked in that unsettling quiet that never really felt restful. He was asleep on the couch, his chest rising and falling with a rhythm so peaceful it felt almost mocking. His laptop screen was still glowing faintly, casting a dim light across the room. I wasn't sure why I walked over, maybe I was looking for something, anything, to distract me from the ache inside. But as my eyes fell on the screen, what I saw made the room tilt beneath me.

The chat was open, Facebook Messenger, his private conversation laid bare. My heart sank as I read the words:

"I get excited to hear from you every morning."

My stomach churned. The words blurred as I read on, catching fragments of their exchange:

"I love waking up to your messages."

A sharp, cold wave rushed over me as the reality sank in. While I'd been mourning James, my child who was never born, sinking deeper into grief, he'd been sending sweet nothings to another woman. I turned to look at him, sprawled out on the couch, blissfully unaware of the storm raging inside me.

Something inside me shattered, a piece of myself that I'd been holding onto slipped away, lost in the deep ocean where so many other fragments of me were already drowning. I felt hollow, weightless, like my body couldn't hold me together anymore.

When he stirred and his eyes fluttered open, I wasn't sure if I had the strength to confront him. My voice felt distant when I finally said, "Who is this woman you've been chatting with every morning?"

He blinked at me, groggy at first, and then his face darkened in an instant. Sleep melted into anger, his eyes narrowing as if I had committed the crime.

"What the hell, Grace?" he snapped, sitting up. "You shouldn't be looking at my private conversations."

"I wasn't looking for anything," I said, trying to steady my voice. "You left the laptop open, right there, in front of me. I didn't go digging. The chat window was open. I saw it."

His eyes burned into me as he scoffed. "Well, you shouldn't be reading my private messages. That's the problem here, not me, not the conversation. You don't respect my privacy."

I felt the ground shift beneath me. My grief for James was still so raw, and here he was, turning my pain into an excuse.

That night, something inside me broke. I had lost James, and now I was losing myself. When someone betrays you while you're grieving, it does something strange to the soul. Your mind wants to run, but your trauma is still bonded. You start clinging to the very person causing the pain, just to stay upright. That's what betrayal trauma does, it ties you to the one who breaks you, making it feel like leaving would collapse what's left of your world.

But deep in the wreckage, something stirred. I wasn't free yet, but I was waking up. The bars of my oppressive cage were still there, but I had begun to see them for what they were.

I wasn't meant to live like this.

And for the first time, I didn't just wonder if I had the strength to leave, I wondered if I could survive if I stayed.

Reflection

Whether it was toilet paper or my ability to have children, he made me feel like I was always falling short, always failing to meet his impossible standards. It wasn't the thing itself that mattered, it was the power he derived from my pain.

I later learned that this kind of behaviour, explosive over small things, constant criticism, moving the goalposts, was part of a wider pattern called coercive control. It's mapped out in what's called the 'Power and Control Wheel', a tool used to help survivors and professionals recognise abuse that doesn't leave bruises. It includes things like emotional abuse, intimidation, isolation, and financial control. That toilet paper wasn't just toilet paper. It was a warning flare, a symbol of a much deeper pattern of dominance. I just didn't have the language for it yet.

Buddy, my Labrador pup, had fought for me in a way my husband never had. Buddy's unwavering devotion reminded me of something I'd long forgotten, I was worth fighting for.

The realisation didn't come all at once, but piece by piece, like a tide slowly pulling away the debris. One day, I would stand on solid ground again. And when I did, I wouldn't just survive, I would rise.

5: Beginning of the End

Before I ever saw the bars of my cage, before the betrayals and the manipulation, there was a moment, a choice. In April 2007, during the Easter weekend, I attended *Confest*, a hippie-style festival in Moulamein, New South Wales.

The serene bush landscape, complete with drumming circles, workshops, and a mud bath, provided an ideal escape from city life. This was my third time at the festival, having previously attended in 2005 and 2006.

On the first day, my friend Cath introduced me to a tall, blonde man with a surfer look, who would later become my husband. She mentioned he had LSD, and I decided to purchase a drop from him. I diluted it in my water bottle and sipped it throughout the morning. As the effects intensified, I felt overwhelmed by the vibrant colours of the leaves and trees dancing in the breeze. Seeking comfort, I asked my friend Kale to slow down and hold my hand. Our group, which included Cath, her partner Con, their three teenage children, and our friend Kale, had come to immerse ourselves in nature and participate in various activities like drumming, dancing, and workshops. Feeling unsteady, Kale guided me to the mud bath area near the steam tent, where nudity was optional.

Sliding into the mud felt like entering a bowl of chocolate mousse, and I couldn't help but laugh at the sensation. As I adjusted to the experience, the man who sold me the LSD joined us in the mud bath. Engaging in conversation, we laughed and got to know each other amidst the warm April weather. After some time, Cath helped me out of the mud bath and into the river to wash off the caked-on mud, which had become like clay on my skin and tangled in my hair. The process was challenging, especially given my shyness and discomfort with nudity, but Cath's encouragement helped me through it.

Entering the steam tent, a long corridor filled with eucalyptus-infused steam, I found myself alone and overwhelmed. The combination of nudity and intensified psychedelic effects heightened my anxiety. Struggling to find a comfortable position, I felt exposed, disoriented. Noticing my distress, the LSD man from the mud bath made eye contact and offered me a seat beside him. His calm demeanour and intuitive response provided a much-needed sense of safety. Sitting next to him, I began to relax, grateful for his kindness during my internal crisis.

This encounter left a lasting impression on me. Despite my recent frustrations with dating and trust issues stemming from past experiences, his genuine concern and the sense of safety I felt with him stood out.

Prior to the festival, I had been disheartened by a series of disappointing relationships. One man, a father of two, abruptly ended our connection, citing his daughter's attachment to me as the reason. Another turned out to be living with his girlfriend, despite portraying himself as single. These experiences had left me wary and disillusioned with dating.

After the festival, encouraged by friends, I reached out to the man from the mud bath. We then met at a house party in Coburg. We spent the evening conversing, getting to know each other better. His laid-back nature and understanding of my struggles with period pain were reassuring.

As the night progressed, I became aware of his drinking and smoking habits. These raised concerns. However, I chose not to judge him hastily, considering my own experiences with self-medication to cope with chronic pain. When it was time to leave, I insisted he stay over to avoid driving under the influence. We spent the night together, an uncharacteristic move for me, given my usual caution and trust issues.

The following morning, after sharing a joint, I felt unprepared for a family lunch and detoured to a friend's house to recover. Reflecting on the situation, I initially decided to end things with him, concerned about the potential influence of his lifestyle on my own struggles. However, after discussing my dalliance with the LSD man with my close friends, Cath and Isla, they encouraged me to give him a chance. So, I reconsidered and reached out to him again. We continued dating, and he remained understanding of my ongoing battle with undiagnosed period pain.

I didn't know it at the time, but cannabis would become my main treatment for endometriosis and adenomyosis. Medicinal cannabis would eventually replace pharmaceutical drugs for me. This was 2007, and it wouldn't be until 2019 that I would finally be diagnosed with the debilitating period pain that had taken over my life. I endured another 12 years of relentless seeking and searching for answers.

"Instinct is a marvellous thing. It can neither be explained nor ignored." - Agatha Christie

Nothing else was offered to investigate, as period pain wasn't taken seriously, and at this point. I was not informed of a surgery called a laparoscopy. That wouldn't happen till my period became a crisis, and I wanted to kill myself for lack of support. Additionally, I was contending with a history of childhood sexual abuse, which further impacted my self-worth and feelings of inadequacy.

Looking back, I recognise this as a pivotal moment where I chose to override my intuition, influenced by the well-meaning advice of close friends. This decision led to a whirlwind relationship that unfolded rapidly, underscoring the complexities that arise when external influences sway personal judgments.

Today, I understand that this was the whisper of intuition, what trauma experts and even law enforcement training now recognise as an early warning sign of danger. But back then, I didn't know how to honour that voice. I had learned to override it, to rationalise, to defer, to people-please.

Reflection

Trusting one's intuition is crucial, especially when external influences challenge personal judgments. As it turned out, those two friends who told me to give him a chance regretted their advice and ended up giving me the most grief about him. Whenever I tried to open up to them about any concerns I had in my relationship, they would just shut me down with, "Just leave him", there was no space to unpack any of my concerns, they just didn't want to know or didn't care. Had I listened to my gut and not to these two girlfriends, I would have ended it with him just as I had done before.

We don't talk enough about what coercion looks like in its early forms, it's not always dramatic. Sometimes, it's overriding your gut to appease others. Sometimes, it's saying yes when your soul is screaming no. Trauma teaches you to doubt your inner warning system. And so, even love begins with betrayal, when it's the betrayal of yourself. I went back on my word. I betrayed myself. I ignored my intuition to walk away. In doing so, I set in motion a story that would take years to undo. I didn't just ignore my intuition, I ignored everything my parents taught me through their actions, sacrifice and silence.

To understand how far I wandered, I need to take you back to where I began.

6: A Legacy of Strength

To understand how I lost myself, and how I found my way back, I had to look at where I came from. My Sicilian heritage shaped not only my strengths, but also the silence I carried, the loyalty that kept me stuck, and the deep sense of duty that blurred my boundaries. This chapter is about that legacy, what helped me survive, and what I had to break free from to become who I am today.

I have come to realise that life is a gift and equally a series of constant challenges, and when we learn from our challenges, both are truly gifts.

Much of my lack of boundaries in my marriage came from my Italian heritage and culture, where men were placed at the top of the pyramid of power. The old traditions expected women give in to men and most men know this. Some honour that with respect and others take advantage.

Breaking that culture and genealogy is key now to my life. I will never again allow a man to dominate me. Because I am strong and now, I would like to share one of my most precious gifts that comes from my parents and their culture.

My Sicilian heritage played a big role in shaping my values, both the fierce loyalty and deep sense of family, but also the silence, secrecy, and pressure to endure things no one should have to bear. Understanding this helped me make sense of why I stayed so long and why breaking free felt like breaking tradition.

A Voyage to New Beginnings

My parents didn't just survive; they carried a world within them.

They left behind the sun-scorched hills of Sicily, the scent of olives and lemons in the air, and the stories of generations before them.

With nothing but what they could carry in their hands and hearts, they set sail for a land unknown, trading familiarity for a future.

They crossed oceans, navigated an unfamiliar language, and started over in a foreign land.

Their bodies carried the weight of war, of hardship, of labour.

And yet, through all of it, they never stopped creating, creating a home, creating a future, creating a life for the family that would come after them.

Their sacrifices were silent, stitched into every meal placed on our table, every dollar saved for a future they could barely imagine.

I didn't see it as a child.

I only saw the strictness, the early mornings, the endless work.

But now, I see it for what it was, love, given in the only way they knew how.

I didn't realise how much of their strength was stitched into me.

I have spent years trying to understand my pain.

The doctors never listened. The system never cared. But when I think of my mother, my father, I realise they, too, knew pain.

Not the kind that doctors dismiss, but the kind that carves itself into your bones.

The kind that comes from war, from hunger, from working your hands raw just to survive.

Their pain was different from mine.

But maybe their strength is the same.

There were moments in my life when I felt like no one saw me.

Like my pain was invisible, my body an afterthought. But maybe that's how Mum and Dad felt when they arrived in Australia, two Sicilians in a foreign land, carrying nothing but hope and a language that no one understood.

They, too, had to fight to be heard.

To be seen.

To survive in a world that wasn't built for them. And yet, they did.

My parents, both of Sicilian heritage, arrived in Australia during the 1950s, seeking a new life filled with opportunities they could not find in their homeland. Leaving behind the rich, tumultuous history of Sicily, they embarked on a month-long voyage by ship, filled with hope and uncertainty. Melbourne, at the time, was a modest city, far from the bustling metropolis it is today. It was here they would rebuild their lives, far from the shadows of the past.

> *"The greatest legacy one can pass on is not material things, but a legacy of character and faith."*
> *- Billy Graham*

Dad was born in Vizzini, Provincia Catania, and Mum in Floridia, Provincia Siracusa. Both towns were steeped in history, surrounded by breathtaking landscapes, and shaped by centuries of cultural influence. However, like many others, they were also places marked by hardship. Sicily's beauty often masked the struggles of everyday life, with its long history of conquests and, more recently, the influence of the mafia, casting a shadow over its proud culture.

Mum: A Childhood Touched by War

Mum's early years were shaped by the turmoil of World War II. She was around five years old when an American soldier, drawn by her curly locks, stopped to marvel at her hair. "Che sono belli questi ricciolini," he said with warmth, his voice filled with wonder. He bought her an ice cream, a rare and treasured treat in those difficult times. It was a simple moment of kindness amidst the chaos, one that stayed with her for a lifetime.

But the war wasn't just marked by fleeting moments of joy. Planes often hovered overhead, dropping bombs, and she and her family would seek cover, bracing for the destruction that followed. For a child, the danger was sometimes masked by the adventure, but the memories of homes reduced to rubble left a lasting impression.

Mum's brilliance shone in school, her mind sharp and eager to learn. She devoured books, soaking up knowledge as if it were nourishment.

At twelve, she still dreamed of classrooms, of ink-stained fingers, of a future where learning was her path forward.

But one day, her mother sat her down.

'Your brother will go to school. You will work.'

Her dreams collapsed in an instant. No argument, no plea could change it.

She cried every day, but the world didn't bend for a girl's tears.

So, she swallowed them.

And she worked.

Her role was to work, helping to support the family and fund her brother's education. She cried every day, but her tears went unnoticed. The decision wasn't personal, it was cultural, a reflection of the gender roles deeply ingrained in society at the time. Even as she carried this heartbreak into adulthood, Mum's love of learning never faded.

At 20, she left Sicily for Australia, sponsored by a friend. The journey on the ship *Oceania* was bittersweet. She celebrated her 21st birthday alone, without her family, and spent Christmas and New Year's in a new land, surrounded by strangers. Though there was music and dancing on board, she hesitated to join, fearing the judgment of others. Gossip could ruin a young woman's reputation back then, and she wanted to protect her honour at all costs.

Dad: Resilience Forged in Struggle

Dad's childhood, too, was shaped by the war. Born in 1938, he was just six years old when he watched two warplanes battle in the sky above his family home. One was shot down, exploding in a fiery crash, scattering debris across the streets. Survival meant constant vigilance. Bombs disguised as everyday items, clocks, coffee makers, even toys, littered the ground, a deadly reminder of the war's reach.

At 10, Dad's classroom became the fields. Instead of ink and paper, he learned the language of sheep and wind, of hunger, exploitation and exhaustion. He was as a shepherd boy, enduring gruelling conditions. On one farm, he faced relentless abuse from the owner, who beat him so severely that his back was left bruised and bloodied. At home, life wasn't much kinder. An innocent mistake, like accidentally hitting an old man with a rock meant for another boy, resulted in a brutal beating from his father, leaving his arm broken.

Despite these challenges, Dad grew into a man of resilience and determination. At 17, he followed his brother to Australia, seeking a fresh start. He carried with him the lessons of survival and a deep sense of responsibility, traits that would define him as a husband and father.

A Sicilian Legacy in Australia

In Australia, Mum and Dad built a life rooted in hard work and sacrifice. They instilled in us the importance of family, education, and honouring our heritage. Their stories of survival and resilience weren't just tales of hardship; they were reminders of the strength that ran through our blood.

Mum often spoke about Sicily with a mix of pride and longing. She shared stories of growing up in Sicily, their culture, their ways of living.

One example that stands out, there was no toilet paper, they used a big rag for the whole family. She shares how she took pride in washing this rag. They didn't know any different, so to her it was her norm. For me my eyes popped out when I heard that.

She shares how they sat around the wireless (radio) as a family, and how there was no fridge, that they would walk to go get a block of ice, wrap it around with a cloth and store it under the bed, to keep it from melting. It truly is a tapestry of wonder how the human conditioning evolves. I grew up immersed in this rich heritage, unaware of how precious it was until I lost it during my marriage. I knew it was precious, but not as much as when I yearned for family and their love. That marriage was like living in a desert, I was thirsty for love and care.

For Dad, his connection to Sicily was quieter but just as profound. He would speak of the mountains of Vizzini, the rivers he played by as a boy, and the family traditions that shaped him. He carried the scars of his childhood, both visible and hidden, but never let them define him.

A Lasting Tribute

Mum and Dad's journey to Australia was more than just migration, it was a testament to their hope for a better future. They overcame the shadows of their past, carrying with them the resilience of their ancestors and the promise of a brighter tomorrow. Their sacrifices laid the foundation for everything I am today. I carry their stories as a reminder of where I come from and the strength that runs through me.

Their legacy is one of love, determination, and unyielding faith. With over 60 years of marriage, they have weathered many storms, always keeping love at the centre as they forged ahead. It wasn't easy. Like so many others, they arrived in a foreign land without knowing the language. Hearing phrases like 'a cup of tea' and 'a sandwich' were entirely new concepts to them. They came from a world of olives, cheese, dried tomatoes, and the communal act of squashing grapes to make wine.

I grew up in a culture vastly different from the one my husband knew. His deeply rooted Australian upbringing was the complete opposite of my Sicilian heritage. I left home at 25, and a relative in Sicily told me I had dishonoured my father by doing so. The husband, on the other hand, had left home at 17. His life was filled with freedoms I could never have imagined, like getting a motorbike as a teenager. I didn't even learn to ride a bicycle until my late teens.

My upbringing revolved around the kitchen and family responsibilities. From a young age, my sisters and I were cleaning and cooking together. Saturday mornings meant cleaning the house from top to bottom, and on Sundays, there was no rest, Dad would have us up early, telling us to clean the windows. There was always work to be done. Yet, amidst the toil, there was family: a table full of food, arguments that gave way to singing and dancing. Work and family were at the core of everything we did.

In contrast, the husband's world seemed to revolve around alcohol. It was such a central focus in his life that it shaped many of his actions and deeply affected our daily lives. He drank during the week as though every day was the weekend, indulging excessively, just as he did with most things in life. His drinking wasn't just casual, it was relentless, a constant presence that influenced his moods, decisions, and interactions.

Ironically, I couldn't escape alcohol either, it was everywhere in my upbringing. But even so, I yearned for simpler, more typical Australian experiences, like having a chocolate birthday cake as a child. Yet, alcohol in my childhood was part of family tradition and culture, woven into celebrations and gatherings. With him, it was different. His relationship with alcohol was all-consuming, spilling over into every aspect of our lives.

Our cultural differences ran deep. I was a Sicilian woman, one of three sisters, while he was an Australian-born, only child who enjoyed freedoms I couldn't fathom. When I first asked him if he understood Italian families, especially Sicilian ones, he lied. He confidently said, "Yes, I've worked at lots of Italian restaurants, and I had an affair with one of the workers, so I know how they work."

At the time, I believed him, naively accepting his words. Looking back, I see how much that statement revealed, not only about his misunderstanding of my culture but about his character. His shallow, selfish and dismissive ways.

Reflection:

While my parents built a legacy of love and resilience, my marriage often felt like the antithesis of everything they stood for. The closeness I cherished with my family became a source of resentment for my husband, creating a rift that was as painful as it was isolating.

My parents built a home out of sacrifice and love.

My husband built walls out of control and cruelty.

My father's hands, once broken from labour, were still gentle when they held us.

My husband's hands, unscathed, left bruises, on my body, on my soul, on everything I tried to hold onto.

My mother's strength was in her quiet endurance.

My husband's strength was in his ability to break me down.

Two worlds. Two men.

One gave me life.

The other tried to take it from me.

I spent so much time in my marriage defending my love for family. The husband would twist it into something ugly, accusing me of being more married to my family than to him. His jealousy was relentless, his anger corrosive, and his words like daggers, constantly tearing at my soul. It became an endless, exhausting battle, arguing, justifying, and trying to prove that my love for family didn't diminish my commitment to him. But no matter what I said, it was never enough.

At first, he claimed to understand Italian families, even embracing the closeness and warmth. He would smile and say all the right things, making me believe he truly valued what family meant to me. But as time went on, the façade crumbled, and he became increasingly resentful and bitter. His resentment turned into a weapon. He berated me, yelling with such aggression that some nights, especially when he was drunk, his rage escalated to terrifying levels.

There were moments when I feared for my life. Nights when he got so drunk that his rage spiralled into uncontrollable violence, leaving me shaking, wondering if I would survive. He attacked the very core of who I am, my deep, unwavering love for my family.

I missed so much during those years. I was isolated, cut off from the people who mattered most to me. My nieces and nephews grew up, and I wasn't there to see it. I grieved those lost moments, the birthdays, the milestones, the small, precious memories that can never be replaced. I cried countless tears over the distance he created between me and my family, over the dark, suffocating world I found myself trapped in.

It was as if he was trying to snuff out the flame inside me, the love I have for others, especially my family. But no matter how much he yelled, no matter how much he tried to break me, he couldn't destroy that love for my family. It flickered, it faltered, but it never went out.

My parents' journey to Australia was a leap of faith, driven by dreams of a better life. Leaving the sun-drenched hills of Sicily, with its ancient traditions and deep familial bonds, they ventured into the unknown. Their stories are etched into my heart, not just as tales of hardship but as testaments to their unwavering hope and resilience.

Mum, with her love of learning and unyielding spirit, embodied the sacrifices so many women of her generation made. Her stories of the war, of seeking shelter as bombs fell and finding joy in a soldier's kind gesture, paint a vivid picture of both hardship and humanity. Dad's journey was equally marked by struggle. From enduring abuse as a shepherd boy to navigating a new country as a teenager, his resilience became the foundation of the life he built for us.

The Challenges of Marriage

In stark contrast to my parents' legacy, my marriage became a battle for survival. While my upbringing emphasised family, connection, and shared responsibility, my husband's world seemed to revolve around indulgence and control. His resentment of my love for my family was like a poison, seeping into every corner of our life together.

He accused me of being more loyal to my family than to him, twisting my love into something he could weaponize against me. I lost precious years with my nieces and nephews, moments I can never get back. But even in the darkest times, the flame of my family's love never went out. It flickered, dimmed, but it never died.

Reflection and Healing

Looking back, I see how my parents' legacy carried me through the storm. Their sacrifices and love became a lighthouse in the darkness, guiding me back to myself. While my husband tried to tear me away from everything, all I held dear, he could never destroy the foundation my parents built, a foundation of faith, resilience, and unyielding love.

> *"Beautiful are those whose brokenness gives birth to transformation and wisdom." – John Green*

My parents' journey reminds me that even in brokenness, there is strength to rebuild. Their legacy lives on in me, in the choices I make, and in the life, I am reclaiming for myself.

My parents crossed oceans so their children wouldn't have to live in survival mode.

They left behind war so I wouldn't have to fight battles just to be seen.

And yet, I did.

I fought to survive my husband.

I fought to survive a system that dismissed my pain.

I fought to survive myself.

But now, I see their legacy wasn't just in their survival, it was in their strength to create something new. And that strength lives in me.

I am their legacy.

And I will carry it forward.

GRACE AMORE

My parents' lives are a testament to this truth. They carried the light of hope and faith through every hardship, passing it on to me. Now, as I continue to heal and rebuild, I honour their legacy by carrying that light forward, for myself, for my family, and for the generations to come.

"The greatest gift we can give to a person in pain is to hold in our own minds the thought that there is a light beyond this darkness." – Marianne Williamson.

I've searched for truth my whole life. I thought I found it in religion, but that wasn't it. I thought I found it in love, but that wasn't either. I even tried to create my own truth through the Lesbian, Gay, Bisexual, Transgender and Intersex (GLBTI) events, but that left me empty. The only thing that ever set me free was Jesus. My personal relationship with Jesus Christ. And that is the truth I stand in now -even when it costs me something. Because no matter what happens, I won't be silent about what I know is real anymore.

7: Descent into the Maelstrom

At first, life with my future husband was intoxicating, a nonstop blur of parties, festivals, music, and drugs. It felt like an escape, but in reality, it was a slow erasure of everything I once was.

Weekends were never about rest, always about the next party, the next high, beach parties, bush parties, drugs and alcohol, then back to work on Monday, running on fumes. Sleep was something for later, recovery an afterthought. I barely noticed the exhaustion setting in, the way my body started disconnecting from itself. The rhythm of our life wasn't mine to set, it was his. And it was relentless.

When I met my future husband, marriage wasn't on my mind.

I had spent years enduring medical dismissal and doubting my own body. So, when I met my future husband, the man who called himself a 'happy camper', his apparent understanding of period pain felt like a miracle. It was 2007, and I had no idea that the thing he claimed to accept about me would later be used against me.

He seemed tolerant, accepting, and compassionate. I wanted so desperately to believe him that I did. It was too good to be true, but I ignored my intuition and doubts. Desperate for acceptance, I bought the lie.

Before meeting my future husband, my relationships had been fraught with emotional abuse. I justified my partners' outbursts, telling myself they stemmed from past wounds I could help them heal. My trauma response shaped me into a people-pleaser, a rescuer, convinced that appeasing the abuser would keep me safe. If I agreed with them, I believed, they wouldn't hurt me. The storm would pass with minimal harm. But this illusion only locked me in the endless cycle of abuse.

From my late teens into my thirties, I had few intimate relationships. Those I did have were tumultuous and boundaryless. The childhood trauma I carried silenced my voice, leaving me unable to advocate for myself. I yearned to be accepted, to be loved. Over time, my unspoken pain began to manifest physically, as endometriosis and adenomyosis. These took hold of my body. Entering relationships, I often abandoned my dignity, leaving myself vulnerable to being used and abused.

For a while, embracing single life felt like liberation. I relished the freedom to pursue my desires without answering to anyone. But as I approached my late thirties, societal and familial pressures mounted. My parents, deeply rooted in Sicilian traditional views on marriage, began expressing their concern over my single status. In their desperation, they even suggested my gay friends as potential husbands, failing to grasp the complexities of my reality.

My confusion about my sexuality, compounded by the unrelenting period pain and past sexual traumas. These made the prospect of marriage feel even more foreign. Doctors had dismissed my pain for years, calling me crazy or prescribing impractical advice: "Just have a baby, it will help." The irony was cruel, as endometriosis can impact fertility, making pregnancy an impossible solution. The constant gaslighting from medical professionals stripped away my self-worth and robbed me of the chance to dream of motherhood.

By the time I met my husband to be, my health was challenging but manageable. I had found ways to push through the waves of debilitating pain that came every month. However, the persistent cycle of questioning my sanity and doubting my body left cracks in my resilience. Each period brought new struggles, moments of isolation, and unanswered questions that doctors dismissed as trivial.

So, when I confided in him about my troubled history with men and the debilitating pain that consumed my life, his apparent empathy felt like a miracle. A man who listened, who accepted me despite my struggles, flaws and all. His understanding seemed genuine, even divine. But his kindness was a facade, carefully crafted to mirror what I wanted to see.

Confusion about my sexuality, compounded by the relentless period pain and the shadow of past sexual traumas, left me feeling unworthy of marriage.

Although I tried to manage my health, my self-worth took a devastating hit. I began self-medicating to dull the emotional and physical pain, trapped in a cycle of questioning my body's integrity and my own sanity. Each month brought more internal battles and moments of withdrawal from the world, a futile effort to protect myself from the constant sense of failure.

When I opened up to my husband to be about my struggles, he seemed to embody everything I had desperately longed for: understanding, kindness, and compassion. I felt hopeful and accepted for the first time within an intimate partner relationship. I didn't feel like a freak, his acceptance of me was paramount, it was a breath of fresh air.

His words painted a fraudulent picture of a supportive partner, someone who could help shoulder the burden of my pain. But it was all an illusion, a carefully crafted facade. He didn't truly understand my struggles, nor did he care to. Instead, he echoed back what I needed to hear, offering hollow reassurance to gain my trust. Our union, a woman battling relentless pain and a man concealing his dark compulsions, became a toxic combination that destroyed us and nearly destroyed me.

Without a safe space to retreat to, our home became a prison without bars due to his insidious control over every area of my life. My personal lockdown began long before the world shut down during the 2020 Melbourne COVID-19 lockdowns, though I hadn't yet grasped the full extent of my entrapment.

At the time, professionals still weren't legally required to identify or act on the signs of coercive control. Today in Victoria, the *MARAM* framework, short for *Multi-Agency Risk Assessment and Management*, requires professionals across sectors to identify family violence risk factors and respond appropriately. But back then, there was no such mandate. I fell through the cracks.

The official government lockdowns would only deepen the isolation, trapping individuals like me in abusive situations with little regard for our safety. A survey of 15,000 women taken in May 2020 by the *Australian Institute of Criminology* showed that one in 12 experienced physical violence from their live-in partner in the first three months of the pandemic, when most Australians were locked down.

After surviving a traumatic dog attack and enduring three agonising days in the emergency room without adequate pain relief, my pelvic pain worsened. Desperate for a sense of normalcy, I forced myself back to work after just five days, even as the physical and emotional toll weighed heavily on me. Meanwhile, the stress at home mounted. My husband's birthday loomed ahead, a date that brought immense pressure, as his unmet expectations would inevitably result in relentless beratement. At one point, I thought to myself that if it weren't for my pup, I might have simply let those dogs maul me to death.

I knew, on some level, that I was being used in my marriage, though I couldn't yet articulate exactly how. My husband's constant blame shifted the focus away from him, making every problem in our relationship appear as though it stemmed from me. I felt like a mouse trapped on a wheel, running endlessly in circles without escape. I sought help from counsellors, psychologists, and even *Relationships Australia*, but none of them recognised the abuse for what it was. Their failure to name the dynamic left me feeling more isolated than ever, as though I was navigating this nightmare alone. I had to change that. I had to reach out to someone for help.

I remember the first therapist I went to. It was early 2011, right after we returned from the road trip, settling into a new life in Cranbourne. East Gippsland. We had moved 1.5 hours away from all family and friends, landing on the other side of town, in a place I never imagined myself living. It wasn't the city, but it wasn't the country either. It was no man's land, a vast, isolating stretch of roads and highways where everything felt too far apart.

I was alone with this man I had married in 2009, alone with the weight of a miscarriage that had swallowed me whole, alone with the memories of the outback road trip we had taken to escape it all. We had worked in remote towns, him as a chef, me either behind the bar, waitressing, or in the kitchen beside him. It was another world, a world that kept me moving. A world that kept me distracted. But now, we were back. And something was shifting in him.

The demands started as soon as we returned. It wasn't just sex with him, it was with others, too. Against my will. He prattled on with justifications, with his expectations of what it meant to be a wife, with his insistence that we go to places I had no interest in. My body recoiled, my gut screamed, but my voice had nowhere to go.

So, I reached out after 2-3 years of marriage. I searched for help. I found a sex therapist 2011, a psychologist, and made an appointment. I counted down the days, waiting for a moment to breathe, to be heard, to say out loud what was happening behind closed doors. The day came, and I sat in the waiting room, stomach in knots, nerves electrified. This was it. This was my chance.

GRACE AMORE

She called my name. Short, stocky, with an expression I couldn't yet read.

I sat down, heart pounding, and before she could even settle into her chair, I blurted it out in one breath: "My husband is making me do things I don't want to do. He's forcing me to go to sex places. Swingers."

I let it all out, waiting, praying, for relief. For validation. For her to say, "That's not okay. You're not alone. I hear you."

Instead, she raised her hand like a stop sign.

"This is not how counselling works, Grace," she said. "We have to build rapport first."

Something in me shut down. My body, my throat, my shoulders, my pelvis, everything that had braced itself for safety suddenly collapsed inward. The words that had fought so hard to surface were silenced again. "I am not safe here." That's all I could hear.

I walked in believing this was my chance to be free. I walked out knowing I was alone.

I said to myself, If I couldn't tell a sex therapist, who *could* I tell? My two closest friends had already dismissed me, they didn't want to know. And now, neither did a professional. I walked away defeated, the cloak of shame wrapped so tight around me I could barely breathe.

That was just the beginning.

I kept reaching out. I kept trying. Therapist after therapist, counsellor after counsellor, psychologist after psychologist. Each time, I hoped someone would see me, hear me, name what was happening to me. But the cage remained invisible, and I remained trapped inside it.

The only reason I was even *allowed* to see therapists was because *I* was supposedly the problem. That's what he told me, over and over. "You're the one who needs help. You're the one who's broken. You're the one who has issues with sex."

And so, I kept searching for answers, even when I didn't have the words for what my body already knew. Even when every attempt to speak up was met with dismissal, correction, and control.

At the very start of my marriage, I reached out. And at the very start, I was shut down. Again and again, until I learned not to speak at all.

I hadn't yet realised I was married to a narcissist with sadistic tendencies, someone who seemed to derive pleasure from my pain. The truth was obscured by his manipulative tactics, leaving me caught in a web of confusion and self-blame.

What I was experiencing was coercive control, a form of abuse that doesn't rely on physical violence but instead uses isolation, surveillance, threats, and humiliation to dominate another person. At the time, I didn't have a name for it. But it was real, and it was eroding my sense of self every single day.

Home life had devolved into a relentless cycle of demands, rigid agendas, and expectations that I could never seem to meet. The weight of it all bore down on me, leaving little room to breathe, let alone find peace. One evening after work, my husband's demeanour shifted unexpectedly. He seemed unusually caring, almost out of character. With an uncharacteristic gentleness, he informed me that he had arranged an in-house massage for me.

I hesitated, caught off guard by the gesture. What was the catch this time? His voice carried an air of sincerity, expressing a desire for me to relax and take some time out for myself, a rare consideration in our daily chaos. He casually mentioned that a masseuse would be arriving at 7 p.m. that night.

It was a weeknight, and my mind raced to keep up. "He is coming over soon," my husband told me, as if it were a simple, thoughtful arrangement. Yet, my body sent warning signals almost instantly. Something felt off, an internal alarm ringing quietly but persistently. Be careful, my instincts whispered. He's up to one of his tricks again.

I felt my stomach churn as I wrestled with the unease. Dare I refuse his offer of an in-house massage? It was difficult to confront this undercurrent of mistrust. After all, on the surface, he was doing something thoughtful, even kind. He had gone out of his way to organise this. But the familiar knot of dread tightened in my chest, an all-too-familiar response to the ambiguity of his intentions.

Something was wrong, and deep down, I knew it. Yet, as with so many moments before, I felt powerless to voice my unease, caught in the web of doubt and confusion that defined our marriage.

There was a knock at the door, sharp and intrusive. My heart pounded as I fidgeted nervously in the lounge, the curtains drawn tightly to mask out the eyes of the world outside. My husband opened the door, and in walked a stranger carrying a massage table. The air in the room shifted, thickening with unease. It's difficult to articulate what happened next because my body responded instinctively, moving into a state of heightened alert. Every nerve hummed with tension as an unspoken warning vibrated through me: Be aware, Grace. Your husband has an agenda.

Confusion mingled with distress as I tried to process the scene unfolding before me. This was my home, my space, a place that once held the promise of safety, now stripped of anything sacred. Piece by piece, I had surrendered safety since marrying him, and tonight, it was to be desecrated again.

The stranger, a *Craigslist* hire; a classified ads website where people advertised all sorts of services, jobs, or items for sale and sex hookups. It was a casual arrangement, not through any official company. a man my husband had invited into our home, approached me with forced reassurance. I felt my body tense, my instincts screaming at me that something was deeply, dangerously wrong.

He explained that he was a legitimate masseuse and insisted there were no hidden agendas. But his words bounced off the fortress of alarm that had risen within me. My sympathetic nervous system screamed louder with each passing second: This is not right, Grace.

I wanted so desperate for this to be genuine, for my husband's gesture to come from a place of care. But deep down, I knew the truth, it was all about him. It always was. Something seedy was unfolding, and I was trapped in its clutches.

Exhaustion blurred my thoughts, the haze of medications further clouding any sense of clarity. Darkness seemed to envelop my mind, shutting down reason and leaving my amygdala in complete control. Fight or flight. Neither seemed possible. I was frozen. Alone with these two men in my own home, I was unsafe. Deeply unsafe.

The last words I recall were, "You need to get on the massage table, Grace, to have the massage." Then the frame of memory abruptly cut to black.

Though my mind went blank, what I know now is this was not simply a massage, it was an act of sexual coercion, arranged under false pretences. It was trafficking within my own home, masked as a favour.

The next thing I remember is the frame narrowing again, closing in on my hurting body stretched across that massage table. Panic gripped me, tightening like a vice around my chest. My body shut down, retreating into a survival mode I had come to know all too well. I left myself there on that table, exposed and vulnerable. I left my body to the wolves.

The details after that moment are hazy, fractured by fear and dissociation. I remember faintly hearing something about "owing someone sex," and that was it. The rest is shrouded in a fog of terror and shame. What became horrifyingly clear later was that my husband had arranged this so-called in-house massage with the unspoken understanding that my body would be the payment for the massage, another transaction in the twisted economy of his desires.

My husband had always organised my life around an unspoken rule: his needs came first. With every seedy and degrading experience, the weight of shame grew heavier, piling like rubble in the trauma centre of my mind. That shame became a mountain, impossible to climb or escape. Meanwhile, the unexplained pelvic pain intensified daily, each wave of it a cruel echo of what I had endured.

The cumulative stress mounted as my body became a battlefield, a site of pain, a vessel for shame, and a silent prisoner. My voice had been stifled, my autonomy stripped away, and I was left tangled in the web of entrapment I had unwittingly married into.

Reflection

Looking back now, I can see how fleeting his 'nice guy' facade truly was. I was so desperate to believe that someone might genuinely care about me, my pain, and my worth. I clung to the illusion because it offered the hope I had been denied for so long. But what I see now is not always what is, he was a wolf in sheep's clothing, his kindness nothing more than a calculated mask that hid his narcissism and his aberrant sexual desire.

The power he wielded wasn't physical but psychological. He tore me apart piece by piece, leaving me questioning my reality, my worth, and my sanity, only to rebuild me into a version of myself that served his needs. George Orwell's words echo hauntingly: "Power is in tearing human minds to pieces and putting them together again in new shapes of your own choosing." That was his power, his ability to dismantle my mind and reshape my life into a prison that I couldn't even see I was trapped in.

"Power is in tearing human minds to pieces and putting them together again in new shapes of your own choosing."
– George Orwell, 1984

But as I reflect now, I see the cracks in his facade were always there. The truth, once hidden beneath layers of manipulation and shame, has surfaced. And though the descent into that maelstrom nearly consumed me, it also began to awaken something within, a quiet but determined voice that would not stay silent forever.

8: Weight of Silence

The days following the massage incident blurred into an overwhelming haze of pain, exhaustion, and confusion. My body felt drained, my mind fractured, but there was no room for acknowledgment, only silence, only survival.

I couldn't explain what had happened, not even to myself. The shame from that night settled in my body like a sickness. Trauma does that, it silences you before you even know what you're trying to say. The husband's shaming and blaming ensured that there was no room for reflection, no space to acknowledge my feelings. My body, already a battleground, carried the weight of yet another violation.

And then, as if my body hadn't endured enough, August 2019 brought another layer of suffering. After the dog attack, everything became a dense fog of stress, pain, and exhaustion, each crisis bleeding into the next.

> *"She had not realised how much she could endure, but she knew now that it was almost more than she could bear." – Edith Wharton, The House of Mirth.*

Work was my safe space even though it was overwhelming, with deadlines and expectations piling up, while managing my health consumed what little energy I had left. My workplace was my haven. My days revolved around endless medical appointments, trips to the pharmacy for prescriptions, and the unrelenting pelvic pain that consumed my body. Each movement was a reminder of the storm raging inside me.

At work, I was barely holding on. I could feel myself unravelling. Each day felt like a slide down a cheese grater. A battle to appear functional while my body screamed for relief.

It was clear, at least to me, that I was having some kind of breakdown.

My body ached, my gums throbbed, and eating or drinking was a chore with the swelling and discomfort from the dog attack.

I was still healing from surgery, face, thigh, and hand all stitched. But no one seemed to notice the toll it took, least of all the man I was married to. I had become invisible in my own suffering.

When I looked in the mirror, I barely recognised myself. The stitches across my face stretched near my left eye, a near miss that could have taken my vision to the bottom of nose. The reflection staring back at me was a patchwork of physical and emotional scars. I felt like a female Frankenstein, stitched together yet falling apart. I was raw and messy, fragile and vulnerable, with no safe place to cry in peace or find a way through the chaotic wilderness of this marriage.

I didn't even have the comfort of my usual walks with Buddy. The dog attack had robbed me of those quiet moments of solace.

Buddy, once my safe space, now limped too. I watched his playful spark dim. We were both survivors of the same attack, he bore punctures in his chest, I wore them on my face. He still looked at me with unwavering love. I held onto that.

The fear of facing another dangerous encounter kept me from venturing out, trapping me further in the suffocating confines of my life. Buddy, too, seemed unsettled, his once lively demeanour dulled by the tension that had overtaken our home.

The web I was caught in felt hazy and suffocating, a seedy entanglement of stress, fear, and relentless sexual demands I couldn't keep up with. My body was no longer my own; it had become a battleground, an object of his control. The pain in my pelvis intensified daily, amplifying the despair. I was exhausted, physically and emotionally, with nothing left to give.

Suicidal thoughts began to take root, creeping in like shadows that I couldn't outrun. The weight of distress pressed down so heavily that it felt as if life itself was closing in on me. I lived in a dark haze, perpetually on edge. Sleep, when it came, was a rare luxury, while the expectation of sex loomed over me like an even darker cloud, suffocating and inescapable.

The husband had an endless abyss of needs such as sex and pornography to fill his insecurities and the dark void.

There was no space in our home for healing, only for his appetite. I was not a partner; I was an object to be used and then discarded. Porn was always on in the background, humming like white noise. I began to internalise the message: I didn't matter.

Like a ghoul that fed on another's light, he never self-reflected on the cause of his behaviours or took any responsibility for his mayhem or madness.

The pressures, demands, and stresses mounted endlessly, with my husband adding fuel to an already raging fire. The more unwell I became, the more intolerable he grew, his complaints and criticism amplifying my despair. My thoughts were no longer my own; clarity had become a distant memory, something I hadn't known since before the marriage.

Driving to medical appointments while heavily medicated felt like navigating a cruel and unrelenting labyrinth. I was expected to function on morphine, Endone, and other opioids, drugs that dulled my senses and left me barely coherent behind the wheel, yet medicinal cannabis, the one thing that actually eased the relentless knife-like spasms in my pelvis, was off-limits for driving.

It felt cruel: the one medicine that actually helped wasn't allowed. Yet society said, "Push through." I was punished for being in pain, then punished again for trying to treat it.

The hypocrisy was maddening. Cannabis had the power to quiet the unbearable spasms, to smooth the jagged edges of pain that left me breathless while driving. Yet, unjust laws criminalised its use in situations where it could have been a lifeline, forcing me to endure each excruciating journey in silence.

Each appointment with each new medical expert I sought brought its own form of torment.

It was like emotional whiplash, every time I hoped to be heard, I was sent away emptier. I stopped expecting help. I stopped expecting kindness.

Explaining my story over and over, hoping for relief but finding none, drained what little energy I had left. One pain specialist charged $200 for a ten-minute consultation, only to dismiss me with a sterile, "I'm sorry for your pain," and no solutions. She handed me a referral and sent me on my way. Another hollow gesture from a system that didn't care. Her indifference was infuriating, a hopeless waste of her education, and a betrayal of the Hippocratic oath. I left feeling used, depleted, and utterly abandoned by the very people meant to help me.

Due to my mounting medical bills, I was advised to access my superannuation. Adding to the chaos, *Australian Super*'s income protection process became another layer of torment, an endless paper merry-go-round designed to stall and exhaust me. Each phone call, each demand for more documents, felt like a calculated effort to grind me down further. I was drowning in bureaucracy, with no life raft in sight.

Adding to this relentless storm was my husband's insistence on attending a birthday party a few weeks after the dog attack.

It was a Saturday night, and though my body screamed for rest, my husband had other plans. He didn't demand outright that I go; that wasn't his way. Instead, he spun it as something for my benefit, a chance to 'get out of the house' and 'take my mind off things.' His words carried the weight of manipulation, the kind that made me doubt myself. This wasn't about going out, it was about submission. The party was a test: would I give in? Would I obey? The cost of saying no had become too high.

> *"For God does not give us a spirit of fear, but of power and of love and a sound mind" - (2 Timothy 1:7).*

I knew there was little room for me to say, "No." The unspoken consequences, his sulking, the cold silence, or the eventual explosion, wouldn't be worth the small relief of a night at home. So I went, even though every part of me wanted to stay.

I wasn't me anymore. Grace was slipping further away with every passing day. Maybe she still lingered somewhere, a faint whisper beneath the weight of shame, stress, and relentless demands. But she was getting harder to find. Harder to hear.

There was no room for reprieve, no space to breathe. Each day felt like a battlefield, and I was losing the fight.

Reflection

This period of my life was so dense with confusion and pain that it felt like trying to think clearly while drinking poison. Every thought was clouded, every decision weighed down by the toxic environment I lived in. Clarity seemed impossible. In this suffocating fog, prayer became my anchor, the one thing I could hold onto. It was the flicker of light, a tiny flame that refused to go out, no matter how faint it seemed at times.

Amid the chaos, one thing stood out, a verse I had taped to our lounge room sliding door: "For God does not give us a spirit of fear, but of power and of love and a sound mind" (2

Timothy 1:7). I clung to those words like a lifeline, reading them over and over, letting their truth sink into my spirit as the husband unleashed his relentless tirade of negativity. That verse was a small light in my darkness, a reminder of the power and love that still existed, even as I felt my strength slipping away.

9: Caught in the Crossfire

The more I tried to hold onto hope, the more the reality of my marriage clawed at me. Silence had become my survival, but it also became my prison.

The silence kept me safe, but it also kept me invisible, even to myself. It muffled my screams, my needs, and my intuition until I didn't know what was real anymore.

The weight of everything, his demands, my pain, the sheer exhaustion of pretending, was unbearable. And still, it wasn't enough for him.

> "There is no greater agony than bearing an untold story inside you." – Maya Angelou (I Know Why the Caged Bird Sings)

This was something I didn't know about when we first met: in the background, he was into swingers' parties. I wasn't. The very idea repulsed me. It made my stomach churn. Just thinking about those kinds of environments brought a wave of nausea.

It wasn't just casual interest; it was a world he was deeply entrenched in. These were not just fantasies; they were expectations that violated every value I held.

Here I was, married to a man whose sexual preferences clashed with everything I believed in, everything I valued. Yet, somehow, I had to meet his needs because he was a man with a high libido.

Why choose someone like me, someone who suffered from excruciating period pain and had no desire for spaces like that? No desire at all. I would have preferred sitting around a campfire under the stars, having a deep and meaningful conversation about life.

Swinging couples was never my thing. I detested even the thought of it; it grossed me out to my core. I remembered seeing a 70s movie once about couples swapping keys in baskets at a party. Panic struck me just watching it; it was scarier than any horror movie I'd seen. Yet, the very thing that terrified me and churned my stomach was something he desired and justified endlessly. He had needs, he told me, and I was his wife, so it was my duty to fulfill them.

The shame grew, and I became smaller. Valued only for the sex I gave him and the whims that I granted. I was living in a marriage where my needs, my pain, and my voice had no place.

I was like wallpaper, present, but never seen. Pretty, polite, and permanently dismissed.

How could I ever tell anyone the truth? The thought of admitting it felt like a betrayal of myself, and yet, every day, I was betraying my body by staying in a marital train wreck.

I reconciled with myself that I had married him and now we had to work through this somehow.

I believed the lie that loyalty meant staying no matter how much it hurt. That 'working through it' meant giving everything, even my soul.

One night, I mustered the courage to say something I'd been holding inside.

It felt like whispering into a void, but I couldn't hold it in anymore. The truth burned in my chest, demanding to be spoken.

"It's like you have an abyss in you that never gets filled," I told him. You could have all the sex in the world, and it wouldn't even touch the sides. I believe it's a spiritual thing."

I braced myself for his usual backlash, but to my surprise, he just nodded and said, "You're probably right." Then, without another word, he returned to the porn site on his laptop. It was one of the rare moments he didn't argue, berate, or lash out. But it didn't matter, his indifference said enough. His agreement was hollow, a reflection of how little he cared about the deeper issues I had pointed out.

Our arguments were usually tit for tat. He called them that, saying I always had to have the last word. But it didn't matter what I said, he never cared about my perspective unless it served him in some way.

His attitude about the dog attack proved just how little I mattered to him. Publicly, he played the role of the concerned and caring husband. After the attack, we had to attend council meetings to raise awareness for safety reasons in our area; to prevent another attack. We met with local council about the owner's taking responsibility for their dogs that were off leash attacking animals and people. The owners were never found.

At the council meetings, he presented himself as someone invested in my wellbeing and the safety of our pup, Buddy. We even ended up on the news, raising awareness about the dangers of unleashed dogs in the neighbourhood. He wore his mask well, fooling everyone into thinking he was a loving, protective partner.

But behind closed doors, the story was different. To me, he downplayed the attack, dismissing my near-death experience as no big deal. I'll never forget the chilling moment he admitted, in a cold and detached tone, that he had heard my screams that day but didn't come running.

"I heard someone screaming," he said casually, like it wasn't worth investigating. "It didn't seem like a big deal." That scream was me. And he knew it. Deep down, I believe he knew. He just didn't care.

My father was furious when he heard this, recognising the husband's cruel agenda. But for me, it was the moment everything shifted. Stunned, I looked at him, my heart breaking as I realised what kind of man I had married. This was the guy who would run to help strangers at festivals. The one who prided himself on being the first to respond to someone in danger. But not for me. Not for his wife. Not for our dog.

He just sat there that day, smoking bongs chocked with marijuana, while my screams filled the stormy air.

He numbed himself while I and Buddy bled. That's who he was. He protected his high before he protected his wife and pup.

It's an eerie, almost surreal feeling to realise that the person who claims to love you could hear you in mortal danger and chose to do nothing. He didn't check where the screams were coming from. He didn't call the police to report someone in distress, he just stayed where he was, completely unmoved.

The delusion of marriage shattered. I had been so naive, such a fool. The chronic people pleaser in me started to wake up, shaking off the fog of manipulation I had lived in for years. Here I was, in 2019, entrenched in a nightmare marriage, wrapped in his web of lies, sexual exploitation, and daily demands. Drunken rages, violence that left no bruises other than those to my already low self-esteem. Relentless emotional manipulation had become my norm.

I gave everything to that marriage, everything, to my own detriment. And for what? I remember apologising to my body. "I'm sorry," I told myself. "I put him before you. I was blind, but now I see."

My eyes were opening to the madness of a marriage I had been trapped in but back then, I was thick in the insanity of his world. Lost in a pit of meeting his endless needs, I couldn't yet see the way out.

I was deep in the darkness, my spirit swallowed by despair. The weight of his demands pressed down on me relentlessly, leaving no room for me to breathe, to recover, or to escape. But even in that suffocating pit, a small flicker of awareness began to grow. I was starting to see him for who he truly was, and with that realisation came the first glimmer of hope that one day, I might break free.

As his birthday loomed closer, the relentless stress of my life felt like it was closing in. My surgery, finally scheduled for September 24th after years of pleading with doctors to take my period pain seriously, was just days away. This surgery, a laparoscopy to investigate endometriosis and adenomyosis. It was a lifeline, my chance to understand the cause of the relentless pain that had consumed my life for so long. Yet, instead of support, all the husband could focus on was his birthday.

Even though his best mate of nearly 20 years, Pixie, was celebrating her birthday at the same time, he acted like it was a minor inconvenience. "It's not the same," he scoffed when I pointed it out. "My birthday is more important."

Not my surgery, not his mate's milestone, just his birthday. In his mind, he was the most important and others just didn't matter to him. He expected to be treated like royalty, demanding admiration and attention as if he were a king. His entitlement was unrelenting, his ego insatiable. Once, he even told me he believed he was God. I stared at him blankly, unsure of how to respond. He hated my faith in God, so I didn't dare contradict him. I let it go, as I had learned to do with so many other things. But his self-centeredness was suffocating, draining the last reserves of energy I had left.

Living with him was like working in a residential care home for high-needs youth, except I couldn't clock out.

It was like running a crisis centre with no off-switch. But the crisis was him. I was the staff, the cleaner, the carer, the scapegoat, all rolled into one.

His behaviour mirrored that of five troubled teenagers rolled into one: violent tendencies, relentless demands, and deeply disturbing, highly sexualised behaviours that put himself and others at risk. His vices, alcohol, smoking, sex, porn, and partying, consumed his life, leaving me to pick up the pieces. Watching him drink can after can of cider, smoke endless bongs, and still remain the same miserable person was soul-destroying. He called it getting 'F.U.B.A.R', Fucked Up Beyond All Recognition, and it was his motto for life.

I understood addiction could stem from trauma, but where was the line where responsibility began? Where was the point where someone decided to stop blaming the world and end the cycle of harm? At the start of our relationship, he had presented himself as mature and independent. But the truth was far from that image. He had me running on the spot putting out all his spot fires. I was running on empty. My emotional and physical fuel tank was bone dry.

A Forced Return to Cruelty

The *Royal Women's Hospital* September 2019 had been a rare sanctuary. The care I received from the compassionate women there, a team that listened, believed, and treated me with respect, was a balm for my battered spirit. They understood my pain, validating what years of gaslighting had denied. I finally had a name for the agony that had ruled my life: endometriosis and adenomyosis. For the first time, I felt seen.

I couldn't return home after hospital. I needed care and there was no care there at all. When I returned to my parents' house to recover, I was surrounded by nurturing hands and kind eyes. My mother and father moved gently around me, bringing me drinks, ensuring I had everything I needed. Their care was a stark contrast to the cold indifference I had grown used to. For two days, I felt what it was like to be supported without demands, without cruelty.

Then, he showed up.

Without warning or consent, the husband stormed into my parents' home, his energy brimming with hostility.

For two sacred days, I remembered what love felt like. I had forgotten that tenderness existed. But that peace was short-lived.

He hadn't called, hadn't checked in, hadn't cared if I had survived the surgery. But now he was here, full of fury. Why? What did he want? My body, still sore from the incisions, tensed instinctively. Something about his presence felt like a violation. I was fragile, vulnerable, but he didn't care. He didn't ask how I was feeling. He didn't even meet my eyes. He was here to collect me like an object, dragging me back into his world. He didn't want to care for me, that much was clear. So why had he come to drag me back?

I felt my body react before my mind could process what was happening. A sharp unease prickled through me as he appeared in the doorway. His eyes burned with anger, his movements abrupt and aggressive. My parents looked at me, confused and concerned, silently asking why he was there. I had no answers.

He didn't explain. He didn't ask. He simply grabbed my things, roughly, carelessly, and barked orders for me to get moving. "Let's go. Traffic's going to be a nightmare," he snapped. It wasn't traffic he feared, it was losing control over me. This wasn't about love. It was about possession.

Reflection

The surgery was supposed to be a turning point, a moment of validation and relief. And in many ways, it was. I finally had answers for the pain that had consumed my life. But the aftermath was a stark reminder of the nightmare I was still living in.

But what no one tells you is that getting answers doesn't immediately bring healing, especially when you're still living with the source of your pain.

The cruelty of it all, his dismissal of my pain, the forced ride home, the lack of care, felt like a new low. Yet, even in that darkness, there was a glimmer of hope.

I should have felt relief. After years of doctors dismissing me, here was the proof: I wasn't crazy. My pain was real. But the validation I had waited so long for meant nothing to him. In his world, my body's suffering was just an inconvenience.

For the first time, I had a name for what was happening in my body. Though it was too late to reclaim the years lost to pain and gaslighting, it wasn't too late to start reclaiming myself.

That day in the hospital marked the beginning of a shift. I wasn't free yet, but I had begun to see the bars of the cage. As I drifted under anaesthesia, that small, quiet voice reminded me: *"You are not alone. This is not the end."*

For the first time in years, I believed it.

I knew I couldn't keep living this way. The surgery was a lifeline, but it was also a mirror, forcing me to confront the truth of my existence. I had spent years carrying his pain, his entitlement, his endless needs. But I didn't want to be his secret keeper anymore.

I didn't want the weight of his abuse to be mine to bear. I was done co-signing his silence with mine.

GRACE AMORE

As Maya Angelou wrote, "There is no greater agony than bearing an untold story inside you." I was done carrying the untold. I done suffocating under his weight. And when I finally named the pain, something inside me began to rise. Not yet free but no longer blind. Not yet flying, but wings stirring beneath the ash.

10: The Torture Chamber

⚠ **Content Warning!**

This chapter contains graphic content including sexual violence, marital rape, psychological abuse, coercive control, and drug-facilitated assault. It also explores the emotional isolation following surgery and the trauma of being violated by both a spouse and an acquaintance.

Please prioritise your wellbeing, if this chapter feels too heavy, it's okay to skip it or return when you feel safe. You are not alone. Support is available: 1800RESPECT (Australia) – 1800 737 732 (24/7 sexual assault, domestic and family violence counselling).

Your safety matters. While this chapter is confronting, it also marks a turning point, a quiet but powerful moment where I began to hear a whisper of hope: there is a way out.

With love and care,

Grace.

The night before, I had lain awake, staring at the ceiling. My mind circled an inescapable truth: He didn't love me. He never had. And yet, I was still trapped, bound to him by a thousand invisible marital, social, and familial chains of belief. That realisation should have prepared me for what came next. But nothing could have.

After the operation, every step hurt. My body was bloated from the anaesthetic gas and tender from the surgery. Each movement sending fresh waves of pain through me.

My parents' home felt like home. My own home felt like a prison. And my husband demanded I go with him. Back to prison.

I was too weak to resist as he grabbed my arm, his grip tight and unyielding. I winced, his touch amplifying the ache that already consumed me.

As we got into the car, terror set in. His anger filled the confined space, crackling like electricity in the air. He spat venomous words at me, blaming, berating, raging. He was so unhinged that I genuinely didn't know if I would survive the drive home. My heart pounded as fear coiled around me like a vice. Would this be the moment his rage finally erupted into something irreversible?

Every bump in the road sent fresh jolts of pain through my body, but he didn't care. He didn't think to offer me water or ask if I was comfortable. His spite and hatred were palpable, suffocating me with their weight. My parents had been so gentle, so attentive. Why couldn't I have stayed with them, safe and cared for? Why had he demanded I come home only to treat me this way?

What was so urgent about taking me home? He didn't want to care for me, that much was clear. His venom and spite felt like punishment, as though my vulnerability offended him. "Don't think you're staying at your parents' house, you're my wife. You go where I tell you."

I had gone from being nurtured by compassionate hospital staff and the safety of my parents' home to sitting in a vehicle with a man whose rage suffocated me. My husband, who hadn't visited me once during my hospital stay, seemed as though he wanted me dead. Not once did he ask how I was. His eyes were cold, deadly. His demeanour shattered any comfort I had clung to after surgery.

By the time we reached the house, I don't even know how I made it inside. I struggled to walk. The painful car journey had drained what little strength I had left. Once inside, I collapsed onto the couch, curling up with our pup, Buddy. Wrapped in a blanket, I tried to make myself as small and invisible as possible. Buddy stayed by my side, his warmth and presence offering the only sense of safety in that moment.

I didn't dare ask my husband for anything, not a glass of water, not food, not even a moment of basic care. And he didn't offer.

It was as though his rage needed no reason, as if the very act of me existing was enough to fuel his contempt. His hatred for me filled the air, thick and suffocating. I was terrified to move, even to breathe.

His fury didn't take long to escalate. Not long after we had arrived, he stormed into the lounge room, flinging open the sliding doors and unleashing a torrent of insults and accusations. His words were sharp, cruel, and full of venom, as though he had been saving them up for this moment when I was at my lowest and most defenceless. That face. That anger twisted; scornful face burned into my amygdala the fear I would feel deep in my body every day.

I don't know how long his tirade lasted. My body went into a state of paralysis, frozen in fear. It was as though I had left my body entirely, the pain and the terror too much to process. I lay there, curled up in a foetal position on that broken couch, like most things in our home, broken and neglected because he never wanted anything repaired or replaced. His money priorities were focused on his needs. Never ours. The darkness of despair swallowed me whole.

I was trapped. Alone with an unpredictable, raging husband, far from my family, with no safe space or privacy to call for help. My phone was nearby, but the idea of texting for help felt like a distant hope. I didn't know if he would check my messages or accuse me of something for even trying. I felt utterly powerless, my body too weak from surgery and pain medications to defend itself. The house had become a mental torture chamber, and I had no way out.

And then, the nightmare reached a new level of horror. Even before I got through the door, I knew I wasn't just returning to my husband's rage. There were others. Rover was one of my husband's friends. He was 50 years old, single bisexual businessman, that went to gay saunas. Rover was heavily into Amal sniffing; he seemed to always carry a bottle on him. It was a gay man's drug. He was tall and very confident, no hair, he carried a boldness.

Rover's van had been parked in our driveway more and more, a silent reminder that my body was never my own. Rover had a van, a sex van. It was set up with a mattress and a TV screen playing porn. He would park in our driveway, his arrival signalling an unspoken expectation.

> *"It was me and a gun, and a man on my back, and I sang, 'holy, holy, holy' as he buttoned down his pants."*
> *– Tori Amos, Me and a Gun*

The husband would regularly tell me, "I was his wife, and I owed him." He would say that in so many ways, repeatedly. "I was to submit to him," through jokes, or serious, or crying and complaining blaming me that he had to masturbate. It was my fault, and I owed him. "As a male, his needs were more important than mine."

The Violation

I thought the worst had already happened. I thought the worst was surviving the car ride, the screaming, the endless demands. But the worst was yet to come. And I never saw it coming.

Somewhere between the surgery in September and the end of that year, I was raped by my husband and this acquaintance. The other rapist was a man named Rover a businessman who travelled frequently. Someone we met at a gay sauna. Rover would come to our event which was for Gay, Lesbian, Bisexual, Transgender or Intersex (GLBTI) community. It was meant to be a safe-space, monthly event which was all about living your truth with love. The event was designed for people to feel accepted and a sense of belonging on their journey of exploration, in a bar in Melbourne's South-East.

The husband wanted to fuck me while he got fucked, and I hated it. I was nothing more than a conduit for their pleasure, a living sex doll.

I didn't have the words then, but now I know.

Under Australian law, what happened to me is called *rape*. Even in marriage, sex without consent is a crime.

It doesn't need to be violent to be illegal.

If it's coerced, through pressure, drugs, manipulation, fear, or if you're unable to say no, it's sexual assault.

I didn't consent. I froze. I endured. That wasn't consent. It was survival. The law sees that now. I wish someone had seen it then.

That Tuesday morning at 9 a.m., I was curled up on the couch with Buddy, my body still raw from surgery, when Rover let himself in, marching inside like a Gestapo soldier with the ugliest of confidence. Without a word, he pulled out a bag of cocaine, cutting a long, deliberate line across our kitchen bench.

The husband and Rover stared at me. Expectant. Waiting.

It was like being surrounded by wolves. I could feel them circling, their hunger palpable.

I knew what was coming.

I don't know how I got up and took the line, but I did, hoping it would numb me. Hoping it will anesthetise my body, dull the pain, and make me disappear for a while. But nothing could dull what followed.

I felt the cocaine rush into my bloodstream, but it didn't bring the numbness I hoped for. Instead, everything became too sharp, Rover's stare. The husband's expectant smirk. The way the room seemed to tilt and blur. I wasn't escaping. I was still here. If anything, it's as though everything became even more heightened. I knew I was fucked. Done. The end of me.

I had taken pain relief earlier that morning, but it was as though nothing was working. The only thing to do was mentally leave my body. The room closed in on me, darkness took over and what happened next, has taken years to find the words to express what happened on that Tuesday morning at 9am.

They took turns, violating me in ways that left permanent scars on my soul. They invaded every part of me except my backside, which they did to each other. The level of degradation and cruelty is something I struggle to put into words, a memory too vile to fully articulate.

One of these people called himself my 'husband.' The other called himself a 'man.' But in my mind, they were not even human. Certainly not part of human-kind. These are the kinds of 'men' that tarnish the male species the world over. It should be man's aim to clean up their image and honour their brand, their reputation.

What made it worse was the overwhelming silence. There was no one to stand up for me, no one to tell these two predators to leave me alone. I had no strength, no voice, and no defence.

Buddy stayed pressed against me, the only living thing in that house that loved me.

When they were finished, I didn't move for hours. I lay curled up in bed, staring at the ceiling, unable to comprehend what had just happened. I felt like I had left my body entirely, as if my soul had shattered and drifted away.

The house was silent, but not the kind of silence that brings peace. It was the silence of a graveyard, a place where something had died. The only sound was my own shallow breathing, and even that felt like too much. But I could still hear their laughter.

The Glimmer

Yet, even in that suffocating darkness, there was a glimmer of hope. For the first time, I had a name for what was happening inside my body: endometriosis and adenomyosis. Though it came far too late to reclaim the years lost to pain and medical gaslighting, it wasn't too late to start reclaiming myself.

As the days passed, I clung to that glimmer. In the face of unimaginable cruelty, it became my lifeline.

One small whisper of hope that maybe, just maybe, there was a way out of the devil's snare.

I thought if I didn't fight, it didn't count. But I know now, that's the lie patriarchy told us. Consent isn't about signing a contract on your wedding day. It's about choice, every single time. And I had none. He used my body like property. That is not love. That is a crime.

11: The Longest Night

The days after the assault blurred into each other, my body aching, my mind fractured. The house felt different, as if the walls themselves had absorbed the violence. I was trapped in a loop of pain and silence, my voice buried beneath the weight of what had been done to me. Psychologically, I knew I was conditioned to silence. I feared for my life and said nothing.

And then, as if nothing had happened, life moved on, at least for him.

The husband had started a job as a chef at a local venue around Christmas. As usual, I wasn't sure how long it would last. He had a pattern: tempers flaring, arguments brewing, and moving onto the next gig before the dust had settled. This new job seemed no different.

It was Christmas time when his workplace offered an open bar tab for staff, a gesture meant to spread holiday cheer.

That night, I stayed home. I was curled up in pain, the weight of post-surgery recovery pressing heavily on my body. The medications barely took the edge off the pain. Buddy, our pup, stayed close, his presence a source of quiet comfort as I drifted between moments of restless discomfort.

The husband no doubt was revelling in an open bar. The more he drank, the more scrambled his text messages became. At first, they were coherent, an update about work or casual remarks. But once the bar tab opened, the tone shifted. His texts turned erratic, barely legible, dripping with drunken carelessness. They came one after another, relentless, filling me with dread.

By midnight, my phone buzzed with his call. His voice on the other end was unmistakably drunk, slurring and sharp. "Come pick me up," he demanded, his words thick with alcohol.

I hesitated, my voice trembling. "I can't. I'm in pain. Please call a taxi."

His response was instant and venomous, filled with insults and rage. "You're a fucking bitch!" he spat, his tone turning menacing. The venom in his voice made my stomach churn. He hung up abruptly, but his threat lingered in the air like a storm cloud ready to burst.

I knew how this would go. The longer he had to stew, the worse it would be. Maybe if I had just agreed, if I had picked him up, none of this would be happening. Maybe I should have forced myself out of bed, ignored the pain, gotten into the car. But I was so tired. So, so tired. And I knew, deep down, that it wouldn't have made a difference. There was no winning with him. Only survival.

Anxiety shot through me like lightning, my body responding to the familiar red alert. My heart raced, and my breath quickened as Buddy stood on edge, sensing the rising tension. Buddy growled low, his stance protective, his body rigid as though an intruder was about to break in. It didn't matter that the husband wasn't physically in the house yet, his presence, his looming rage, invaded the space, suffocating me even from a distance.

I tried to lie down and rest, but my body was frozen with fear. My heart pounded so hard I could feel it in my throat. I hadn't healed from surgery, my health was declining after the trauma of the rape, and now his relentless demands were draining what little strength I had left. My mind was a foggy mess, unable to think clearly as the pain medications dulled everything but the terror. It felt like slaughter of the lambs, me, the lamb, waiting for the inevitable.

Hours passed. Around 2 a.m., Buddy's low growls began to rumble, his posture stiff as though preparing to protect me from an intruder. I froze. My senses heightened. Then I heard it, the unsteady shuffle of his footsteps. He had walked home from the venue, two hours in the cold, anger festering with every step.

The door opened, and there he stood. His eyes were wild, his movements unsteady, swaying drunkenly as he stumbled into the room. He hurled insults my way, the venom dripping off every word.

Buddy's growls grew louder; his body poised like a warrior ready to attack. "Buddy, it's me, it's Dad," the husband crooned, trying to feign friendliness. But our pup didn't buy it. His stance didn't waver, his instincts sharp.

I stood frozen in the corner, feeling like a spectator in my own life. It was as if I had left my body, watching the scene unfold from above. My heart pounded in my chest as fear gripped me like a vice. Buddy remained my only shield, standing between me and the man whose anger burned like a wildfire.

The husband's tone shifted rapidly, swinging from mock affection for Buddy to deadly threats toward me. His blackened eyes met mine, filled with a hatred that seemed bottomless. "You're dead," he muttered, his words cutting through the air like a blade.

It was after 2 a.m. now, and the chaos only grew louder. I *saw* the fury on his face before he exploded again, his fist punching a hole through the door, splinters flying, the jagged edges catching the light. The *sound* cracked through the house like a thunderclap, echoing off the walls, a physical manifestation of his rage. He cracked open another cider, the sharp hiss of the can splitting the silence, then *gulped it down* and lit the bong, the acrid *smell* of smoke clinging to everything. His *voice* was relentless, curses, insults, slurred threats, bouncing from room to room, swallowing the quiet of Christmas night.

I *felt* the tremble in my hands, my breath shallow, chest tight. My whole body was on edge, bracing. My *fingers hovered* over the screen of my phone. I thought about calling the police. The logical part of me, the part that analysed, reasoned, calculated, ran through every possible outcome. *Would they come? Would they believe me? Would it make things worse?* The fear screamed louder than the logic. My mind raced with questions, but my body *froze*. I knew what retaliation looked like, and it was worse than tonight.

By 4 a.m., he was still stomping, crashing, swearing, each step a *vibration through the floorboards*, each slam a jolt through my nervous system. The house felt *alive with tension*, every wall holding its breath. Buddy stayed by my side, his low growls grounding me in the *here and now*, reminding me I wasn't entirely alone. But the fear was suffocating. The air felt *heavy*, thick with threat, like the house itself was warning me, *anything could happen*.

> *"Beware; for I am fearless, and therefore powerful."*
> *– Mary Shelley, Frankenstein*

It was hard to believe this was Christmas. Hours earlier, he had been out drinking with his coworkers, revelling in the freedom of an open bar, while I lay curled up at home, fighting through waves of pain. Now, his volatility consumed the night, transforming our home into a battleground.

As dawn approached, I stared blankly into the fading darkness. The weight of his unpredictable anger, the hole in the door, and the threats that hung in the air settled heavily on my chest. This wasn't just another night; it was another descent into a deeper, darker pit, one that I wasn't sure I would survive.

The shadows of Melbourne's looming lockdown crept closer, promising an even greater isolation than I already felt. And yet, even in the chaos, Buddy's unwavering presence gave me the smallest glimmer of hope. While the darkness of the mire of anger threatened to swallow me whole, there was still a flicker of light, a fragile reminder that I wasn't entirely alone in the abyss.

I didn't have a name for it then, but looking back, I understand now what my body was trying to tell me.

The human body is wired for safety, for connection. But in that house, there was none. The nervous system doesn't just process pain, it stores trauma. And without safety, the body holds onto it like a secret.

"The true self needs limbic resonance to feel safe." Psych mechanics explain, 'Limbic resonance is defined as a state of deep emotional and physiological connection between two people. The limbic system in the brain is the seat of emotions. When two people are in limbic resonance, their limbic systems are in tune with each other.' (Psych Mechanics 2024. https://www.psychmechanics.com. Sourced 3 August 2024).

My understanding is that limbic resonance is about connection with others, as we are socially wired for relationship. Shapiro highlights in her book 'Still Writing: The Perils and Pleasures of a Creative Life' (2014), "The blessing is next to the wound."

The brain is connected to an intricate autonomic nervous system, heart, and integral body parts that impact behaviour. Shojai and Polizzi in their book *Trauma* encourage the reader.

"Releasing trauma takes time. Before you freak out, take a deep breath. This is a good thing. Every time you use a new therapy or therapist, embrace some ancient wisdom, or a natural remedy, or give yourself a new self-nurturing practice, you let go of a little pain which allows more light into your life" (pg. xviii, 2010).

The light will eventually become brighter, and the darkness dimmer and dimmer, until it no longer has a presence. As Shojai and Polizzi explain ...

"It's not the event that's traumatic; it's our response to it." In a section called 'Sage Wisdom' (pg.12. 2010), they reassure with a message of hope: 'There's this beautiful relationship between the body and the psyche where when we're in a situation that feels too much for our psyches to bear, the body says, "I'll take that, so you can keep going, so you can survive this."

Understanding Sexual Coercion and Consent in Australia

I wish someone had told me this at the time. I wish I had known what was happening wasn't just wrong, it was criminal. In Australia, marital rape is a crime. It doesn't matter if you're married, dating, or living together, you have the right to say no. Consent must be freely given, and you can withdraw it at any time.

Under Victoria's Crimes Act 1958, it is illegal to engage in sexual activity with someone who:

- is coerced, threatened, or manipulated
- is asleep or unconscious
- is too affected by alcohol or drugs to make decisions
- submits because they feel they "owe" it or are afraid to say no.

This includes within marriage. Being someone's wife does not mean you give up the right to bodily autonomy.

There are also laws in Victoria that recognise coercive control, a pattern of behaviour that isolates, manipulates, and removes your sense of safety or agency over time. It's subtle, layered, and incredibly damaging. And it's real.

If this chapter brought anything up for you, please know there is help available:

1800RESPECT (24/7) – 1800 737 732

Sexual Assault Crisis Line (Vic) – 1800 806 292

You are not alone. What happened to you was not your fault. And there is a way out.

With all my heart, Grace.

Reflection

As I look back on that night, the cruelty, the relentless rage, the suffocating fear, it's hard to grasp how I survived. The contrast was staggering as he had spent hours celebrating with his coworkers, enjoying the freedom of an open bar, only to come home and unleash his fury on me. The weight of his hatred, his threats, and the violence that loomed over every moment was almost unbearable. Yet, somehow, I endured.

The quote I chose for this chapter, *"Beware; for I am fearless, and therefore powerful,"* from Mary Shelley's *Frankenstein*, resonates deeply with this experience. It reflects the destructive nature of the husband's rage, his fearlessness in unleashing harm without regard for consequences. His power came from his lack of care, his absence of empathy, his willingness to cross lines no one should ever cross. In many ways, he embodied the monstrous, unchecked force Shelley described in her work.

But the quote also speaks to the subtle power within me that night. Though I was terrified, weak, and in immense pain, I remained. I didn't collapse under the weight of his cruelty, and I didn't retaliate in kind. Instead, I clung to what little light I had left, Buddy's loyalty, the hope that the night would end, and the faint belief that even in the darkest moments, survival was still possible.

The monstrous nature of his actions made me feel like a lamb led to slaughter, but in surviving that night, I began to see that I could still endure, still hold on, even when the darkness threatened to consume me. The 'fearless power' Shelley describes doesn't only belong to those who destroy, it also belongs to those who face the storm and refuse to break.

12: Chains of Control

The night after Christmas, something in me changed. I had spent years trying to reason with his rage, to soften his blows with silence. But as I lay awake in the wreckage of Christmas night, I realised, his power wasn't just in his fists or his words. His control ran deeper. And it was everywhere.

I told myself that if I stayed quiet, if I didn't provoke him, he would stop. But silence didn't save me. It only made him stronger. As time passed, silence turned into surrender. If I just gave up a little more, my faith, my friends, my finances, maybe then he would love me or leave me. Maybe then, the storm would pass.

His rage wasn't confined to drunken nights. It seeped into everything, my choices, my money, my very sense of self. That night was terrifying, but the real horror was knowing that I had nowhere to turn. He had cut me off from everyone, everything. Even my own bank account wasn't mine anymore. The husband took control of everything, and I lost control of everything including my own body and my life.

Fear was my constant companion. That night, as I lay in bed, the echoes of his threats still rang in my ears. But even as the house grew silent, the weight of his control never lifted. I wasn't just afraid of his fists or his drunken rages, I was afraid of the slow, quiet way he was erasing me.

I had become so isolated. Piece by piece, I let go of the things that once brought me joy, comfort, and purpose, believing it might ease the tension in our marriage.

One Sunday morning, I sat on the edge of the bed, debating whether to go to church. My hands shook as I reached for my shoes. I could already hear him in the other room, scrolling through porn, making it clear that my faith was nothing but a joke to him. If I left, there would be consequences, a cold shoulder, a cruel remark, another layer of distance between us. So, I stayed. And after that, I stayed again. Until one day, I realised, I had stopped going to church altogether.

I stopped volunteering. I distanced myself from family and friends and abandoned the gym and my health groups, spaces that had once been a lifeline for me. It seemed like everything I did upset him, so I thought if I let it all go, if I gave up the things that mattered to me, maybe it would calm the storm. Maybe things would get better.

But they didn't.

"In chronic abuse, incidents are just fragments: they rarely give precise shape to the whole. It's the atmosphere victims live in that keeps them in a state of high alert. Over time this climate of constant abuse and threat can end up shredding the nervous system." - Jess Hill, 'See What You Made Me Do: Power, Control and Domestic Violence

It started with Sunday church. Coercive control, as described by researcher Evan Stark, refers to patterns of domination that strip away a person's freedom and sense of self.

He hated it so much that I stopped going altogether, thinking it would help ease the tension. But it wasn't like he had plans for us to spend that time together, he didn't want me at church, but he didn't want me at all. Those hours became his sanctuary, not mine. He spent them glued to his computer, obsessively scrolling through porn sites, arranging hook-ups, and planning degrading acts he expected me to perform. Acts that repulsed me to my very core.

The laid-back guy I had first met was long gone. In his place was an angry, volatile man-boy who held no accountability, only judgment and endless bitterness. Our marriage became a relentless cycle of blame, if only I changed, if only I did things differently, then everything would be better. At least, that's what he told me. To say my marriage was stressful is an understatement. I felt like Sisyphus pushing a boulder uphill every single day.

The heaviness wore me down. I cried a lot, in the shower where no-one could see. I cried in the car on the way to work, in the rare quiet moments I had alone. But there was no resolution, no breakthrough. Just the daily torture of his angry tirades about how horrible the world was and his seething hatred of God. And because I had faith in what he mocked as an 'invisible God,' I became his target. I was the fool to him, the idiot who believed in something he found laughable.

I thought I had sacrificed enough to make things better, but nothing I gave up was ever enough.

What on earth was I living in? I asked myself that question over and over. Is this normal in a marriage? Are wives meant to honour and obey their husbands every whim? Is marriage meant to be this hard? But the shame of my reality kept my lips sealed. How could I possibly speak to anyone about this? The thought of exposing the truth, my truth, felt unbearable, like an invitation to judgment and rejection.

Judgment and rejection become a problem because they threaten our core need for belonging and safety.

"A deep sense of love and belonging is an irreducible need of all people. We are biologically, cognitively, physically, and spiritually wired to love, to be loved, and to belong." - *Brené Brown, The Gifts of Imperfection.*

In her work, she explains that the fear of judgment and rejection threatens our ability to feel safe in connection, which is why people often hide their true stories or silence their pain.

Additionally, psychologist Carl Rogers, a pioneer in person-centred therapy, wrote: "The curious paradox is that when I accept myself just as I am, then I can change.", Carl Rogers.

His work highlights how judgment, even perceived judgment, prevents healing, whereas unconditional acceptance fosters true transformation.

Stephen Porges, the founder of Polyvagal Theory, who teaches that: "Safety is the treatment.", *Stephen Porges.*

He explains that our nervous system is constantly scanning for cues of safety, and rejection or judgment signals *danger*, which shuts down our ability to connect, heal, or express ourselves.

For someone who has already been silenced, dismissed, or abused, the idea of *exposing the truth* can feel like standing naked in front of a crowd, waiting to be either embraced or condemned. It's not just a fear of being misunderstood, it's a fear that your deepest pain will be used *against* you.

Your nervous system, already wired for survival, associated truth-telling not with healing, but with *danger*. Because in your past, truth wasn't met with empathy. It was met with minimisation, shame, or more abuse. So, keeping it in felt safer than letting it out.

The thought of exposing the truth, *my* truth, felt unbearable, like an invitation to judgment and rejection. And that wasn't just fear talking, it was memory. Judgment and rejection had always been dangerous to me. Polyvagal Theory teaches us that when safety is compromised, the nervous system stays in a state of defence, freezing, fawning, or shutting down altogether.

I grew up in a culture of silence, where abuse was ignored, and pain was swept under the rug. Later, I lived in a marriage where I was mocked, gaslit, and shamed for even having needs or a voice. So, the idea of telling the truth didn't feel freeing, it felt like putting myself at risk. My nervous system had learned that speaking up led to more pain, not less. Judgment meant being dismissed. Rejection meant being left to suffer alone. I kept the truth inside, not because I didn't want to heal, but because I didn't yet believe it was safe to be seen.

I swallowed my despair. I buried my questions, my doubt, my anger, everything that made me who I was. Piece by piece, I surrendered myself, dying slowly to the life I once knew. I handed over my power to a wolf in sheep's clothing, deceived into believing that maybe this was just how things were meant to be.

And so, there I was, alone in a house steeped in darkness, cut off from everything and everyone that once made me feel alive. My life had become a hollow shell, the weight of it pressing down on my chest like a stone. I didn't know how much longer I could carry it.

Living with him meant surrendering autonomy in nearly every part of my life, even in matters as personal as finances.

According to the *Australian National Research Organisation for Women's Safety* (*ANROWS*), financial abuse is a common tactic of control in abusive relationships, where one partner restricts the other's access to money, employment, or financial decisions.

He often invoked his friends in finance during conversations, using their expertise as leverage to justify why I should pay my money into his home loan rather than my own. "It's smarter to put the money into the home you're living in," he'd say, framing it as logical and sound. But the advice wasn't impartial; it was another strand in his carefully constructed web of control.

I never stopped questioning the madness. Deep down, I knew something was very wrong in the marriage. But it was so hard to see clearly when his voice was constantly imposing itself on my thoughts. Every time I tried to think differently or offer another perspective; he'd put me down. "You don't know what you're talking about," he'd sneer. "I know better than you." His daily barrage of condescension and dismissal was relentless, designed to erode any confidence I had in my own judgment.

Still, I did everything I could to maintain a sliver of clarity. I sought ways to see things from a different perspective, holding onto the hope that there was a way out of this madness. But his grip was suffocating, his control a constant force, and the battle to hold onto myself became harder with each passing day.

If he discovered that I had put money toward my own home loan instead of his, his fury would ignite like a firestorm. He'd lash out with cruel words, calling me names and berating me for what he saw as outright defiance. "You don't listen! Every time we take two steps forward; you take us two steps back!" His voice was full of venom, cutting into me and leaving me questioning my own decisions. He'd insist, over and over, that he knew better than me, that I was incapable of making the right choices, and that all I needed to do was follow his lead.

Being far from my family and isolated within the confines of our marriage, I had no one to turn to for advice or support. There was no one to help me see the bigger picture, no one to tell me that his behaviour wasn't normal. Without a sounding board, I was left to navigate these decisions alone, under the weight of his constant criticism. The loneliness was suffocating, and slowly, I began to doubt myself. Maybe I wasn't good with finances. Maybe I was wrong, and he was right. Maybe I just needed to do what he said.

Over time, I gave up trying to manage or even understand my own money. Every effort to take control was met with his anger, and it became easier to let go than to endure another storm. But with each concession, I lost more than just financial independence, I lost pieces of myself. My autonomy slipped further and further away, leaving me feeling powerless and disconnected from my own life.

I never fully understood why I wasn't allowed to pay off my home loan. Whenever I tried to ask questions, he'd call me stupid, his impatience cutting through any confidence I had left. The embarrassment was overwhelming, and I withdrew deeper into myself. There was no safe space to seek clarity or ask questions about my own finances. I began to dread any financial discussions, knowing they would end in humiliation.

Even during bank appointments, he made it impossible for me to advocate for myself. If I asked a question, his eyes would roll dramatically, his sighs heavy with disdain. Under his breath, he'd mutter insults, calling me names that stung like a slap. In front of the bankers, he'd belittle me, telling me to hurry up, making me feel like a fool for trying to understand. His interference robbed me of any opportunity to learn or gain control over my financial situation.

Bit by bit, I lost not only my voice but also my belief that I could manage my own life.

I remember working tirelessly, hoping to carve out something for myself amidst the chaos. I made a decision that felt hopeful, a chance to invest in my own growth by paying for coaching. It was a glimmer of light in the darkness, a step toward clarity and learning in a life that felt increasingly out of my control. For the first time in a long time, I saw a path to better understanding myself, to finding my voice again.

When I signed up for coaching, it felt like breathing fresh air for the first time in years. It was something just for me, a choice I made, independent of him. For the first time, I felt a spark of control over my own life. But like everything else, it didn't last. His fury was swift, volcanic. And just like that, the small light I had found was snuffed out.

When he found out, his rage was volcanic. He despised the idea of me seeking help, of me learning from someone else, and he poured all his hatred onto my coach. His anger wasn't just about the money, though that was his excuse, it was about control. He couldn't stand that I had taken an independent step. The tirades were relentless, his accusations brutal. "You're irresponsible," he yelled. "You can't afford this. You're making life harder for both of us!"

His wrath left no room for reason, no space for me to explain why this was important to me. The barrage of insults and guilt became unbearable, and eventually, I stopped the coaching sessions. Another small piece of myself had been stripped away. Another attempt to grow, to heal, was extinguished by his wrath. I was left hollow, questioning whether I had made a mistake by trying to prioritise myself.

It felt like no matter what I did, nothing was ever good enough. Every decision I made, every effort to move forward, became another excuse for him to tighten his grip. He used each moment to remind me of my supposed failings, to hammer in the idea that I was powerless in his world. Bit by bit, I lost the ability to fight back, to defend myself against the endless wave of criticism and control. Desperation replaced hope, and the walls of his dominance closed in around me.

Reflection

Financial abuse was a pervasive and insidious part of our marriage. He had a way of using others, bankers, friends, anyone with a financial background, to back his narrative and pressure me into doing what he wanted. It wasn't direct threats; it was manipulation cloaked in 'advice' that always seemed to come from an external source. When I hesitated or tried to assert my own judgment, he would cut me down with sharp words that chipped away at my confidence.

Looking back, I can see how those constant put-downs were designed to erode my sense of worth and capability. It worked. Bit by bit, I stopped trusting my instincts, convinced that he must be right, and I was wrong.

By the time I left my last job, all my salary packaging had gone into his home loan, $30,000 of my hard-earned money. When I brought it up, hoping he might acknowledge it as a contribution, he dismissed it entirely, minimising the amount and its significance. "It wasn't that much," he said, as if to erase the effort and sacrifice behind it.

This financial abuse didn't just hurt me in the marriage; it left me severely limited when I finally got out. I had no financial safety net. In the throes of the 2020 lockdown, with no income coming in and mounting medical needs, I had no choice but to take $10,000 from my super just to survive. Even then, he had already sold the house and taken the settlement money along with most of our belongings.

He showed no concern for my situation, not for my medical needs, my homelessness, or the fact that I was too unwell to work. If it hadn't been for my parents stepping in, I don't know where I would have ended up. On the streets? Or worse, dead from the unrelenting toll on my body and spirit.

This reflection isn't just about the financial abuse but the devastating ripple effects it had on my life. It stole not only my resources but also my sense of security and stability.

Research from organisations such as ANROWS (Australia's National Research Organisation for Women's Safety) shows that survivors of financial abuse often face long-term economic instability, even after leaving the relationship, due to coerced debt, lost income, and depleted superannuation.

I lived that reality. By the time I left my last job, all my salary packaging had gone into his home loan, $30,000 of my hard-earned money.

Yet, even in that reflection, I see resilience. I see the strength it took to survive, to endure, and to eventually find a way forward. Financial abuse was one of his tools, but it wasn't the end of my story. It was a chapter, a dark one, but not the conclusion.

I had nothing left. My money was gone. My faith was ridiculed. My body was breaking under the weight of years of abuse. The chains weren't just around my finances; they were wrapped around my very soul. I felt like I was disappearing, dissolving into nothing.

13: Through Death's Door a New Beginning

After years of surviving on his terms, something inside me had given up in 2020. The weight of his control had drained me of everything, my faith, my finances, my sense of self. Now, my body was following. I was shutting down, fading away, and I barely had the energy to care. But God wasn't done with me yet.

At first, I thought it was just the stress. My body ached constantly, and no amount of rest seemed to ease the exhaustion. My stomach twisted in knots, rejecting food. I had been losing weight, but I barely noticed until I looked in the mirror and saw someone unfamiliar staring back. Something was very wrong.

"Through Death's Door to a New Beginning" – Epigraph.

A Foreboding Alert

The day I learned about COVID-19, something stirred deep within me, a quiet, foreboding alert in my spirit. I couldn't pinpoint exactly what it was, but the unease was undeniable. It felt as though an unseen evil had been unleashed, cloaked in the guise of a global crisis.

In Victoria Australia, under MP Dan Andrews, the 48th Premier, and nationally under MP Scott Morrison, the 30th Prime Minister of Australia, fear and control seemed to dominate governance. The shifting rules and ever-changing restrictions mirrored the dynamics of my marriage. Just as I never knew what to expect with my husband, his mood swinging unpredictably, his words cutting like a knife, the government's sudden impositions felt like psychological warfare.

GRACE AMORE

A Prison Inside a Home

At home, the abuse had become suffocating, and the imposed lockdown amplified my already unbearable isolation.

Losing my job in March 2020 was devastating. Work had waited six months for me to recover and return to work, but due to the high demands of the work, my position had to be filled, and so I received a letter of termination due to medical reasons. This letter was like receiving a funeral notice for my death, as I was going to be at home 24 hours with my abuser in Melbourne's lockdown. Financial abuse had already drained me, and now, without an income, I was even more vulnerable.

Research by Australia's National Research Organisation for Women's Safety (ANROWS) shows that during the COVID-19 lockdowns, financial abuse intensified for many women, particularly those already isolated by controlling partners. The pandemic's economic strain, combined with coercive control, created a heightened risk environment for those experiencing domestic abuse.

The house that should have been a refuge was a nightmare. My sisters called it 'the dungeon,' a fitting name for a place where doors didn't close properly, except for the bathroom and toilet. Any attempts I made to repair or improve the house were belittled by him.

His words defined every corner of my existence. "You're a defective female for not giving birth." "You're worthless." "You'll never amount to anything." He dictated who I was, what I thought, and how I felt, leaving no room for me to have an identity outside of his control. I remember standing in front of the mirror one night, staring at my reflection. His words whispered through my mind like a curse. "You're defective." "You're worthless." I traced the shadows under my eyes, the sharpness of my collarbones. Who was I anymore? Maybe he was right. Maybe I really was nothing.

Patricia Evans' words echoed in my mind during those moments: "The verbally abusive person tries to control the partner by defining the partner." He didn't just define me; he erased me. I didn't know who I was anymore.

Fear of Escape

There were times I thought about calling the police. But the idea filled me with dread. Could I even speak through the fear? What if they didn't believe me? What if they left, leaving me to face his fury alone?

I picked up my phone, my fingers hovering over the screen. If I called, would they believe me? Or would they leave me here, trapped with him? I imagined the moment they walked away, the door shutting behind them, leaving me alone with his fury. My stomach turned. If the police left without helping, I wouldn't survive the night.

The thought paralysed me. I pictured sitting in the back room, trying to make myself invisible as his rage filled the house. His voice, venomous and loud, reverberated off the walls, drowning out my own.

What would happen if the police came? Would they see through his charm, or would they leave me in even greater danger? The unknowns froze me in place.

Survival in the Shadows

So, I stayed silent, enduring the chaos, waiting for him to exhaust himself into unconsciousness. It was a miserable kind of survival. The nights stretched endlessly, and the fear of what might happen next consumed me.

Even as I fought to find a way out, the shame of my situation weighed on me. His words, "You're nothing. You're worthless.", were like chains, tightening with every outburst. The very thought of explaining my reality to someone else felt insurmountable.

GRACE AMORE

The Lockdown's Mirror

As Melbourne went into lockdown in 2020, the parallels between my marriage and the government's actions became chillingly clear. Isolation, fear, and coercive control were the tools of both my husband and the state.

In Victoria, coercive control is increasingly being recognised in legal and policy frameworks. While not yet a standalone criminal offence at the time, growing recognition has led to its inclusion in family violence risk assessments, such as under the MARAM framework. It reflects non-physical abuse like isolation, threats, and micro-control that erode autonomy.

Under the guise of protection, countless people were trapped in unsafe environments, with no reprieve or escape.

The media, complicit in spreading fear, amplified the isolation. Families turned against one another, friendships fractured, and communities were broken apart. The government's actions reflected the patterns of abuse described in the *'Power and Control Wheel*,' weaponising fear to strip away autonomy and creating silence and dissent.

Despair and Deterioration

By May, my health had deteriorated drastically. I lost 20 kilos at an alarming rate, unable to keep food down. Vomiting and diarrhea were constant, and I felt like I was wasting away.

I had spent years trying to shrink myself, to survive in the shadows of his control. But now, my body was screaming for an escape my mind had long been too afraid to take. I wasn't just breaking, I was dying. And then, God spoke.

One night, as I lay on the couch, I had a vision of my death, riddled with cancer, slumped lifeless. God's voice cut through the darkness: "Grace, if you don't leave this house, you will die in three weeks. You need to stay alive to tell your story."

These words came after I saw a vivid and terrifying vision of my own death. In the vision, I was slumped on the couch, riddled with cancer, lifeless and alone. My husband stepped past me without a second glance, his indifference a chilling reminder of how little he cared. The sight was haunting, but it was the clarity of God's voice cutting through the darkness that shook me to my core.

This moment was pivotal. It was as though God Himself was reaching into the abyss, pulling me back from the edge. His instructions weren't just about survival; they were about reclaiming life, breath, and hope.

A Lifeline: Psalm 23

In my darkest hour, when I could no longer see a way out, God gave me clear instructions: "Get your headphones. Play Psalm 23 on repeat with sound healing instruments. Let the vibrations feed life into your spirit. Keep your headphones in 24 hours a day to block out your husband's deathly dribble."

After years of surviving on his terms, something inside me had given up. The weight of his control had drained me of everything, my faith, my finances, my sense of self. Now, my body was following. I was shutting down, fading away, and I barely had the energy to care. But God wasn't done with me yet.

In the midst of chaos, God's voice broke through, offering clarity and a way forward. Psalm 23 became a sanctuary, leading me toward the peace I had been yearning for.

It was a glimpse of light.

Psalm 23 became my lifeline, the words resonating deep within my spirit:

> *"He makes me lie down in green pastures: He leads me beside still waters. He restores my soul." – Psalm 23; 2-3.*

GRACE AMORE

As I listened to Psalm 23 on repeat, accompanied by sound healing instruments like the didgeridoo, I felt something begin to shift. The imagery within the psalm, the green pastures, the still waters, transported me to a sanctuary far away from the prison of my marriage. I began to visualise a serene place where streams of water flowed gently, trees and palms swayed in the breeze, and sunlight danced through the leaves.

The sound of the didgeridoo added a grounding, earthly resonance, vibrating deeply throughout my body. It felt as though those vibrations were reaching into the parts of me that had been frozen in fear, unlocking places of tension I hadn't realised were there. The combination of scripture and sound brought me moments of reprieve, moments where the madness around me receded and my spirit could breathe.

I could hear the water, see the lush greenery, feel the soft breeze on my skin, and be transported to a space that was safe, calm, and nurturing. This vivid imagery, paired with the deep, earthly vibrations of the didgeridoo, created a sensory sanctuary that helped my mind and body escape, even if only for moments at a time.

This practice didn't fix everything, but it gave me something essential: a break from the relentless chaos. It was a way to create space within myself, to reconnect with the promise that God was still with me. My nervous system, long trapped in a state of terror, began to find brief moments of calm.

Psalm 23 was more than a prayer; it became a vision of hope. Each verse reminded me that even in the valley of the shadow of death, I was not alone. God was leading me beside still waters, restoring my soul, and showing me that there was a life beyond the nightmare I was living.

The healing vibrations of the sound instruments combined with the sanctuary of the psalm's imagery felt like lifeblood to my weary spirit. It reminded me that there was a world outside of the prison I was in, a world full of life, peace, and renewal.

This simple act, immersing myself in Psalm 23 and its imagery while letting the deep, resonating sounds wash over me, became the first step in reclaiming my sense of self. It wasn't just a momentary escape; it was a lifeline, a whisper of hope in the midst of overwhelming darkness. Through this, I began to believe that my story wasn't over. God was still with me, guiding me to freedom, to healing, and to a life beyond the nightmare.

I wore the headphones constantly, day and night, even as my ears began to ache. It didn't matter. Each time I heard the words of Psalm 23; they became more than just a prayer, they became a promise. The vibrations seemed to touch places within me that had been locked away by fear and despair. It was as if God was drip-feeding life back into my broken spirit, one verse at a time.

I didn't expect the practice to magically or spiritually fix everything, but it gave me something essential: the ability to breathe, to slow my racing heart, to create space between myself and the chaos that surrounded me. My nervous system, long trapped in a state of relentless terror, began to find moments of reprieve.

Psalm 23 was more than a prayer or a song; it was a thread connecting me to God's unwavering presence. Each verse reminded me that even in the valley of the shadow of death, I was not alone. It was a profound reminder that God was leading me beside still waters, restoring my soul in ways I couldn't yet understand.

This simple act, putting on the headphones, immersing myself in Psalm 23, and letting the healing vibrations work through my body, became the first step toward freedom. It was a lifeline, a whisper of hope in the midst of overwhelming darkness. Through this, I began to see that my story wasn't over. God was still with me, guiding me, and giving me the strength to take the next step forward.

Sue: A Friend in Darkness

The husband was cautious not to allow me to have friends other than the one's he had. There was Pixie from Bairnsdale way and would stay the weekend at times. Like all my friends, I knew Pixie through the husband. She and I became good friends, there was a time during the lockdown period while still married she came over to stay, and I broke down in her arms. He just watched and went off for his bong. Pixie had known him for nearly 20 years and never knew what was going on in my marriage. I never told her. The husband ensured that I didn't have any privacy with her, he was always there.

Most of my friends came from the 'sex' world. It was an incestuous world.

Around this time, Sue, a dear friend, became a beacon of light in my suffocating existence. Her visits were orchestrated by God, bringing moments of hope and reprieve when I felt the most trapped. Sue was not just a friend; she was an angel who heard my cry for help and answered with unwavering conviction.

I met Sue through my husband. They had first crossed paths while working in the film catering industry, a world that was fast-paced, chaotic, and filled with fleeting connections. Yet, Sue was different. She had a warmth that cut through the noise, a steadiness that felt rare. In the darkness that surrounded me, she became a light, a presence that offered me something I hadn't realised I was starving for: kindness without condition, friendship without pretence.

Sue would bring over leftover food from work. This act wasn't just about the food; it was like having family come over. It was the warmth and love she brought with the food that made the difference. Each meal she shared carried with it a quiet reassurance, a reminder that I wasn't alone.

Looking back, I realise that meeting Sue was no accident. She was meant to be there, to remind me that light can still break through, even in the deepest darkness.

Sue's faith in God's love was evident in everything she did. She saw my despair, even when I couldn't fully articulate it. Despite my fragmented words, she understood the urgency when I said, "Stream, Nimbin, hemp embassy, take me to Nimbin."

What made me crave Nimbin? It wasn't just a place, it was a memory of healing, of being seen, of something spiritual washing over what felt unspeakable. After my first miscarriage in the first year of our marriage, I was shattered. We were meant to be going on a road trip while pregnant, but instead, we left in the wreckage of that loss. Our daughter, whom I named Violet, though he never called her by name, had passed from an ectopic pregnancy.

On the day we lost her, his friends arrived with their newborn and stayed over, as though nothing had happened. I felt erased, suicidal, like I no longer existed. Our first stop on that road trip was Nimbin, where an Indigenous man approached me in the main street, looked me straight in the eye, and said, "You need to come with me."

He took us to a sacred birthing site deep in the rainforest, where three streams meet, where women once went to give birth on country. There, he held a ceremony for me. I was guided into the water, covered in ochre, and told I was surrounded by the grandmothers and aunties of the past. He invited me to release my grief. I wept, I wailed, and something heavy lifted. The suicidal thoughts dissolved. Something ancient, deep, and holy moved through me. That place held healing in its waters.

Years later, when I was unravelling again, I cried out to Sue, "Stream, Nimbin, Hemp Embassy, take me to Nimbin." I wasn't just seeking a location. I was seeking a return to that sacred space where my grief was first witnessed and honoured, where I was told I was safe. Where I remembered I wanted to live.

Without hesitation, she responded with compassion and determination: "I'll get you there." She didn't need long explanations or justifications. Her eyes told me she knew exactly what I needed, and she was prepared to do whatever it took to help me. In that moment, as Sue said, "I'll get you there," I felt a flicker of relief that I had been seen and heard. Validated.

I knew in my bones, in my spirit I had to get to Nimbin, it was as though the three streams were calling out to my womb. To be washed clean again, but this time, not just grief of 3 babies but also the shame that weighed me down like death.

For the first time, someone truly saw my pain and was willing to act on my behalf, no matter the cost. Sue and I sat with the husband and told him that Sue was driving me to Nimbin, but I don't think he took it seriously because he seemed to shrug it off, even though we had asked how much fuel he would think it would cost to drive to Nimbin.

Sue's role in my escape was pivotal. She didn't just offer a listening ear; she organised her entire life to make the journey possible. Driving me to Nimbin, New South Wales, was no small task. It was a 20-hour drive, an extraordinary act of love and sacrifice. Her conviction for God's love fuelled her actions, and her unwavering support reminded me that I wasn't alone, even in my darkest hour. It is hard to put into words what it felt to be validated.

Her presence woke me up to the reality of my abusive marriage. Through her kindness and gentle persistence, I began to see the truth: my husband's actions were not love, and staying with him would only lead to my destruction. Sue's clarity and steadfastness were a lifeline, pulling me from the fog of manipulation and despair.

In that trip June 2020 with Sue, I saw how harmful my marriage had been. The man I had once trusted had isolated me, demeaned me, and erased my sense of self. But Sue's actions, her conviction for God's love, and her determination to help me escape, made one thing clear: I could never go back.

"The verbally abusive person tries to control the partner by defining the partner. The partner may be told what they are thinking and feeling, and told what they need and want, and even told what they are doing and why. The partner is often told what they are, and are not, in negative ways." - Patricia Evans, The Verbally Abusive Relationship: How to Recognise it and How to Respond

Reflection: Drip-Feeding Life

Looking back, the words I received from God, "Drip feed life into your spirit" were a turning point. They reminded me how close to death I had come and how vital it was to fight for my survival.

Sue's unwavering faith and God's presence were my anchors. This was more than an escape, it was the start of a journey back to life, to healing, and to the realisation that my story wasn't over.

Patricia Evans' quote ties it all together: I had been defined, controlled, and erased. But through God's grace, I began to reclaim my identity. The chains were breaking.

God was still writing my story. And this was just the beginning. This was not just the end of my captivity, it was the beginning of my rebirth.

As I felt the distance between my husband and I, my body still trembled from withdrawal, my mind clouded by exhaustion. But something stirred deep within me. It wasn't just escape, it was a longing for something more.

Not just survival, but healing. Not just freedom, but safety. I didn't know what that felt like anymore. But I was about to find out.

Experts in trauma recovery highlight that reclaiming one's nervous system regulation, such as through music, breath, or safe relationships, is foundational for healing. Psalm 23 paired with sound instruments offered not just spiritual comfort but also somatic relief for my overwhelmed nervous system.

14: Sanctuary in the Storm

Water. It had always called to me in moments of deep pain. The beach walks during lockdown, the way I let the waves carry my sorrow, the sound of rain tapping on my window as I lay in bed after another fight.

Now, in Nimbin, New South Wales, the rainforest hummed around me, and all I wanted was to submerge myself, to let the past be washed away, to feel my body truly belong to me again. My soul cried out for renewal, and my bones ached to be free from the weight of my marriage. I felt so dirty I wanted to sit in a stream for a year and have all the filth of that life be washed from my body. I yearned to be in resonance with another human being.

"Safety is communicated through the physiological state of another person, especially through tone, eye contact, and posture, engaging our social brain." Limbic resonance in this context means that through social cues and emotional alignment, people co-regulate and feel safe, which is critical in trauma healing."
- Steven Porges.

A Safe Place to Scream

For years, I had lived in a state of hypervigilance. My nervous system was always on high alert, scanning for danger, waiting for the next verbal assault or cruel dismissal. But now, sitting in the stillness of the rainforest, I felt something different, a presence, a warmth I hadn't known in years. Safety. And safety wasn't just about physical distance from harm; it was about the presence of someone who truly saw me.

Sue was more than a friend, she was like an angel social worker, sent to pull me out of the suffocating darkness of my marriage. Her unwavering faith in God and her deep care for my well-being were evident in everything she did. She didn't mince words when it came to my situation. "You can't go back to that marriage," she told me, her voice firm yet compassionate. She saw the truth of my pain and refused to let me minimise it.

That Sunday night, the pain poured out of me. I screamed so loudly into the rainforest around the cabin that it felt as though the trees themselves absorbed my agony. For the first time in years, I felt safe enough to release the grief, anger, and despair I had held inside. The lush, green oasis of the cabin became a sanctuary, a sacred space where I could finally breathe, cry, and let go.

The Cost of Healing

Detoxing from pharmaceuticals was a battle. I knew I could feel my kidneys crying out to stop all the pharmaceuticals. That I was going to die if I continued to take these synthetic drugs, as my body had had enough. it would be hard, but I didn't realise just how brutal it would be.

Withdrawing from opioid-based pain medication after prolonged use isn't just uncomfortable, it's traumatic for the body. The body goes into survival mode. The vomiting, cold sweats, tremors, spasms, and disorientation aren't signs of weakness; they are the body's response to suddenly losing the chemicals it had come to rely on for basic functioning and pain regulation.

The next morning, Sue had to return to Melbourne for work. I was heartbroken to see her go; she had been my lifeline. Sue left from Lismore, catching a bus back to Melbourne. I was supposed to drive her, but my car wouldn't start that morning, a strange occurrence that felt almost supernatural. The cabin owner kindly drove Sue to Lismore, ensuring she made it to the bus, while I sat dazed in the back of the car, battling the nausea and fog of withdrawal.

Alone in the cabin, I faced the hardest week of my life. The detox hit my body like a freight train. I looked like a skeleton of myself. It hurt to move, every step feeling like my body was being torn apart. Spasms wracked my muscles, contractions gripped my abdomen, and the pain was unbearable. My body didn't know what had hit it, I was in a washing machine of withdrawals. Showering required too much energy. Vomiting and diarrhea left me weak and depleted. One night, I vomited so violently and so often that I genuinely didn't know if I would survive until morning.

A Husband's Betrayal

While I was battling for my life in Nimbin, my husband was sleeping with an acquaintance in our bed. I would later find out they weren't shy about their affair, flaunting it without a shred of decency or respect. This revelation would come later, but even then, the seeds of understanding were taking root. Each betrayal made it clearer that going back to him was not an option.

A Desperate Moment

At one point, I realised I desperately needed toilet paper. My mind was so clouded by withdrawal and pain that I didn't think to ask for help. I forced myself to walk to the shop, but on my way back, the pain overwhelmed me. I collapsed onto the grass in the park, my body gripped by violent contractions. Three strangers approached me, concern in their eyes. Their kindness was humbling, and heartbreaking. These three strangers showed me more compassion than my husband ever had.

Somehow, I dragged myself to Nimbin's small hospital. The staff noticed how erratic I was, laughing one moment, crying the next. A nurse called my younger sister, Angela, for insight into my mental health baseline. Angela was amazing. She asked the most basic, human questions: "Has she eaten? Has she showered? Has she had anything to drink?"

A nurse named Nicole, the same name as my niece, sat with me. She brought me a sandwich and a warm Milo, gently encouraging me to eat and drink. Her kindness broke me. I wept, telling her how much I missed my nieces and nephews. She cried with me as I opened up about everything, the pain, the betrayal, and the gratitude I felt for Sue.

What Nicole did was trauma-informed care in its simplest, most powerful form. She didn't try to fix me. She didn't give me advice. She just showed up. Trauma-informed healthcare begins with human connection, being seen, being fed, being spoken to gently. That's what heals. It's not always the medication or the treatment plan; it's often a warm Milo and a nurse who sees you.

The Drive Home: A Supernatural Journey

By Wednesday night, my body was weak, trembling from the sweats, spasms, and relentless pain. Then, a terrible body memory slammed into me, the rape after my surgery by my husband and his acquaintance. The memory was so vivid it felt like I was reliving it. I screamed out in pain, the rainforest absorbing my cries. That night, through the tears, I sensed something in my spirit: my mum needed me home.

Four days later, on Monday, I began the 20-hour drive back to Melbourne. My father had considered flying to get me, but Melbourne's lockdown rules were tightening. The journey home felt impossible, but I clung to a quiet prayer: "With God, all things are possible."

I forced myself to eat small meals, stocked up on tissue salts, magnesium, and plant-based medicine. The freezing winter air kept me awake as I drove, my body screaming for rest. I found two places to stop and sleep, both owned by incredibly kind people who encouraged me to keep going. Their kindness was a balm to my weary soul.

As I neared Melbourne, exhaustion nearly claimed me. My eyes were heavy, my body pleading for rest. At one point, I swear an angel sat next to me, guiding the wheel.

There's a spiritual phenomenon that trauma survivors often describe, a moment where something unseen steps in. Whether you call it God, an angel, or divine protection, many who've been through life-threatening experiences speak of a presence that helped them hold on. For me, it was real. I believe it was God keeping me alive, whispering, *you will not die here.*

The semi-trailers ahead of me felt like they were sent to keep me on track, making sure I didn't fall asleep. I was barely hanging on, but I knew I had to make it home. I repeated my prayer like a chant: "With God, all things are possible."

Finally, after what felt like an eternity, I arrived at my parents' house at 9 p.m. When my mum saw me, I knew something had happened to her. She had taken a major fall down an escalator, but she was okay. So was I. A miracle on both sides.

This chapter of my journey marked the beginning of a new chapter, one where I would fight to reclaim my life, my health, and my freedom. It was the end of one battle and the beginning of another. The next part was facing my husband.

Reflection: The Power of Safety

Steven Porges wrote, "Safety is communicated through the physiological state of another person."

According to Polyvagal Theory, our nervous system is constantly scanning for cues of safety. It listens not to words, but to *tone*, *body language*, and *presence*. That's why Sue's kindness, Nicole's eyes, and the rainforest's stillness did something no medication could, they helped my nervous system feel safe enough to begin healing.

In Nimbin, I finally understood what that meant. Sue, family, the kind strangers, the nurses, even the rainforest itself, each had given me moments of safety. Moments where my nervous system could finally begin to heal.

For the first time, I believed that healing was possible. That life could be different. That I wasn't beyond saving.

I had made it home. I had survived. But I wasn't free yet. The final battle was still ahead.

.

15: The Reckoning

As I packed my things from the cabin in Nimbin, a deep sense of foreboding settled in my gut. I had glimpsed freedom, but I wasn't free yet. Melbourne loomed ahead, a battlefield waiting for my return. The weight of unfinished business, of finalising the marriage, of navigating his manipulations, all of it pressed down on me. I took one last deep breath of the rainforest air, trying to hold onto the stillness, knowing I was walking straight back into the storm.

Nimbin had given me a taste of what safety felt like, but safety is not the same as freedom. I wasn't free yet. The reckoning was waiting for me, the final unravelling of the marriage, the truth of what I had sacrificed, and the cold, hard realisation of what I was walking away from. But I knew, deep down, that I could never go back.

From the sanctuary of Nimbin into the chaos of Melbourne's 2020 lockdown, my body was a battlefield of triggers. I had come from a quiet, peaceful town into Melbourne, where the nerves seemed on edge, every breath heavy with the weight of survival.

It's fascinating how quickly the world was told to isolate, mask up, and keep their distance, fear pumped into every message, millions spent reinforcing the idea that we were all under threat. And all in the name of health. But was it really about health? From the very start, my gut screamed otherwise. A complete and utter farce. That was my gut from the get-go with this 'plan-demic.'

Yet, amid the chaos, I had an even bigger battle to fight, planning my escape from my marriage. But with my health unravelling faster than ever, one question haunted me: How could I possibly pull it off?

Amongst the madness I had to find a way to organise my escape out of the marriage. The question loomed, "How could I do it when my health was in such rapid decline?"

Returning to Cranbourne was surreal.

I knew I had to keep focused on the task of finalising the marriage, without using the word divorce, as with all things it's important that the idea comes from him and not me. He must feel in control. Otherwise, he could make life worse than the hell it already was. I had to be careful and strategic, especially being as unwell as I was. Tactful, vigilant and alert were my three keywords for 'operation escape.'

Many survivors in coercive or high-control relationships report having to develop "safety planning" strategies that prioritise the abuser's perception of control to avoid retaliation. These are common survival mechanisms when navigating coercive control dynamics, especially during illness or crisis.

Returning to Cranbourne wasn't a step backward, it was a calculated move. I knew I could never truly go back to the life I had in that house. But I also knew I couldn't just walk away without a plan. My body was unwell, my nervous system fried, and he was unpredictable. My plan wasn't dramatic, it was quiet, internal, strategic. I had to finalise the marriage without using the word divorce, because with him, control was everything. If he felt it was his idea, things would be smoother. If not, the fallout could be dangerous. I focused on essentials, what needed to be retrieved, what loose ends had to be tied, what emotional bait I had to sidestep. Tactful. Vigilant. Alert. That was the mantra. I wasn't returning to rekindle or confront; I was returning to *complete*. To gather the last pieces of my old life before stepping fully into my new one.

Safety planning, as described in domestic violence literature, often requires a strategic, quiet form of resistance. It involves minimising perceived threats to the perpetrator's control, which can prevent escalation and provide space for the survivor to act.

When I saw Buddy, I was so happy but also sad. My conscious triggered my love for Buddy but unconsciously I anticipated losing him. I knew we were in a transition where I may not see Buddy ever again.

In many cases of intimate partner violence, pets become part of the coercive control system. Abusers may use them to manipulate, isolate, or threaten their partners. Studies have shown that 1 in 4 survivors delay leaving an abusive relationship out of fear for their pet's safety.

There he was bounding toward me, and I lathered him with my love. Though it had only been a short time away, maybe about 2 weeks, it felt like an eternity had passed.

With my body going through such extreme changes, the days seemed to have stretched and blurred under the strain of detoxing, and being back in the house felt like stepping into another reality. Hugging Buddy, stroking his soft fur, was a brief but grounding moment of comfort amidst the chaos.

In the short time away, the husband had been up making changes, big changes. I quickly learned that while I was away, the husband had made a monumental decision without me: the house was up for sale. He and his mother had discussed it, and he decided to sell the property and move up north to Queensland.

Nothing was ever clear with him. He never said outright that I was going with him, and he never said I wasn't. It was all left in the air, just enough implication to keep me guessing, to keep me emotionally entangled. At one point, he mentioned that once the settlement came through, he'd get me a new car. It sounded like a gesture of care, but I knew better. He hadn't even given me $50 when I needed it. His promises were never real, they were tools to manage me, to string me along just enough so I wouldn't break away completely. Everything was vague, strategic, unspoken. That was how he operated: silence, suggestion, and control cloaked as generosity.

The announcement hit me like a slap. There was no discussion, no consideration for me or the reality I was navigating. This decision, like so many others, was made entirely in his self-interest, a reminder of just how invisible I was in this relationship.

Yet, as shocking as the news was, I felt a strange flicker of opportunity. If the house was being sold, maybe this could be my chance to finally break free.

Yes, leaving for Nimbin was the beginning of my emotional and spiritual breaking free, it was where the fog started to lift and where I heard, for the first time, a clear and loving voice calling me to live. But the news of the house being sold brought a different kind of a flicker opportunity. Nimbin cracked open the spiritual chains; the house sale offered a possible exit from the physical entrapment. As shocking as the news was, I felt that strange sense of hope: "Maybe this is it. Maybe I can finally walk away." It wasn't one moment that set me free, it was a series of them, each chipping away at the walls until the door finally appeared.

But first, I had to summon the strength, both physically and emotionally, to confront him, navigate this transition, and take the steps needed to close this chapter of my life.

It was clear: the reckoning had begun.

> *"Darkness cannot drive out darkness; only light can do that." - Martin Luther King Jr.*

It was a shock to return and see the husband fixing and painting the house, preparing it for sale. This was the first time I had ever seen him make an effort to repair anything. We had lived in Cranbourne for ten years, and during that time, he had never bothered to fix a door hinge, a broken handle, or even patch up a hole he had punched in the wall during one of his rages. But now, here he was, in a mode I had never witnessed before.

He painted the house as if erasing the years of neglect. I watched as he patched the holes he had punched in his rages, covered the stains of our fights, and prepared the house, not for us, but for his next chapter. The house had never been a home. I realised then, I had only ever been an occupant, not an equal.

The realisation hit hard: it took selling the house to motivate him to fix it, yet it had been perfectly acceptable to live in a broken, neglected space all those years. It wasn't just the physical repairs; it was the messages behind them. The house was never going to be a home; it was simply a place to inhabit until it served his next purpose. Seeing this was a harsh wake-up call, one that underscored just how little care or respect he had for the space we shared, or for me.

The husband had even arranged for Amos, a good friend to stay over and help with the renovations, along with his beloved fur baby, Minty. I had always adored Minty, she and Buddy got along famously, their playful energy a rare bright spot in the house. But as I stood there, it struck me how much had changed in the short time I'd been away. It felt like I had stepped back into a completely different space, one where decisions had been made and plans set in motion without any input from me.

Of course, that wasn't new. He had always gone ahead and made decisions on his own, leaving me out of the process entirely. But this time, it felt especially stark, like I was a bystander in my own life, watching him prepare for a future that didn't include me.

It was during this time, in July 2020, that I began staying at my family's beach house in Rye, on the Peninsula.

I went from Cranbourne to Rye as things got finalised. The word divorce was never mentioned, I didn't dare mention it, as everything had to be his idea. I had to play the role of everything is fine.

He didn't say much about me going to Rye. There was no question, no concern, no checking in, just silence. But then, out of nowhere, he threw in a comment that said everything: "If you want a booty call, call me." That was the only thing he had to say about my time away. No acknowledgement of the separation, no curiosity about how I was doing. Just a crude, dismissive remark that reduced me to a body, not a person. It was his way of keeping a hook in me, sexualising the distance, belittling my autonomy, and pretending as though none of it mattered. But to me, Rye *did* matter. It was the first place I could breathe again.

Nestled close to the ocean, it became a sanctuary of quiet and solitude, especially during the lockdown. The stillness of the area was a stark contrast to the chaos I had just come from. I needed the relief from this self-obsessed new renovation chaos. For the first time in years, at the beach house, I had the space to breathe, reflect, and begin putting my thoughts on paper. This is where I started writing my story, this book.

Being at the beach house gave me the freedom to voice my side of the story without the constant interruptions or judgments of the husband. Writing became a way to reclaim my narrative, to express the pain and truth I had kept locked away. For once, I wasn't being bulldozed by his endless opinions, demands, pressures, or relentless bullying. The act of writing was more than cathartic; it was a defiant declaration of my existence and my truth. It was the first step in finding my voice again.

The husband had taken charge of everything, as usual, without consulting me. He had arranged for a large storage container to be parked in the driveway, and I watched as he carted most of our belongings into it. The container was set to be transported up north to his mum's house in Queensland, where he was clearly planning to live with her and her husband.

As I stood there, I couldn't bring myself to say the word divorce, even though his actions made it obvious he was already making tracks to start a new life without me. The unspoken reality hung heavily in the air, yet I stayed silent, unable to voice what we both likely knew was inevitable. It was a surreal experience, watching my life being packed away piece by piece, while the words I wanted to say remained trapped inside. I've had since come to understand that when you change and make a new decision, that life changes in accordance with your new vision. It was starting to become evident that my new decision had bought my ticket to freedom. I was merely waiting for my ship to set sail.

The sale of the house went through within the next month, and by early October, we had to have everything organised, our paperwork, accounts, and the remnants of a life we had shared for 13 years.

It felt surreal to dismantle everything we had built together, but I knew there was no room for error. I had to be meticulous. Every detail needed to be sorted, every loose end tied up, because I knew him too well. He would seize on any unfinished business, any overlooked account or document, and use it as ammunition to manipulate me back into his world. His ability to twist and weaponise even the smallest thing was something I had lived through for years, and I was determined to give him no leverage this time.

This wasn't just about closing a chapter, it was about ensuring my freedom, safeguarding myself from the constant cycle of control and manipulation. Every piece of paper I filed and every account I closed was a step toward reclaiming my life. With everything going on, I didn't dare speak of divorce. Like everything in that marriage, it had to be *his* idea. I knew better than to risk setting him off or giving him any excuse for rage. During this period, he did have an outburst, one afternoon, when we were alone. His aggression flared up as he snapped, claiming he had been abused because he was bullied at school and bled, and that my abuse by my grandfather didn't count because there wasn't any blood.

The absurdity of his comparison left me speechless. It made no sense, and I didn't bother engaging. He was angry with the world, always playing the victim, and I was too unwell to waste my limited energy.

The pain was constant and consuming. Walking was difficult from the knife-like pain shooting up my groin. Sitting hurt. My pelvis felt like it was being sliced from the inside, jolts, jerks, contractions, and stabbing sensations that came without warning. My lower abdomen was bloated and tender, with pain radiating down my legs. I wasn't sleeping. I had headaches, nausea, and menstrual cramps that hit randomly throughout the month. At times, I couldn't stop crying, not just from the physical agony, but from the emotional weight of it all. The pain was relentless, and I was surviving hour to hour.

I was just hanging on, trying to preserve every ounce of strength I had to get through each day. Engaging with his rages, his twisted logic, and his need to diminish my pain would only drain me further, and I couldn't afford that. I chose silence, not as a surrender, but as an act of self-preservation.

Trying to cut all loose ends with him was utterly draining.

Research from *Australia's National Research Organisation for Women's Safety* (*ANROWS*) shows that survivors of financial abuse often experience long-term instability due to coerced debt, loss of income, and drained superannuation, exactly the impact detailed here.

It was exhausting, requiring every ounce of energy I had to navigate this period. He was moving up north with our pup, Buddy, while I was staying in Melbourne, Victoria. By early October 2020, when the house was sold, he found himself temporarily without a place to go due to yet another lockdown.

Experts in trauma recovery note that survivors often feel compelled to maintain some access to a shared connection, such as a pet or home, especially in the early stages of separation, when emotional and financial vulnerabilities are highest. For two weeks, he stayed at the family beach house with his brand-new $70,000 Utility, purchased through the settlement.

In the weeks leading up to the sale of the house, Cranbourne had become a hub of chaos. He was dealing and trading drugs, with a steady stream of people coming and going, and who knows how much sex he did on the side, it was as though there was no lockdown. In contrast, the beach house, where he stayed temporarily after the sale, was eerily quiet, almost unsettlingly so. Despite the turmoil in Cranbourne and the strange calm of the beach house, I knew I couldn't allow myself to get drawn back into his world. Every decision I made, every step I took, was with the sole purpose of breaking free and reclaiming my life.

During this period, there was nothing coming into my account, no income, no rent payments, no *Centrelink*. It was a stark and devastating reality. I remember asking myself, "What is going on in my life that all financial flow has completely stopped?" It was as though every stream of support had dried up, leaving me to confront the full weight of my financial situation alone.

This financial void forced me to reflect on how much I had sacrificed for the husband. For the first time, it hit me that in the last two years of my role as a Local Area Coordinator, my salary packaging had gone directly into paying off his home loan. The realisation left me feeling like an absolute fool. I had trusted him so deeply. I believed him when he justified that his home loan had to be paid off first, not mine. I had been so naïve, so blinded by trust, that I gave him the benefit of the doubt.

I vividly remember asking the *Australian Taxation Office*, with the husband standing right there, how much of my salary packaging had been used to pay off his loan. The answer hit like a punch to the gut: $30,000 over two years. Instead of acknowledging the sacrifice I had made, he dismissed the amount, spitting out, "It's only $10,000 because of tax." His indifference was a slap in the face, a harsh reminder of the kind of man I had married.

I felt a deep sense of shame and embarrassment, not just for how much I had trusted him, but for realising I had married someone who seemed to have the heart of Mr. Burns from *The Simpsons*, greedy, self-centred, and utterly lacking in empathy. The weight of these realisations was crushing, but they were also the wake-up call I needed to see just how much I had lost by being with him.

At one point, the husband casually pulled a wad of cash from his pocket, flaunting the profits from an illegal drug sale and showing me just how much money, he was making. Meanwhile, I had no income, no income protection, and no support from *Centrelink* due to delays and complications with my application.

I owned a unit, but because of lockdown rules, my tenants were given a grace period to delay paying rent, leaving me without even that small source of financial stability. All my resources stopped, and I was left wondering how we could be married, with a settlement having just come through, yet I was struggling to survive while he lived in abundance.

A day or two before he left, I asked him for help. I explained my situation: *Centrelink* was having issues processing my details, and I didn't know when the tenants would be able to pay rent. I was struggling to make ends meet, and I hoped he might offer some support. His response was shocking. He had a new $70,000 Utility, had spent over $20,000 on an add-on for camping, and even bragged about buying toy race cars for himself and his father-in-law. He also had two massive bags of cannabis with him, ready to sell on his way up north. Yet when I asked for help, he clutched his chest dramatically, going pale and grey, claiming he had to pay off the remainder of his mum's home loan.

To add insult to injury, when I asked for some cannabis for my chronic pain, knowing that it helped calm my spasms and provided relief, he had the audacity to tell me, "Prices have gone up to $300 an ounce." He wasn't offering it to help; he was trying to sell it to me, his own wife, who had no income and was using cannabis to manage pain instead of pharmaceutical drugs. I laughed in his face, unable to comprehend how low someone could go.

It made my head spin. I thought to myself, "How sad can someone be to exploit their own wife, who has no financial support, after losing her livelihood and suffering so much?" The husband's greed and lack of empathy were laid bare in that moment. It was a stark, heartbreaking reminder of the kind of person I had married. How embarrassed was I to still be married to a man who wouldn't even give me $50 for petrol after receiving over $400,000 from the sale of the house? A house that I helped to finance!

The realisation left me feeling ashamed, not just of him, but of myself for choosing to marry someone capable of such coldness. If the roles had been reversed, I knew I would have helped him without hesitation, but with him, there was no generosity, no compassion.

This was such a stark contrast to how he had been in the beginning. Early in our relationship, he had insisted on paying for everything, going out of his way to show he could provide. I remember him getting offended when I offered to pay for something myself. Having been single and independent for so long, I was used to paying my own way, but he was adamant, it was his role to cover the expenses. At the time, it felt like care and love, even though it was unfamiliar to me.

Now, looking back, it was clear how far he had fallen from the man he pretended to be. The disparity between who he was at the start and who he had become, or perhaps who he always truly was, was glaring. The man who once insisted on providing for me was now unwilling to part with even $50 for petrol, despite having so much at his disposal.

This time was highly emotional, and I tried my best to keep it together, resisting the urge to get reeled into his endless manipulative stories. Yet, regrettably, I caved in to his pestering and relentless sexual demands. I didn't want to give in, I wanted to be left alone, but he wouldn't stop. I found myself wondering, "What it would take for him to finally leave me in peace?"

Due to the husband selling the house and lockdowns, he had nowhere to live. I allowed him to stay at my parent's beach house straight after the house was sold. I was clinging onto Buddy, finding it hard to say goodbye to Buddy. As it was lockdown period and he had Buddy, I wanted to spend as much time with buddy as possible.

His time at the beach house was relentless, his presence suffocating. The stress rattled me to my core, making every moment feel like a battle for my sanity. Yet, amid the chaos, I held on to the small comfort of spending the last days with Buddy, my hero pup who had saved my life twice.

The husband slept inside the beach house, while I stayed in the garage, cuddled up on another bed with Buddy. It was bittersweet, these stolen moments with Buddy were precious, but they were tinged with the devastation of knowing I would soon lose him. I knew I wasn't well enough to look after Buddy, and I didn't have a place of my own to give him a stable home. Saying goodbye to my boy, who had been my constant companion and protector, broke my heart.

I remember the day they left vividly. Buddy sat in the passenger seat, his big, soulful brown eyes gazing out the window as if pleading, "Mum, why aren't you coming with us?" It was as though he understood something was deeply wrong. His expression, filled with confusion and sadness, pierced through me like a dagger. I stood there in the driveway, trembling with uncontrollable grief as I watched him drive away with Buddy's head poking out the window, staring back at me. The image seared itself into my mind.

My heart shattered into a million pieces as the car disappeared into the distance, taking Buddy away from me forever. It felt like the final blow, a loss that compounded every other loss I'd endured, the three babies I'd lost during my marriage, my two precious fur babies, Frida and Matisse, and now Buddy. Even my ex-husband had experienced the loss of his fur baby early in our relationship, but nothing could prepare me for this. I had hit my quota for loss.

As Buddy vanished from sight, I fell apart completely. The sobs wracked my body, and it was as if I was going in and out of myself, unable to anchor to anything solid. I stood there, shaking, consumed by an ocean of grief that I couldn't control, my heart utterly torn apart. The realisation that I would never see Buddy again was unbearable, a pain so deep it felt as though my soul had been ripped in two.

GRACE AMORE

Buddy and my husband went to stay with Anser and Kevin on their farm as they made their way up north, leaving Victoria. I first met Anser in 2007 when he was my team leader at a training organisation in Melbourne CBD, and I had just stepped into my first role as a teacher trainer for the Diploma of Community Welfare, teaching international students. At the time, I had been working part-time in drug and alcohol recovery at the *Salvation Army* in St. Kilda. Looking for full-time work, I enrolled in teacher training part-time while continuing my role in recovery services and eventually transitioned into teaching.

From the moment I met Anser, he made me laugh and feel completely at ease. He had a way of turning even the most mundane days into something fun and memorable. We shared so many laughs in that workplace. I still recall the time we had chair races down the corridor (no students around, of course). What stood out most about Anser was his generous heart and his profound love for birds. Back then, he lived in Melbourne but dreamed of owning a farm where he could breed birds, lots of birds. And he made that dream come true.

Anser's farm became a sanctuary, not just for birds but for a whole menagerie of animals. Dogs, sheep, and countless other creatures filled the property with life and vitality. Over the years, he had so many animals that I lost count. It was truly a haven, a place where animals thrived under his care and love.

As the days to their departure drew closer, I called Anser and arranged for my husband and Buddy to stay on his farm as a stop on their journey. My intentions weren't for my husband; I did it for Buddy. I knew Anser's farm was a loving and nurturing environment, and it gave me a sliver of peace amidst the immense heartbreak. I took some comfort in knowing that Buddy would experience joy and warmth there, even if only for a short time.

The thought of Buddy being surrounded by Anser's warmth and the company of other animals was a small consolation during an otherwise devastating moment. While I couldn't keep Buddy with me, knowing he'd be cared for in such a safe, loving environment helped ease the unbearable ache in my heart, if only just a little.

Lockdown added a deeper layer of solitude to this coastal town of Victoria. It was beyond quiet; it was eerie. It felt apocalyptic, as though everyone had left the planet, leaving only me in this vast emptiness. The street where the beach house was located didn't have an official name that reflected the times, but I started calling it 'Quarantine Street' because it felt so fitting. Hardly a soul passed through, and the stillness outside mirrored the desolation I felt within. For the first time in my life, I came to know what it was like not to see or speak to another person for days on end.

Going from the chaotic, fast-paced life I had been living, filled with constant demands, drama, and noise, to this profound stillness was a shock to the system. It wasn't just the absence of sound or people; it was the stark contrast to the relentless turbulence I had grown accustomed to. The silence magnified everything, forcing me to confront emotions and memories I had spent years burying. How strange it was to experience such a sensation, to be enveloped in an almost otherworldly quiet. The solitude was all-encompassing.

16: Pixie And The Ascension 2020

One of the things the husband would say throughout our time together, right from the start, "If you and I ever break up, I can see you and Pixie remaining friends forever." Now after that quote, nearly two decades on, he's not wrong.

I spoke with Pixie; I couldn't be on my own as I was suicidal, the grief of losing my babies out of the marriage and fur babies. I was beyond distraught and so lost in emotions.

It was during this time that I decided to drive up to East Gippsland to visit Pixie. The drive itself felt like an event in its own right, navigating the ever-changing restrictions and not knowing which roads might be blocked. It was like trying to traverse an alien planet, with each checkpoint and detour adding to the surreal chaos. The strangeness of it all mirrored the turmoil I felt inside.

> *"If you and I ever break up, I can see you and Pixie remaining friends forever." – The husband*

As it was during the lockdown with multiple police checkpoints along the way, I was stopped by police. A policewoman approached my car and asked where I was going. Her question hit me like a tidal wave, and I burst into tears, overwhelmed by the sheer weight of it all. Through my sobs, I told her I was seeking refuge at a good friend's home after coming out of domestic abuse. Her compassion was immediate and tangible. She stepped closer, her presence warm and reassuring, and gently let me know about services I could contact if I needed help. It was as though she wanted to give me a hug, and in that moment, her kindness was a balm to my frayed nerves. It reminded me that even in the midst of madness, there were still people who cared.

SAVING GRACE

I can't imagine what the policewoman saw as I drove up to her on that road. My car was crammed with belongings, and I was a shaking, an emotional mess. Her kindness stayed with me, lingering in my mind as a glimmer of hope and helping me muster the strength to continue the drive to Pixie's home. By the time I arrived, I was completely beside myself, exhausted, broken, and overwhelmed.

It was November 2020, and the world was still in upheaval. Victoria, especially Melbourne, had become a surreal echo of wartime for my parents, a stark reminder of chaos, restriction, and uncertainty. The atmosphere was heavy with an oppressive strangeness, making everything feel even more bizarre.

I was so emotionally and physically messy that I could barely function. One moment, I'd burst into uncontrollable tears; the next, my body would jolt with spasms. Involuntary screams escaped me, loud and raw, as if my nervous system couldn't contain the tension any longer. I was a complete mess; my nerves shattered beyond words. The fragility of my state was undeniable, yet somehow, through all the chaos and pain, I had made it to Pixie's home, a sanctuary, if only for a moment.

I was deeply grateful to have support and validation from Pixie and her family. Her mum, grandmother, husband, and two little girls welcomed me into their home with open arms. Their kindness felt like a balm to my shattered spirit, and I was profoundly thankful for the safe haven they provided.

Pixie gave me her caravan to stay in, a space she had lovingly transformed into a magical refuge. It was beautifully decked out, filled with her artistic expressions that radiated creativity and joy. The cozy bed and enchanting ambiance made it a sanctuary, a place where I could begin to exhale, even if just for a moment.

This caravan had been Pixie's business for six years hosting Children's Parties and attending markets and festivals with her hand made faerie treasures and air brush face painting, along with running her weekly laughter Yoga club. This caravan had been transformed throughout the lockdown; it had gone from a purple Pixie Palace to a Rainbow Hippie's Palace covered in Pixie's art. She was living in the Palace while also going through her own separation from her husband of seventeen years. She also had no escape apart from the caravan during the lockdowns, although her husband wasn't a narcissist, unlike mine which I was about to discover with Pixie in an in-depth conversation.

One night, Pixie and I were sitting outside under the stars, surrounded by the stillness of her property. The air was crisp, and the atmosphere felt safe enough for me to open up in a way I hadn't before. I started sharing, for the first time, the details of the husband's behaviours, his manipulations, outbursts, and the relentless way he made everything about him.

According to the DSM-5, Narcissistic Personality Disorder (NPD) is marked by a pattern of grandiosity, a need for admiration, and a lack of empathy. Survivors of narcissistic abuse often describe relationships with such individuals as psychologically destabilising and emotionally exhausting, due to tactics like gaslighting, love bombing, and emotional invalidation. (American Psychiatric Association, 2013)

Pixie listened intently, her face thoughtful, and after a pause, she said, "Grace, it sounds like something a narcissist would do."

I blinked, confused. "What's a narcissist?" I asked.

She hesitated for a moment and then said, "I'm not quite sure, but let's Google it."

As Pixie and I sat under the night sky, she pulled out her phone and started reading. "Let's check something," she said, her voice cautious yet steady. What she read changed everything. Each line felt like a knife slicing through my past, cutting away the fog, revealing the truth I had been too buried in to see. This wasn't just a bad marriage. This was something far more insidious.

She searched for the term. The first article that came up began to explain traits like manipulation, lack of empathy, and a constant need for control and attention. As Pixie read aloud, my heart sank. The words mirrored my reality in a way that left no room for denial. This was the first time I had a name for what I had endured. It was a moment of both clarity and heartbreak, realising the depth of his behaviours and how deeply they had affected me.

Naming abuse is a crucial step in recovery. In trauma psychology, the ability to identify the patterns of harm, such as gaslighting, coercive control, and chronic invalidation, can help survivors move from confusion to clarity. Recognition is often the first step toward reclaiming power.

(Herman, J. L. (1992). Trauma and Recovery)

Pixie and I scrolled through the article titled *"11 Signs You Are Dating a Narcissist, Here's How to Know for Sure"* from *Cosmopolitan*, written by Julia Pugachevsky and published on November 10, 2018. The tagline, *"Because you deserve better,"* hit me like a lightning bolt.

As we read through each point, I felt as though someone had been secretly documenting my life. Every sign, every trait listed in the article had a story in my marriage to match. We paused after each one, and I shared my experiences with Pixie, recounting moments that aligned so perfectly it was unnerving.

One by one, the points brought my past into sharp focus:

The manipulation.

- The lack of empathy.
- The constant need to be the centre of attention – admiration.
- The way he would dismiss my feelings, twisting reality to suit his narrative.
- Question my reality, values, beliefs and memories.
- Sexual coercion – relentless nagging, wouldn't take no for an answer, only when it suited him. He would complain if I said no – he would use it later in a drunken rage.
- Financial control
- Arguments about my family, made it a nightmare to see them
- Made my work a problem because I love working with people, saying I give too much to them.
- Spirituality – faith, he couldn't stand my faith in God. Would publicly humiliate me
- The power and control were crazy

The article explained:

They did everything to win you over in the beginning.

If you're deeply confused as to how someone who used to text you nonstop and told you they loved you by date two suddenly seems rude and distant, that might be your first sign.

"Narcissists are masters of love bombing, where they make a potential partner feel as special as they possibly can," says Dr. Suzanne Degges-White, Ph.D., chair and professor of counselling and counsellor education at Northern Illinois University. And narcissists might be better at wooing you than someone who actually loves you, because they're motivated by winning you over instead of actually getting to know you. What can seem like the most romantic gestures or thoughtful gifts can simply be them studying you to know exactly how to be the 'perfect' partner to you.

"Narcissists are adept at winning affection from their targets early on, but they have trouble maintaining long-term relationships," Degges-White says.

They're wildly selfish when they can get away with it.

When you're past the honeymoon stage of the relationship or simply around other people, a narcissist will be the most courteous, attentive partner. But when no one who matters is looking (which, down the line, includes you), they'll very openly put their needs above yours. "Narcissists see people as objects and often leave their romantic partners feeling more like an accessory than a living, breathing, feeling partner," Degges-White says. She notes that a good sign to look out for is their motivation for buying you gifts–do they do it out of nowhere, for no reason, other than to make you smile? Or do they shell out on special occasions only or shower you with flowers after they screamed at you during a fight? The first is a sign of a genuinely caring partner who thinks of you. The latter is someone buying your affection, so you'll stay even when they're a total nightmare to be around.

They care more about your image as a couple than the relationship itself.

A narcissist's self-inflicted pressure to be flawless doesn't end with them–once you're his or her partner, you're obligated to fulfill the 'insta-perfect ideal' of the power couple he or she wants to be.

"When a narcissist feels that they're losing face publicly, it creates a lot of inner distress because they cannot tolerate failure, and public humiliation is the worst type of failure [to them]," says Degges-White. She adds that their ego is very fragile, so any perceived 'attack' on their reputation makes them furious.

For example, say you get into a small, calm argument while you're out at dinner. Instead of addressing the conflict, a narcissist will get angry that you're 'embarrassing them' in front of people they'll never see again. What started out as you asking them to please text when they're running late turns into a huge fight at home because you 'ruined the whole night' by bringing it up in public.

"Narcissists don't focus on growth in a relationship, because their own self-assessment confirms to them that they are already significantly evolved and accomplished," Degges-White says. They will always prioritise looking like a picturesque couple over actually addressing your needs.

They're constantly nitpicking everything you do.

When they first met you, they loved EVERYTHING about you. Now, those same things–the sound of your laugh, your penchant for wearing Doc Martens, your love of bad reality TV–are a problem. "Narcissists tend to hold some specific image of what they want their partner to be like and they don't 'challenge you' to grow, they try to force your 'growth,'" Degges-White says. "What they are really trying to do is control your behaviours and your choices."

A warning sign: your partner being convinced that his or her point of view on how you should behave is 1000 percent right. Another thing to look out for is if they always criticise how you behave around friends–you made a joke that didn't land or accidentally cut someone off and you're a terrible, selfish person because of it.

Degges-White also notes that someone who actually cares about you checks in with you that you're on the same page about things you want to improve and work on (which **is** important in a relationship). They calmly discuss how they feel and reach a compromise with you instead of berating you for not falling in line.

It's literally impossible to argue with them.

The reason fights with narcissists are so volatile and deeply confusing is actually very simple: They're never wrong. Degges-White says that while a narcissist may agree with your complaints in the dating phase of the relationship, that all goes away in time. "Disagreements and arguments are often highly lopsided–their partners plead with them to see things from another perspective, but narcissists are unable to accomplish a feat of this level of emotional maturity."

This is simply because narcissists believe they are done growing and that their version of the truth is ultimate and infallible. You could have screenshots of what they said to you earlier and they'll still find a way to say that's not reality or what they meant.

Degges-White says that narcissists are more likely to threaten breakups or give harsh ultimatums if you refuse to concede and apologise, even if you have serious doubts about being wrong at all. It's the ultimate form of gaslighting, and it happens all the time with them.

They're masters at making you think, you're the dramatic one.

As if explosive fights weren't bad enough, narcissists also have a knack for convincing you that you're actually the drama queen who starts all the conflicts, all the time.

"Narcissists are manipulators who have no qualms about twisting a partner's words or actions in a way that would make the partner feel guilty or remorseful about things they have no reason to feel bad about," Degges-White says.

Just by bringing up an issue, you're "blowing everything up again." By calmly standing your ground and explaining your perspective, you're 'stubborn' or 'angry' or 'crazy' or 'selfish.' They'll never get that they're the ones who refuse to compromise in any capacity and draw out fights because they can't handle ever being wrong.

They have a roster of 'crazy exes.'

Narcissists don't really have friends as much as collector's items. They use their charm to form tons of surface-level friendships but do no work to maintain them, according to Degges-White.

"To be in an authentic relationship requires that a person is able to let down their guard," she says. "Narcissists are terrified of being seen as human as that would crack open the image that they try to project as 'superhuman.'"

A narcissist will blow people off with no explanation, counting on them to continually reach out to hang out. They'll never truly be there for a friend if it inconveniences them and doesn't make them look charitable or kind. And of course, that leaks into their romantic relationships.

They lash out when they realise, they are replaceable.

By now, it's pretty common knowledge that if a guy calls his exes crazy, he's the one with the problem. And maybe 'crazy' isn't so much used as 'difficult,' 'had issues,' 'loved drama' when describing all their past partners.

"Narcissists who are especially good at winning the affection and praise of others are likely to also have a lot of broken relationships," Degges-White says. Makes sense–being self-obsessed with your image is not exactly the foundation of a healthy relationship.

But she also says that narcissists want to be perceived as the victim in all their relationships, embellishing their great qualities while vilifying their exes to achieve that image. Anytime a narcissist's first comment on past relationships is what the ex did wrong over what they both might've struggled with is a good sign they haven't learned anything.

Dating them makes you feel worse about yourself.

Narcissists are often dubbed emotional vampires for a good reason: they need your constant attention and affection to feel ok (but ironically, treat you like trash once they get their fix).

So naturally, when you go out with your friends more or spend some time on your own (very normal things), they panic. "If you try to claim some space for yourself, the narcissist may feel that you are trying to strip away part of their own identity," Degges-White says. "When you back away, they're going to try that much harder to reel you back into their lives."

In order to regain their sense of self-worth, narcissists may start showering you with gifts or simply being warmer and more affectionate when you come home late. And tiny things, like forgetting to wear the necklace they bought you, can trigger this (or just another huge fight).

They lash out when they realise, they are replaceable.

Eventually, you'll probably be put off by a narcissist's exhausting behaviour and start to emotionally pull away for real. And that's when they get mad.

According to Degges-White, when they feel that they are losing you for good, they can do everything from flirt or cheat with someone to make you jealous, to threatening to leave first so they don't lose face.

Their actions are callous because your only value was to be an accessory, and now that you maybe aren't, bye bye. To them, it's better to be an outright asshole and break your heart over being the one who's been left, because it gives them the sense of control they simply can't live without.

Dating that makes you feel worse about yourself.

Based on everything on this list, you can probably guess that a narcissist is not going to make you feel great about yourself over time. The repeated criticism over the smallest issues, gaslighting in arguments, and inability to ever admit fault inevitably takes an emotional toll on someone who is empathetic and, in the relationship, to try and make it work.

"You may begin to accept that you are less than your partner and begin to belittle yourself and accept criticism as deserved, whether it really is or not," Degges-White says. This creates a codependent relationship: "The relationship can become something like a yoyo–you try to get some distance, but get sucked right back into the old patterns," she adds.

The only way you break the cycle is when the narcissist leaves you out of boredom or anger, or you spot these signs and get out of there (and possibly seek therapy to heal from the emotional damage). If you're reading this list and something in your gut just sank, know you deserve better and don't need to stay in this. There's a lot of love out there for you, but it'll never come from this person.

As Pixie read aloud the article, it was the first time I began to truly understand what I had been living with for so long. It was an awakening, a shattering of the illusion I had tried to maintain about my marriage. The husband I had been living with was relentless and sadistic, driven by excessive and unrealistic wants that constantly questioned my reality, beliefs, and values.

On that clear November night, Pixie read each paragraph aloud with care, pausing to give me the space to reflect and voice what had been buried under layers of shame. With each point, the fog began to lift, and I started to articulate the insanity I had endured.

It was liberating to speak without him hovering over my shoulder, silencing me with his presence. Even though my body betrayed the trauma with involuntary twitches, ticks, and spasms, sounds jumping out unbidden, I felt a glimmer of release. For the first time, I was able to give words to the unspeakable.

Pixie listened to me, holding space for me to process the truth of my experiences. Her compassion created a safe haven for me to begin confronting the reality of my life.

That night was more than just an awakening; it was the beginning of reclaiming my voice. The shame started to peel away, leaving room for clarity and a faint but growing sense of empowerment. It was a step toward understanding not only what had happened to me but also the strength I held in beginning to tell my story. It finally dawned on me that I wasn't crazy. I wasn't the 'drama queen' and all the labels I was given by my husband. The husband was a conniving narcissist, and I became his prey.

That night, Pixie opened my eyes to something I had been living with for so long but didn't know how to name. All I had known was the constant, overwhelming feeling that I was the crazy one, that everything wrong in the marriage was somehow my fault. But there, under the stars in her safe and nurturing space, we began to unpack my marriage with new words that brought clarity and verification: narcissism, gaslighting, love bombing, discarding.

'Gaslighting' is a form of psychological manipulation where the abuser sows seeds of doubt in the victim, making them question their memory, perception, or sanity. It's often used by narcissistic or coercively controlling individuals to keep their partner off-balance and compliant. (Stark, E. (2007). Coercive Control)

It was as though a veil had been lifted. For the first time, the chaos of my marriage had a language, and with each term Pixie read aloud, the pieces of my story started to fall into place. Each word carried weight, giving form to the intangible, oppressive dynamics that had kept me silenced and unsure of myself for so long. Together, we began naming what I had endured, and in doing so, we began dismantling the lie that I had been the problem.

The relief was immense, but so was the grief. Grief for the years spent doubting myself, for the love I had poured into someone who used it as a weapon, and for the identity I had lost in the process. Naming the abuse was painful, but it was also liberating, it allowed me to see the truth for what it was on that clear New Moon night. It took me a long time to realise I was a victim, that what happened to me wasn't my fault. He took advantage of my trust, my kindness, and my silence, and for years I carried shame that never belonged to me.

I was married to an entitled narcissist, a covert, sadistic, and malignant narcissist with sociopathic tendencies. It was on that unforgettable night, 30th November 2020, under a new moon, with Pixie around the campfire in her backyard that everything began to shift.

As we talked, 13 shooting stars lit up the sky behind her, streaking across the night in a dazzling display, as if the universe itself was bearing witness to our awakening. One falling star for each year of my ridiculous excuse for a relationship. The night sky glittered with shooting stars, filling the air with a sense of awe and a stirring deep within my soul.

Pixie, too, was going through her own life transitions and awakenings. Pixie too awakened to the husband's narcissistic ways. She had known him for 19 years and had no idea what he was really like in the marriage with me

In that shared space of transformation, something sacred unfolded. It wasn't just about naming the abuse or seeing the truth of my marriage for what it was; it was about reclaiming pieces of myself I thought were lost forever. Together, we began to name the insidious patterns of covert, sadistic, malignant narcissism and sociopathy that had infiltrated my life, gaslighting, manipulation, love bombing, and discarding. For the first time, I started to make sense of the chaos, to see how these traits had been woven into the fabric of my marriage.

Survivors of narcissistic abuse often experience what's called "narcissistic abuse syndrome", a trauma response involving anxiety, dissociation, and hypervigilance. Naming the abuse is not just cognitive, it is neurological. The brain begins to reorient from a state of confusion to one of coherence, a critical step in healing the nervous system. (van der Kolk, B. (2014). The Body Keeps the Score)

We sat outside under the stars and falling stars. The campfire crackled between us, its warmth mirroring the connection and safety I felt in Pixie's presence. Even though my body still trembled with involuntary spasms, I felt a growing stillness within, a clarity that I hadn't experienced in years.

That night was epic, profound in its symbolism and beauty. The stars seemed to dance with us, marking a turning point in both of our lives. It wasn't just an awakening for me; it felt like a cosmic reminder that even in the darkest moments, light has a way of breaking through. The truth I uncovered that night became the foundation for my liberation, a first step toward reclaiming my power and my voice.

Pixie's caravan, which she affectionately called the Hippie's Palace, became my refuge for the week, a magical safe space filled with her vibrant artistic expressions and warmth. It was a sanctuary where I could start to piece myself back together. For Pixie, too, it was an awakening. She came to know that she too was manipulated by him in ways she was only beginning to see clearly. The pieces started to fall into place, the penny dropped, and for the first time, I saw my marriage through new eyes. That night, as we sat under the stars, we both woke up to the truth of who he was: a narcissist. The veil lifted, revealing the toxic web of manipulation, gaslighting, and control that had almost cost me my life.

It wasn't just my awakening; it was hers as well. That night was a shared reckoning, a moment of profound clarity that bonded us in a way words can't fully capture. Pixie saw him for what he was and stood with me in solidarity as I began to understand the depths of the darkness I had endured.

A year later in 2021, almost to the day, we reconnected again, this time in Melbourne. Pixie came to me, bringing her unwavering support and understanding as I continued to navigate the storm of breaking free. Together, we began the journey of healing, reclaiming, and rebuilding.

It was late December 2021 when Pixie invited me to a Melbourne rally, a freedom rally. It would be the first time I ventured out among so many people in a long while. Initially, I was hesitant, overwhelmed by the thought of the noise, the crowds, and the flashing lights that could easily trigger my complex post-traumatic stress disorder. The idea of my body's jolts, yelps, and spasms occurring in such a public space was daunting, and I was close to declining her invitation.

Just as Pixie was about to leave for the rally, I felt the small, quiet voice of God urging me to go. It was as though God was gently nudging me out of my comfort zone, whispering that this moment held something significant. Pixie's encouragement added to that push, and I decided to join her.

The effort to get out of my safe space and step into the bustling crowd felt monumental. Each step toward the rally was a leap of faith, not just in God but also in myself, trusting that I could face the intensity of the world again, even for a little while. This rally marked more than just a protest; it was a step toward reclaiming my place in a world I had retreated from for so long.

It was overwhelming, a flood of emotions washing over me all at once. Elation, awe, and a profound sense of connection coursed through me as I stood among the massive crowd. There were half a million people, all united in purpose, speaking up for our rights. The energy was palpable, a mix of determination and hope that seemed to ripple through the air. We marched from Victoria's state parliament, down Bourke Street and up to Flagstaff Gardens, carrying Australian flags and placards bearing 'My Body, My Choice' slogans, while chanting "kill the bill", "sack Dan Andrews" and "Aussie, Aussie, Aussie, oi, oi, oi".

Yet, it was jarring to later see how the media downplayed the rally, portraying it as though only a handful of people had attended. The reality was undeniable, there were hundreds of thousands of us gathered in unity, a sea of voices standing together. It was an incredible experience, one that reminded me of the power of collective action and the strength found in community. For the first time in a long time, I didn't feel isolated or alone. Instead, I felt part of something bigger, something meaningful.

At one stage, the overwhelming emotions and the sheer intensity of the crowd became too much. My body responded with pelvic pain, a sharp, familiar reminder of the trauma it carried. Needing to self-regulate and create a sense of safety for my nervous system, I found a spot on the grass near a big tree in the park. With my back to the crowd, I lay down, praying quietly as I tried to centre myself. Around me, rows of police lined the area, their watchful eyes on the speakers and the masses gathered in protest.

GRACE AMORE

As I lay there, focusing on my breath, I felt a deep urge rise within me, a primal need to release the madness that had been locked inside for so long. It wasn't just the chaos of the rally or the ongoing tension of lockdown; it was the unvoiced agony of the marriage, the years of manipulation, and the unrelenting crazy-making of life with him.

I whispered to my body, "You have permission to let it out." Taking a deep breath, I allowed myself to surrender to the moment. From the depths of my soul, a primal scream erupted, a wail so raw and visceral it carried all the messiness, pain, and madness that had been trapped inside. Each cry seemed to reach into the darkest corners of my being, pulling out years of anguish. It wasn't just a scream; it was a release, a letting go of what no longer served me, even as the pelvic pain surged.

For the first time, I wasn't silencing myself. I wasn't holding back. I was giving my body the space to process and release everything it had endured. And as the echoes of my screams faded into the noise of the rally, I felt something shift, a small but significant step toward healing.

I let out about three rounds of visceral, primal screaming, each one deeper and more freeing than the last. It felt like I was peeling away layers of grief, rage, and anguish that had been locked inside me for years. By the time I couldn't scream anymore, my body felt noticeably lighter, as though I had let go of a heavy burden. It was truly liberating; a profound release of pent-up emotions I hadn't even realised I was carrying.

Primal screaming and body-based expressions of trauma are recognised in somatic therapy as ways the body naturally attempts to release stored trauma. This is especially common in survivors of long-term emotional abuse, where the nervous system has remained locked in a fight, flight, freeze, or fawn state. (Ogden, P., & Fisher, J. (2015). Sensorimotor Psychotherapy).

As I sat up to catch my breath, I noticed a woman approaching me out of nowhere. Her face was tense, and without hesitation, she blurted out, "Shut up! You're making us all look crazy or mad." Her words stung, cutting through the moment of release I had just experienced. But instead of retreating into shame, I looked at her directly and said, "What do you expect after being in lockdown and enduring family violence?"

Before I could say more, Pixie stepped in, her voice firm and protective. "She has PTSD," Pixie said, advocating for me without hesitation. The woman paused, seemingly caught off guard, then turned and walked back into the crowd, her criticism fading into the background.

The nearby police, stationed in a row, briefly turned their heads in the direction of my screams. They glanced over, perhaps trying to gauge what was happening, but quickly turned back to focus on the crowd. They didn't intervene or approach; it was as though they understood, on some level, the chaos that many of us were carrying inside.

The incident could have been another moment of silencing, another time when my emotions were dismissed or invalidated. But instead, it became a moment of empowerment. Pixie's support reminded me that I wasn't alone, and my voice, raw and unfiltered, was valid. This small exchange reaffirmed that I had every right to release my pain, no matter how uncomfortable it made others feel.

It's funny, in a way, because just minutes before I lay on the grass, I had greeted a police officer with a casual "Hello, how are you?" He reciprocated politely, a brief but human exchange in the midst of all the tension. Little did either of us know that five minutes later, I'd be on my back, screaming from the depths of my soul, releasing years of pent-up shame from the marriage and the sheer insanity of lockdown.

The juxtaposition of that calm, everyday interaction and the raw, visceral release that followed felt surreal. It was as if my body had been waiting for permission to finally let go, and in that moment, I allowed it. From a polite 'hello' to a primal wail, the contrast captured the chaos and unpredictability of what trauma does to a person, and the release I so desperately needed. I never expected to do that amongst so many people in daylight on the grass. It was a complete permission for the body to release the pain.

Reflection

The 2020 lockdown marked another pivotal moment in an already transformative year. Finding my voice after the husband left with Buddy was an uphill battle. I was waking up to the cruelty I had endured in the marriage and coming to terms with how deeply ingrained my chronic people-pleasing tendencies had been. The grief and loss felt insurmountable at times, leaving me barely hanging on. I wavered between the desire to end my life and the persistent call to speak up and share my story.

The small, quiet voice inside urged me not to give in, telling me to get my story out into the world instead of succumbing to despair. While I may not have gained anything tangible from the settlement, I received something far more valuable, the sisterhood I found through the husband, with Sue and Pixie. Their support, love, and presence were gifts money could never buy. I realised I was wealthy in other ways, surrounded by people who cared and loved me deeply.

Amidst the grief and loss, I could see that I was abundantly blessed with love in my life. This realisation became an anchor, a reminder that even in the darkest times, there was light to hold onto.

After he drove away with Buddy, with everything, I stood there in the driveway, trembling. The world around me blurred. My body felt like it was collapsing in on itself, like my bones had turned to dust inside me. I wanted to scream, but nothing came out. I had nothing left to give. Not a cent. Not a word. Not a single tear. I felt like I was watching my own funeral unfold, the burial of who I once was. And then, silence. A silence so vast it swallowed me whole. I wasn't just grieving a marriage, I was grieving my babies, my body, my own existence. That's when I knew, before I could rebuild anything, I had to come back to myself. But I had no idea how.

Complex grief occurs when multiple losses compound over time, particularly in abusive environments where the grieving process is obstructed or denied. Trauma-informed care recognises this layered mourning and emphasises validating all aspects of the survivor's loss, including identity, fertility, safety, and voice (Neimeyer, R. A., & Harris, D. L. (2011). Grief and Bereavement in Contemporary Society).

17: Reclaiming Rights to My Body

I had abandoned my body long ago, because being inside it meant feeling, and feeling for me was unbearable. My body wasn't mine. It was the husbands. A thing to be used. A thing to be ignored. A thing to endure.

"Trauma lives in the body, not just the mind. Healing must reach both." – Bessel van der Kolk

This echoes the findings of Dr. Bessel van der Kolk in *The Body Keeps the Score*, a foundational text in trauma recovery that explains how the body stores unprocessed trauma and why somatic healing practices are essential.

When he left, when Buddy was gone, when the money was gone, all that was left was this wreckage of a body, this trembling, aching thing that had carried me through years of rape, manipulation, and gaslighting. My body had been his, now it was a stranger to me. I had to find a way back, but I didn't know where to start.

After he left, my body only craved one thing, water. I couldn't explain it, but I needed to be near it, needed to hear the waves, to feel the pull of the tide. Maybe it was because water is the only thing that can hold grief without breaking. Maybe I needed something vast enough to take in everything I carried. But no amount of water could wash away what he had done.

Before he left, before he took Buddy, before he disappeared with everything I had, he violated me one last time. Saying no wasn't safe. It never had been.

I whispered the word "stream" as in a river, over and over, as if saying it might bring me relief. My body had been defiled, abandoned, broken, but maybe, just maybe, the ocean could show me how to come home to myself.

> *"The body never lies." – Martha Graham*

There I was, in the depths of Melbourne's lockdown madness, separating from a husband who raped me one more time before he left. I'm sorry, body. Please forgive me. Once again, I was violated, just before he moved interstate with most of our belongings and the entire settlement. The shame and pain were unbearable, tearing through me like shards of glass, leaving me shattered and hollow. In those moments, all I wanted was for the agony to end, for the earth to swallow me whole.

I tried staying with my parents in Melbourne, but I wasn't coping. I felt an overwhelming yearning to be near water; it was the only thing my body seemed to crave. From July 2020 to September 2021, I lived at the family beach house with a few spurts in Melbourne, but my body was drawn to the soothing presence of the sea. I remember repeating the word "stream" over and over, as if saying it would bring relief. I had lost all appetite for food, and my body was a tangled knot of shame and pain, with no words to express it. All it wanted was to lie down and sleep forever.

With a trail of loss and grief, I cried for the babies I had lost during that marriage. But amidst the sorrow, I was grateful they had not been born into a world where their father prioritised sex, drugs, alcohol, and partying over everything else. I had believed we could work through things together, but he was never interested in working through anything. The weight of that realisation only deepened the ache within me, leaving me to carry it alone.

I remember one night in November, waking abruptly around 2 a.m., during the brief time I stayed at my parents' house in

Melbourne. I felt like I was losing the plot, the grief of losing three babies and three fur babies was overwhelming, and I was barely holding on. The sorrow I hadn't been allowed to feel during the marriage, came crashing over me, suffocating and relentless, making it hard to breathe. When he left the state of Victoria, my body spiralled into an intense overload of emotional grief, as if years of suppressed pain had suddenly been unleashed all at once.

On the phone with *1800 Respect*, I was hit with a shock wave of realisation, how much I had worked, sacrificed, and given of myself to a husband who had used my body to the brink of death. The unspoken stress poured out of me in uncontrollable sobs, tears flowing endlessly as if my body could no longer hold itself together. The floodgates of grief opened with a vengeance, and for a moment, death seemed to beckon me, inviting me to sleep forever. All I wanted was to be with my babies, curled up with Jesus, safe in His arms.

It was a harsh and jarring awakening. The *1800 Respect* worker stayed with me in the mess, gently reassuring me with words that slowly brought my breath back to a steady rhythm. It was like a massive wave of panic had washed over me as I fully grasped the extent of what I had given to this man I had called my husband. The weight of that truth was almost too much to bear.

While staying with my parents in Melbourne during November, I painted a butterfly and titled it '2020: The Great Awakening.' It felt symbolic, though I was far from feeling transformed. My time there was brief before I returned to the family beach house on the Peninsula, near the ocean and that glorious beach, a place that offered a semblance of peace amidst the storm.

It was an incredibly hard time, fresh out of a marriage that had stolen my innocence and shattered my sense of loyalty. My husband had been entitled and spiteful, leaving me broken in ways I hadn't yet begun to comprehend. I looked sick, nothing more than a skeleton of myself, weighed down with shame. The thought of death was oddly comforting, offering an escape from the unbearable pain I carried. It was a shock to the system to go from a house that had so much traffic to everything stopping. Once he left, I was left with the new world I was in, of coming back into the family. But how and where exactly did I belong now. The Grace I was going into that marriage was not the one that came out. This Grace after the marriage, felt so dirty she was tainted with a cloak of shame. She had no place in the family, she was now set apart, a social pariah.

During this time, my sister Angela reached out to the local mental health triage, as I often spoke of wanting to die. This intervention led to a diagnosis of *Complex Post-Traumatic Stress Disorder* (C-PTSD), a name that finally gave context to the overwhelming chaos I felt inside. I was also diagnosed with other stress-related disorders. In short, I was utterly shattered, my mind and body in disarray, struggling to find a way through it all.

It was an incredibly difficult time, compounded by the lack of widespread education about trauma and the impact of leaving an abusive marriage. The blame I received from some people only deepened the shame etched into my body, leaving me feeling even more isolated. It was one thing to be free of being married to a maniac, it was another to be answerable to everyone about why I didn't leave earlier. The judgment was suffocating, almost deathly in its weight. Every attempt to explain myself seemed to make things worse. It was hard being in the marriage and it was just as hard coming out of the marriage into this new world. Of course, lockdown compounded everything. The insane rules kept changing daily under the tyranny of Dan Andrews, deepening the isolation of family violence and all that came with it. At the time I felt like the plan-demic turned people into judging, finger=pointing critics.

How could I possibly explain marrying someone who had seemed so laid-back and easy going, only to have him transform into an aggressor on our wedding night? I was trapped in a well of madness, desperate to make sense of what had happened to my brain and body during those years. The confusion and shame were unbearable, and I found myself searching for answers, grasping for any understanding of the chaos I had endured.

During my time at the Peninsula, during lockdown the silence there was almost eerie, but at the same time it offered a sense of solitude that I desperately needed.

During this time, in 2020, I discovered the *Institute of New Paradigm Intimacy* (INPI), led by the remarkable Victoria, through Judith's son, Jeremy. He was completing a course focused on learning to listen to the body, and I was instantly intrigued when he shared what he had been studying one warm November evening. As we sat together with my dear friend Judith, Jeremy's mum, he demonstrated what he had learned. Judith and I had first met in 2014 during our studies in the *Bachelor of Community Mental Health, Alcohol, and Other Drugs* program in Berwick. Jeremy's insights into implementing boundaries and creating a sacred, safe space for others resonated deeply with me, leaving a lasting impression.

Somatic therapy focuses on listening to the body's cues as a way to heal from trauma. These approaches are gaining recognition in trauma-informed care, especially for survivors who have felt silenced or disconnected from their physical selves.

Jeremy calmly and gently guided me through an informal process, creating a relaxed environment that offered my body unspoken permission to exist exactly as it was, in all its messiness, twitching, and jolting fragility. I was not in a good place, and my hypersensitive body craved reassurance and safety to feel even a semblance of ease.

In this space, there was no judgment, only acceptance. It felt like drinking fresh water after enduring a long, parching drought. Having lived with a husband who acted as the court, judge, and jury, subjecting me to daily demands, harsh words, relentless pressures, and sexual violations, my body was pleading for me to finally learn how to listen to it.

I was captivated, intrigued, and eager to learn more about this approach to working with the body and trauma. The idea of fully accepting the body, exactly as it is, without judgment, was breathtaking. That night sparked a journey of discovery, revealing just how disconnected I had been from my body throughout my life. My experience with Jeremy was profoundly transformative; a stepping stone in rebuilding the trust between my body and me. The fact that it was a male guiding me through a safe and supportive process of reconnecting with my body after leaving my marriage was monumental. After my husband, I struggled deeply to feel safe around men. Even the sound of a male voice, whether in hypnosis or meditation, would trigger me. It had to be a voice that exuded calm and safety for me to even begin to listen.

This experience illuminated just how much I needed to listen to my body; it was time to truly honour and care for the temple I live in. The course became a pivotal part of my recovery and healing, offering me the tools to begin rebuilding trust in my body. I am deeply grateful to Victoria for creating such a transformative program, one that guided me toward a path of self-discovery and renewal.

The Institute of New Paradigm Intimacy is rooted in trauma-informed, consent-based frameworks that empower individuals to reclaim autonomy over their bodies and sexuality through experiential learning and body-based practices.

Growing up, listening to the body wasn't encouraged. Instead, I was met with dismissive comments like, "Don't be stupid, you can't feel like that," or "You're so sensitive, you take everything to heart," or "Everyone gets period pain, what's so special about you?" The refrain was always the same: "Just take a *Panadol* and get on with it."

It was a paradigm that dismissed the body rather than honouring it, a world dictated by male doctors who told me what I should feel in my own body. They insisted my period pain wasn't real, that I was overreacting, or even crazy. Their solution? "Just go have a baby, and the pain will go away." As if having a child was as easy as going to the shop and buying a bottle of milk. Yet how could a man, who had no experience of periods or the intense, sudden pain that came with them, tell me what I was feeling?

I vividly remember one morning at home when I was about 20 years old. A sharp, unexpected wave of pain hit me, and I instinctively went to the kitchen cabinet for *Panadol*. That was the unspoken expectation, to silence the pain and move on, as if my suffering was irrelevant.

I didn't have the language for it. My dad would say, "You need to eat first," but all I could focus on was the sharp, stabbing pain in my pelvic region, one of the signs my period was coming. There was no time to eat; the pain would escalate quickly, leaving me in tears. I had no name for what I was experiencing, only an overwhelming sense of craziness that made me question my sanity. Those thoughts eventually spiralled into suicidal ideation and self-harm.

The course Jeremy shared struck a raw and tender nerve within me. It spoke volumes, resonating with the parts of me that had been silenced, dismissed, and denied for so long. It was a revelation, a glimpse of what it might feel like to finally be seen and understood.

There was an overwhelming amount of grief and loss surrounding my body and everything it had endured. From the sexual abuse I suffered at an early age to the repeated violations throughout my life, it was as if my body had become a battleground I had long since abandoned. This course revealed just how disconnected I had been from it, living so far away from the essence of myself.

I realised that the chronic people-pleaser in me had been operating in a constant state of trauma response, doing whatever I could to keep myself safe. But the harsh truth was that people-pleasing hadn't kept me safe at all. Instead, it had caused even more harm, leaving me vulnerable and disconnected from my own needs and discounting my boundaries.

I had been living in survival mode for so long that listening to my body felt entirely foreign. My husband had claimed ownership of my body, leaving no space for my voice or experiences. When he hurt me, I would tell him, "You're hurting me," and his response was always the same: "I'm not hurting ya; I didn't do it that hard."

One of the cruellest things he would do was squeeze my nipples so hard it would bring me to tears. The pain was excruciating, yet he showed no remorse, no acknowledgment of how much he was hurting me. That dismissive comment would drive me crazy inside because it didn't matter what I said, he didn't care. There was no empathy, no accountability, only blame. He twisted reality until it felt insane, making me believe that the pain I felt was my fault or all in my head. The shame silenced me; I was too embarrassed to tell anyone how much daily pain he was causing to my body.

His cruelty went beyond the physical; it stripped away my dignity, making me feel like I didn't matter, that my voice and body were insignificant. It was as though he thrived on the control, on reducing me to nothing.

At this point, my body didn't trust me at all. It had endured so much harm and violation that it was a complete mess, physically, emotionally, and spiritually. My husband had hurt my body in ways that felt impossible to speak about. During sex, he would hit me on the back of the head, spit on me, strangle and choke me, all while justifying his actions as 'BDSM' and acronym for bondage and discipline, dominance and submission, and sadomasochism.

He was drawn to dark, degrading acts that left me tainted with shame, as though a part of my soul had been stripped away each time. I didn't know how I could ever tell anyone about the sexual darkness I endured in my marriage. The weight of that shame was unbearable, silencing me even further.

My body was crying out for safety, care, and compassion, things it had been denied for far too long. It needed constant reassurance, a promise from me to protect it, to never again put it in harm's way. Rebuilding that trust felt overwhelming, but I knew it was the only way forward.

I signed up for the course, which was scheduled to begin in early 2021. I was determined to learn how to listen to my body in a way I had never known before, to reconnect with it and finally give it the attention and care it deserved.

While waiting for the *Institute of New Paradigm Intimacy* course to begin, I signed up for another course in the interim called *Love Out Loud*, which I heard about from a good friend at work Narelle, who was with the *National Disability Insurance Scheme* (NDIS). Narelle had been a dear friend and a source of immense comfort during some of my darkest moments.

When I was at my wits' end, crying in pain in the lunchroom or wherever I broke down, she would sit with me, offering unwavering support. No matter how broken I felt, Narelle naturally held space for me, her presence a lifeline when the weight of home life and the failure of pain meds to provide relief became too much to bear.

It was in those moments of safety, as I crumbled under the pressures of my reality, that her kindness made all the difference. Narelle's heart is big, kind, and caring, and I am forever grateful for the comfort she brought into those vulnerable times when my body was screaming out in pain.

When Narelle told me about *Love Out Loud*, I decided to sign up and entered my first *Zoom* space after leaving the marriage. I felt raw, messy, and vulnerable, carrying an incredible amount of pain that often left me on the floor, struggling to manage the spasms wracking my body. It was a tender and fragile time, but this step felt like the beginning of something new, even amidst the chaos within me.

The *Love Out Loud* space provided much-needed validation and encouragement, meeting me exactly where I was in all my messiness. It gave me a sense of being seen and supported during a time when I felt utterly broken.

Around this time, I had also signed up for the *Graduate Certificate in Domestic and Family Violence* through *RMIT* online. However, the *RMIT* cyberattack made it incredibly difficult to continue, and looking back, I see it as a blessing. My body was not up for such an intense course, it was crying out for care, not more demands.

I was in the throes of intense emotional and physical pain, plagued by suicidal thoughts and an overwhelming sense of shame. I constantly questioned my worth, wondering how I could possibly live with the weight of so much brokenness. My body needed rest, gentleness, and healing far more than it needed another challenge to bear.

Once *Love Out Loud* finished, I began the course with the *Institute of New Paradigm Intimacy*, and over the next six months, I embarked on a transformative journey of learning about my body. Although the course was longer than six months, I did not do it for the qualification, my intent was for healing purposes.

This was no ordinary course. Led by Victoria, an exceptional woman, it opened a new paradigm of learning to listen to my body with compassion and love. Through sound, movement, music, breath, and touch, I began to understand what it meant to connect with the somatic world. It was groundbreaking to realise that my body had its own language, constantly speaking to me through sensations and responses. For the first time, I was learning to listen to what my body was saying, and it laid the foundation for a deeper understanding of myself and my healing journey.

It was in this course that I first heard the words, "Give yourself permission to just be, and know that all parts of you are welcome." Those words were liberating. For the first time, I felt a sense of freedom to embrace myself fully, messiness, pain, and all. It was a profound shift, an invitation to let go of judgment and simply exist as I was. I found learning to sit with without judgement towards my body, was a step into liberation. Freedom to just be, with all the ticks, spasms, sudden screams and contractions that left me breathless, all was welcome.

Another person in the course that was pivotal in helping me with reconnection was Emily. She was a support person in the course as was Jeremy and both were pillars of strength in their own unique ways, giving my body the safety and permission to move through whatever was present at the time. Although this was all through *Zoom*, it was incredibly powerful to experience.

At the same time, I immersed myself in painting, endlessly covering canvases with water, pouring all my emotions onto the canvas, as if the water could hold and release the grief I carried. It was a cathartic process, a way to give form to the feelings I couldn't yet fully articulate.

During this time, I also ceremonially burned the belongings my husband had left behind, things he didn't want but had burdened me with. Alone at the beach house, I set them alight, symbolically releasing the remnants of his control. I screamed, a lot. I screamed to release the pent-up emotions that had been stifled throughout my marriage. It was raw, primal, and necessary, a way to give voice to years of unexpressed pain.

I listened endlessly to audiobooks on narcissism, Polyvagal Theory, the brain and body, healing from childhood sexual abuse, and trauma.

Titles like *The Body Keeps the Score* by Bessel van der Kolk and *Daring Greatly* by Brené Brown became lifelines, offering scientific and emotional language for the pain I was trying to process. They helped me realise I wasn't alone, and I wasn't crazy.

These books became my guides, offering understanding and language for what I had endured. I also turned to other works of Brené Brown for her insights into understanding shame, which had been a constant weight on my heart and mind. I dived into understanding narcissism, family violence and childhood sexual abuse and what it does to the brain and body at an early age, and how it can lead to abusive adult relationships, just as I had experienced.

Prayer became a lifeline. I talked to God daily, pouring out my heart, praying for peace of mind, and asking Him why I had to stay alive. Those conversations with God, though often desperate and tear-filled, were a source of solace and a thread of hope that helped me keep going, one step at a time.

Each audiobook I listened to, each prayer I whispered, brought me a step closer to reclaiming myself, a piece of the puzzle falling into place in my journey of healing and rediscovery.

At the same time, I sought treatment from a local healer named Jo, that I came to know through Narelle. She had a gentle, intuitive approach to helping me work through the physical trauma and pain I carried. Her place felt like a sanctuary, a safe space that nurtured my body and soul. Jo's three amazing dogs were part of the healing process, bringing comfort and calm that words couldn't express. Uncannily, one of her dogs resembled Buddy. The likeness was striking, and it felt like a tender reminder of him, bringing both a bittersweet connection and a sense of comfort during the sessions. Her treatments were pivotal in my recovery, offering my body the support and care it desperately needed.

During the first six months of 2021, I filed for divorce, thanks to the support of my Aunty Aurora, her son John, and their family friend Nat. Nat informed me that I could file for a single divorce without needing anything to do with him, a revelation that brought me immense relief. I wanted nothing to do with my husband; I wanted him cut off from every area of my life.

Even during the INPI course, he continued to harass and taunt me. I couldn't understand why, after we had gone our separate ways, and he had moved to another state, he was still trying to hurt me and cause further pain. Then, one night, I received a dark and spiteful email about a girl who was supposedly having his baby. The email was cruel and nasty, filled with hateful words that tore me down, calling me a horrible person and mocking me for everything I had endured. It read like pure hate mail, dripping with malice, designed to cut me as deeply as possible.

Knowing he was having a baby with someone else while continuing to harass me was another level of cruelty. It felt like he was still trying to assert power over me, even from a distance, refusing to let go of his control. Filing for divorce was not just a legal step; it was an act of survival, a way to sever ties and reclaim my life from his darkness.

It wasn't a straightforward process, as my husband tried to dispute the dates and prolong the divorce. I told the lawyers that this was typical of him, his need to control and manipulate every situation. I pleaded with them, explaining that I desperately needed to be freed from this man who had nearly killed me more than once.

Even as the divorce proceedings continued, he still found ways to contact me, refusing to leave me alone. His harassment felt relentless, and I eventually involved the police, asking them to tell him to stay away and leave me in peace. I had to change all my accounts, update my information, and take every step I could to ensure he couldn't interfere in my life.

I was immensely relieved when the judge ruled in my favour, agreeing with my dates of separation.

Many survivors don't realise that in Australia, you can file for divorce as a single applicant without the consent of your ex-spouse. This legal pathway can be vital for those leaving abusive relationships where ongoing contact is unsafe.

The Husband had to show up for a court date online during lockdown but as he didn't, it was settled and finally, on July 13, 2021, I was officially divorced.

What a day of joy that was, exhilarating, liberating, and deeply empowering. It marked the end of one of the darkest chapters of my life and the beginning of reclaiming my freedom.

But even after the divorce, he still tried to make contact, finding ways to disrupt the peace I had fought so hard to achieve. It was as though he couldn't bear to let go of the control, he once held over me. Each attempt felt like a shadow of the past trying to pull me back, but I held firm in my resolve to keep him out of my life for good.

During the period from December 2020 to July 2021, I cried out to God in desperation, asking, "Why do I need to hang around this earth?" The weight of shame consumed me, and I would sob uncontrollably, pleading, "I don't know if I can go on."

In that dark place, I reached out to a family friend, Kale, and sent him a goodbye text. It was a simple message: "Thank you for everything, and goodbye." I had reached the point where I couldn't see a way through. I felt utterly alone, with not a single soul around. The world felt eerily empty, with people wearing masks and avoiding eye contact, their heads down as they walked. It was as if I didn't exist, as though I was invisible.

The lack of face-to-face connection was crushing me, draining the last bit of life I had left. After sending that text, I seriously considered how I could take my life. It was a moment of complete hopelessness. I never heard from that friend again after my goodbye text, which only deepened the isolation I felt.

Reflection

Making sense of what happened after my husband left at the end of October 2020 with our dear pup, Buddy, felt like untangling a ball of knotted twine. While knowing he was driving far away, moving interstate, brought a sense of relief, the emotional aftermath was overwhelming. He was the kind of person I needed to keep as far away from me as possible, yet the damage he left behind still haunted me.

That period was tumultuous. I was a twitching mess, a skeleton of myself, my body on high alert, jumping, jolting, overwhelmed by excruciating pain. Emotionally, I was tossed around like a small boat in a storm, plunging in and out of despair. In the midst of the chaos, I clung to the one thing that kept me grounded: God.

I found comfort in Jesus, though the desire to die often battled with the flicker of hope. The thought of writing this book and using my story to help others became a guiding light, a reason to hold on. Through this journey, I realised I was reclaiming the land rights to my own body, a body that had been mistreated, silenced, and controlled for so long. Each step was an act of healing, a declaration that I belonged to myself again.

And then there was my love for my nieces, nephews, and family. I couldn't bear the thought of scarring them with the memory of their aunt or daughter ending her life, found dead at the family beach house. That thought anchored me to this world, pushing me to keep fighting, even when the storm inside seemed too fierce to endure.

There were many moments when I hit my lowest points. When my husband, even from interstate, continued to taunt and harass me, it rattled my fragile nervous system. I had to change everything, my accounts, my contact information, cutting him out of my life was the only way to silence the suicidal thoughts that plagued me.

This meant severing ties with nearly everyone connected to him. I had to let go of all but three close sisterhoods, Sue, Pixie, and Judith. My body instinctively knew it needed to sever every connection. I even had to say goodbye to his dear mother, whom I had loved deeply, though that decision nearly broke me. I also had to let go of Buddy Boy, whose absence felt like another loss I could barely process.

That marriage swept through my life like a hurricane, leaving destruction in its wake. All the emotions I hadn't been able to express during those years came rushing out. I burned the things he left behind, things he no longer wanted, and screamed, cried, painted, and wept beside the ocean. The waves, though silent, felt like a comforting presence, holding space for my grief.

"How am I ever going to make sense of this?" I often asked myself. The weight of it all felt impossible to untangle, but with each wave, every brushstroke, and every tear, I slowly began to piece myself back together. Guided by God's love and the angels who soothed my aching soul, I began a daily practice of tuning in to my body, asking it what it needed and learning to listen to its quiet whispers. Reclaiming myself was a process, but one that was essential for my healing.

Even as I learned to listen to my body, the silence pressed in. I had spent years in a marriage that stole my voice, but now, without him, without Buddy, without the noise of survival, I was left with nothing but silence.

No distractions. No chaos. Just me.

And that's when I realised, he was gone, but his shadow still lived inside me. I was physically free, but my soul was still drowning.

18: Echoes of Silence

Even after I left him, after I was finally alone, I realised something unbearable: he was still with me. Not physically, but in the way my body braced for chaos, in the way silence pressed against my chest like a weight I couldn't shake. I had never known peace, not really.

And then, suddenly, nothing. No one. No sound. No movement.

> *"Silence is not the absence of something, but the presence of everything." - Gordon Hempton*

The silence should have been a relief. But instead, it felt like suffocation. The walls of the beach house, once comforting, now felt like they were closing in. The quiet was too much. My body still twitched, spasmed, jolted, releasing years of trauma, but now, there was no chaos to drown it out. No one to blame. Nothing to distract me from the reality of what had been done to me.

For the first time in years, I was truly alone with myself. And I didn't know how to handle it.

I had left him. I had taken back my body.

But why did it still feel like he was everywhere?

Why did my body still jolt when I heard a loud noise? Why did I still flinch at the thought of a male voice? Why did the silence feel just as oppressive as his presence?

He was gone, but his fingerprints were still all over me.

The trauma didn't leave with him. It stayed, woven into my muscles, my bones, my breath. It whispered to me in the silence, in the way my body curled in on itself at night, in the way I still didn't feel safe in my own skin.

I wasn't free yet. I was just beginning to understand what it meant to truly escape. Every one of my behaviours were conditioned. He filled my neurons! A traumatised brain is like a battlefield wired for survival. Abuse conditions it to expect danger, flooding the body with stress hormones and locking it in fight, flight, freeze or fawn mode. Over time, the brain rewires itself, fear becomes the default, trust feels risky, and self-worth erodes. It's like running on a glitchy survival program where even safety feels suspicious. Healing? That's about rewriting the code, teaching the brain that peace isn't a trap, love isn't a lie, and strength isn't just about enduring pain.

Part one of any transition from trauma is about transforming the trauma coding within the brain. Part two is readjusting to a life without the threat of trauma ever returning.

Coming out of a marriage steeped in family violence left me reeling, not just from the abuse itself but from the shock of the transition. I went from a house that was never quiet, filled with constant traffic, the hum of drugs being sold and traded, and the chaotic rhythm of those who sought out the drugs. Life that was anything but peaceful, to a silent and isolated existence on my own. Previously, the traffic was constant, the house always buzzing with noise, with my husband's dealings keeping everything in motion. Then, suddenly, it stopped. I was left in a world that was eerily silent, far removed from the noise that once consumed me.

At the Peninsula, the lockdown silence reverberated through me like a heavy fog, pressing down on my chest and leaving me gasping for connection. It wasn't just the physical absence of my husband and the life I had known, but the emotional void that followed. The silence was deafening, the stillness unsettling. My body, still in shock from the trauma of years of abuse, began to react to the quiet in ways I couldn't control.

Jolts and spasms wracked my body, as though the trauma itself was trying to break free. It felt like my body couldn't escape what had been done to it, and yet, there was nowhere for it to go. Although mum and dad came up for a few days whenever they could.

It was hard with all the restrictions because my parents were more than 5kms away. When they did come, they were an anchor, my lifeline, physically and emotionally.

Exhausted by the constant physical jolts, I sought help at the *Rosebud Emergency Department*. The doctor and nurse were kind, patient, and understanding. The doctor explained something that stayed with me, he said that the jolts were the trauma leaving my body. It was a small but profound moment of validation, as if my body's response to the trauma was finally being recognised. I told him that I was on my own, separated from family violence, missing human connection.

Going to the emergency department wasn't just about the physical jolts, it was about seeking a connection, a safe connection, with another human being.

Trauma experts like Bessel van der Kolk and Stephen Porges speak about *limbic resonance*, the way our nervous system responds to safety through connection with another. When someone makes eye contact, uses a gentle tone, or simply sits with us in stillness, it sends signals to our brain and body that we are safe. It's why I longed so deeply for resonance, for someone whose presence alone could help my body come down from years of high alert. It's why trauma survivors often need connection more than explanation. Co-regulation through safe human connection (limbic resonance) helps shift the body from survival mode to restoration.

The silence swallowed me whole. My body jolted and twitched, struggling to release trauma, but I had nowhere to go, no one to hold on to. Then, in the quiet of the night, something shifted.

Tilly, a loving cat came to me. She was there in my sleep, speaking to me in a way only the heart can hear. "Take care of my brother and me" she begged. It wasn't just a vision. It was a lifeline. I saw her face, her big almond shaped eyes with love pouring out of them, calling me to adopt her and her brother Banjo.

The next day, I called the *Peninsula Animal Rescue*, and they told me there was a brother and sister, six months old, who needed rescuing. Their situation was tragic, their owner had tried to burn down their house, and they were in a family violence situation. I knew, without hesitation, that I needed to adopt them. I registered to adopt Tilly and Banjo, and on June 11, I brought them home.

When I met Tilly, I saw her exactly as she had appeared to me in the visitation. It was as if she had come to guide me, to remind me that even in the deepest loneliness, I was not truly alone. Banjo, too, was a lifeline. Together, they became a source of comfort, companionship, and healing during the long, solitary days of lockdown.

Tilly and Banjo were more than just pets; they were a part of my healing journey. In the midst of the quiet and isolation, they brought me connection, love, and the reminder that despite everything I had been through, I was capable of caring, of nurturing, and of rebuilding. Their presence helped anchor me, giving me something to hold on to when the loneliness threatened to swallow me whole.

Reflections on Isolation and Loss of Connection

In the days after I left, the house that had once been filled with constant traffic, people in and out, the noise of his drug dealings, the quick exchanges that never allowed for peace, was eerily silent. It was like I had stepped out of one world into another; one so stark and cold it felt like it was suffocating me. The constant hum of chaos had been my reality for so long that the quiet was foreign. My mind struggled to catch up with the stillness, but my body felt the shock immediately.

I'd spent years in that toxic environment, a life that revolved around his needs, his unpredictability. There had been no space for me to breathe freely, no space to claim myself. Yet, paradoxically, the isolation that followed, being completely on my own, in a house without animals, without my partner, felt like a betrayal. A betrayal of the life I had thought I knew, the connections I had thought I had, even if they were built on lies. It was as though I was left in the debris of what had once been a frantic, if painful, semblance of connection, and now, I was lost in the void of silence.

Even as I sat in the silence of lockdown, surrounded by the empty rooms, I found myself yearning for connection. Not the false connections of those years, but genuine, authentic interaction, someone to sit with me, to hear my pain, to truly see me. But each time I thought of reaching out, I felt too broken, too exposed. How could I invite anyone into the mess I was in? How could I possibly explain the rawness, the fragility that had taken over every part of me?

The daily shifting of lockdown rules only deepened the madness. Each day brought a new restriction, new limitations on where I could go or what I could do, and it felt as though my world was shrinking with each passing hour. One day, something would be allowed, only for it to be banned the next, and it only added to the confusion and sense of helplessness I was already grappling with. How was I supposed to rebuild when the very foundations of my reality were changing every day?

To add to the chaos, I kept receiving text messages about alcohol sales, reminders of the substances that had played such a huge part in my husband's life and that still lingered as a temptation, a reminder of the life I was desperately trying to leave behind. Each message felt like a cruel joke, a reminder of the life I was trying to escape, the choices I'd made to keep going, even when everything in me screamed to numb the pain.

And the pain didn't ease up. In fact, it felt like my body was revolting against me. I was experiencing regular contractions, like the kind you feel when you're giving birth, sharp and intense. It was as if my body was holding onto the trauma, unwilling to let go. Each contraction left me breathless, as though I couldn't catch my breath or my bearings. The physical pain was a constant reminder that my body had been through more than anyone could see. It was as if every part of me was being purged, but I couldn't escape the weight of it.

During this time, when I could bring myself to drive, I would head to the lookout by the ocean, just 10 minutes away by car. The vastness of the ocean before me seemed to represent both the endless possibilities and the depth of my emotions. I found solace in looking out over the water, the waves crashing relentlessly against the shore, much like the waves of grief, anger, and despair crashing within me. The ocean was vast and open, a mirror to my inner world, deep, turbulent, but with the promise of something more, something beyond the pain I was living in. It was as if the ocean was offering me a space to breathe, to just be, while it held the storm inside me.

It was in this silence that I turned to writing. The book became my lifeline, a way to express the emotions that had been locked inside me for so long. Writing became my refuge, my outlet. Every word, every sentence, was a way to release the pain, the anger, the fear. It was as if the book itself became a space where I could finally make sense of everything.

But even in this newfound space for expression, the loneliness was overwhelming. There were times I missed human contact so deeply, but fear of judgment kept me isolated. I found myself longing for a connection, but I didn't know how to reach out without feeling exposed, vulnerable. I couldn't bring myself to trust anyone, not after everything I had been through. Even though I had people who loved me, who supported me, I still felt alone in the silence.

When my 16 sessions with the *Centre Against Sexual Assault* (CASA) ended in July, I was devastated. My counsellor had been an anchor during such a turbulent time and losing that support felt like one more layer of isolation. I was left to find my own way, searching for therapeutic support. Unfortunately, I came across a number of counsellors who seemed disconnected from my reality. The contractions hadn't begun just after I left the marriage; they had been increasing in intensity throughout the marriage, growing out of control as the abuse escalated.

The pain was becoming unmanageable, as was the emotional toll. My body, already carrying the weight of years of trauma, was reacting in ways I couldn't control, signalling to me that something was deeply wrong, but I had no space to understand or process it at the time. It was only after I left that I realised how much the trauma had affected me physically. My body was screaming for attention, yet I felt helpless and alone, unable to escape the pain.

In an attempt to find healing, I sought out therapy and counselling. But even in this, there were more challenges. One psychologist in particular, seemed disconnected from my reality. She decided to experiment with *Eye Movement Desensitisation and Reprocessing* (EMDR), attempting to bring up memories of sexual abuse while I was already in a suicidal state. She knew I was alone, struggling to survive, yet never followed up with me afterward. I was left in a worse state than when I first came to her, overwhelmed by the intensity of the trauma that was reawakened.

At what cost does one search for support? It's all well and good to look for a counsellor or therapist, but when you're already at the edge of despair, the wrong support can be more harmful than helpful. The emotional toll of trusting someone only to be left feeling worse than before was devastating. The search for healing became another battle, one where I often felt more isolated than ever.

These experiences only deepened my sense of isolation and confusion. I was left questioning everything, myself, my worth, and whether I would ever find a way out of the storm.

It was time to leave the Peninsula. I was sad to leave the water, the ocean, and the beach, the place that had offered me so much solace during my darkest times. The sound of the waves, the vastness of the sea, had become my companion, my quiet sanctuary in a world that had felt too loud. But as much as I loved it there, I knew I needed my own space, a place where I could heal without the constant reminders of my past.

The decision to leave the Peninsula was bittersweet. The beach had been a refuge, a place where I had found moments of peace amidst the chaos, but it was time for me to create a new chapter. I needed to carve out a space where I could rebuild, truly start again. The silence of the Peninsula had been both a comfort and a challenge, it was time to embrace a new environment that would allow me to grow, to heal, and to fully reclaim my life.

Leaving behind the familiar was hard, but I knew that it was the right choice. I was moving towards something that was mine, something I could own and control, something that wasn't tainted by the past. The water, the beach, and the ocean would always be a part of me, but now it was time to step into the next phase of my journey, alone, but stronger.

Leaving the beach house was also difficult because it wasn't just mine, it was for everyone in the family. It had been a place where memories were made, a shared space that held both joy and sorrow. But staying there, after everything I had been through, no longer felt like an option.

Reflection

Leaving the beach house was not just a change of location; it was a symbolic act of moving away from the past and toward a new beginning. The ocean had been my refuge, but as much as I longed for its calming presence, I knew that I could no longer remain in a space that was not truly mine. It wasn't just about the silence or the physical distance; it was about reclaiming my space, my voice, and my sense of safety. The decision to leave was filled with grief, but also with hope, hope that by stepping away, I was stepping toward something more empowering.

One thing that kept me going through the transition was a small, quiet voice I'd often hear, urging me to visualise what my new life could be like. While I was at the Peninsula, I spent countless hours imagining my new home in Melbourne, not just in my mind, but through all my senses. I could feel the warmth of the sun on my skin in a space that was mine, smell the fresh air, and taste the sweetness of a life I was finally creating for myself. I made a scrapbook of images, pictures that represented everything I dreamed of, peace, safety, and a sense of belonging. Each image in that scrapbook was a step closer to the new life I envisioned, and each day it gave me the strength to keep moving forward.

The beach house, once shared by my family, had been a reminder of what I had lost. It wasn't just the ocean that I was leaving behind; it was the life I had imagined. But in leaving, I was finally giving myself permission to heal in a space that was solely for me. I needed to create a sanctuary, a place where I could rebuild from the inside out. This move, though difficult, was an act of self-preservation and self-love. It was the beginning of forging a future that was mine to shape.

GRACE AMORE

The silence had been deafening. But maybe, just maybe, it was trying to tell me something.

I couldn't live in the past anymore. I couldn't keep circling the pain, letting it swallow me whole.

I needed to move forward. I needed to rebuild. I just didn't know how yet.

But the ocean whispered to me, again and again: "Keep going."

19: Rebuilding My Sanctuary

After months of suffocating silence, I finally had a place to call my own. But when I walked into my new home for the first time in September 2021, my stomach dropped. The house was in ruins, trash piled high, walls stained, a space that had been left to rot. I had dreamed of a fresh start, but instead, I found devastation.

Standing in that broken home, I saw myself reflected back, shattered, damaged, in need of restoration. Could I rebuild this place? Could I rebuild myself? I didn't know. But I had to try.

> *"The world breaks everyone, and afterward, some are strong at the broken places." - Ernest Hemingway*

Moving into my new home with my furbabies, Tilly and Banjo, was the beginning of a long, arduous journey toward reclaiming my life. The house I moved into had been left in complete disarray by the tenants, who had used the space as a dumping ground. There was trash scattered everywhere, and the damage to my house was heartbreaking.

I wasn't just rebuilding walls and floors; I was rebuilding my life. Each layer of grime scrubbed away, each piece of broken furniture removed, was like stripping away the past, peeling back the layers of hurt and betrayal.

It wasn't easy. Some days, I didn't think I had the strength. Thankfully my dad came to help. As my dad tore out the old carpet and laid down new floorboards, as my sister and friends painted over the stains of the past, I began to see it, hope.

A home. A future. A sanctuary.

But through the devastation, a quiet hope began to stir. My dad, steady, dependable, showed up, just as he always had. He tore out the old carpet, laid down new floorboards, and spent endless hours at *Bunnings*, picking up whatever was needed. Every nail he hammered, every broken thing he fixed, wasn't just restoring the house, it was restoring me.

My sister Angela, my niece Elizabeth, her fiancé Jeremy, and my friends Sue and Lorene painted over the stains of the past, their brushstrokes layering fresh beginnings onto what had once been ruins. Each gesture, each moment of effort, reminded me that I wasn't alone. They were building something solid, something safe. And with every piece of the house that was rebuilt, I began to feel the possibility of rebuilding myself.

My father's efforts, unwavering and filled with care, became the foundation of what would slowly transform into a safe space for me. His commitment to restoring the home wasn't just about fixing walls and floors; it was about giving me a chance to rebuild my life, to create something solid where everything had once been broken.

My sister Angela, my friends Sue, Lorene, my niece Elizabeth, her fiancé Jeremy (now husband), and their friend Marco rallied together to help paint, restore, and clear out mountains of rubbish and grime. The work was incredibly physically demanding, and the emotional toll was overwhelming. But as I watched the community of family and friends come together, it felt like more than just a house being restored, it was a sense of belonging and peace slowly being rebuilt. The act of working side by side, of showing up for me in my darkest moments, gave me strength I didn't know I had. I am deeply grateful to everyone for their time and efforts. I couldn't have done it without them. Their support helped transform the chaos into something that resembled hope, and it was in this process that I began to truly reclaim my life.

Sue, in particular, played a huge role in this process. She transported 15 bamboo trees across Melbourne to be planted along the fence line for privacy, something I will forever be grateful for. Those bamboo trees became more than just a barrier; they were a symbol of the safety and sanctuary I was creating, a place where I could finally breathe, a place that was mine. The process of turning the house into a home took several months, about three to six months, but in that time, it began to feel like a haven, a space where I could heal, where Tilly, Banjo, and I could find peace.

For the first time in years, I was beginning to feel safe. My home was slowly taking shape. My body was still hurting, still trembling from the past, but at least now, I had a space that was mine.

And I had Tilly and Banjo. They were my heartbeat, my reason to keep going.

The brain heals from trauma through neuroplasticity, the ability to rewire and form new connections. Healing involves processing the trauma, reducing stress responses, and building resilience through supportive relationships and positive experiences. Therapy, mindfulness, and self-care can help regulate emotions and restore balance.

Family plays a crucial role by providing a safe, loving environment where the individual feels heard and validated. Supportive family members can help by encouraging healthy coping mechanisms, fostering open communication, and reinforcing positive behaviours. Their presence and understanding help rebuild trust, strengthen emotional regulation, and promote overall healing.

But grief has a way of sneaking in just when you think you can breathe again. Just as my house began to feel like a home, grief came crashing back in.

On New Year's Day 2022, I lost Tilly. My girl. My heartbeat.

GRACE AMORE

She had been found a couple of doors down, her body still and lifeless. Poison, they said. My sister Sandra and her daughters, Nicole and Elizabeth, knocked on every door, trying to find answers. But nothing could bring her back. Nothing could take away the unbearable ache in my chest.

I collapsed, sobbing, the walls of my newly rebuilt home suddenly suffocating me. The house I had fought to turn into a sanctuary now felt empty, haunted by absence. I wanted to die. The grief was unbearable, another loss in a life already filled with too much pain.

In those moments, the house felt less like a sanctuary and more like a reminder of everything I had lost. Each room, each corner, seemed to hold the weight of my grief. The physical restoration of the house mirrored my own struggle to rebuild, but it wasn't easy. Yet, even through the heartbreak, I had to remind myself that Tilly had been such an important part of my healing process. Her love and presence had given me comfort, and now with her gone, I was beyond distraught, more loss to bear.

Amidst the devastation, I was grateful to Lorene, who had painted a portrait of Tilly while I was at the Peninsula. Lorene had come to visit during 2021 and, knowing how much Tilly meant to me, she captured her essence beautifully in the painting. That portrait became one of the few things I could hold onto, a reminder of my little girl's spirit and the love she had brought into my life. It felt like a tribute to her memory, one that would help me keep her close even as I navigated the depths of this new loss.

I knew I needed something to anchor me into life after Tilly passed in 2022. The weight of grief, combined with the ongoing physical pain from the contractions, the jolts, and the trauma flashbacks, left me feeling lost. I needed something to keep me alive, to keep me grounded, to give me a reason to move forward. So, I turned to God, crying out in desperation, asking for a sign, something that could guide me through the darkness.

I was drowning in grief, searching for something, anything, that could anchor me. I had lost too much. My body was failing, my mind was breaking, and I didn't know how to keep going.

Then, I found the *School of Faith Australia*. It wasn't just another course; it was a chance to find meaning in the wreckage. A lifeline. A way to stop feeling like I was spiralling into nothingness.

I signed up in February 2022, even though I felt like a mess of shame and sorrow. I didn't know if I was strong enough to face my faith, to face God after everything. But something inside me whispered, try.

I was still grieving, still struggling with the pain and trauma, but something in me told me this was the right path.

The *School of Faith* offered a weekend intensive in Melbourne, and even though I felt like a mess of shame, grief, and loss, I signed up. My body was still struggling, and I was far from being in a good place emotionally. The flashbacks and physical pain made every moment feel like a battle. But I showed up, not knowing how I would recover from the weight of it all.

That weekend away in Melbourne was nothing short of transformative. Even in my fragile state, I felt the love, support, and sense of community that I so desperately needed. It wasn't an instant fix, and the healing didn't come overnight, but that weekend was a lifeline. It became a moment where I could feel God's presence, reminding me that even in my brokenness, there was hope.

In life's darkest moments, when everything feels broken, God offered me hope as a guiding light. Through faith, He reminds me that no pain is permanent, no struggle is without purpose, and no heart is beyond healing. His love provides strength to endure, His wisdom brings clarity, and His grace offers renewal. Even in the midst of despair, He plants seeds of hope, through prayer, through the kindness of others, and through the quiet reassurance that we are never alone. With God, brokenness is not the end but the beginning of something new, stronger, and filled with purpose.

Though the pain didn't vanish, that weekend planted a seed of hope in my heart. I knew I wasn't alone, and for the first time in a long time, I felt like I could take a step forward. It was a reminder that despite the pain, despite the loss, there was still a path forward, one that led to healing, restoration, and a future that was not defined by what I had lost, but by what I could still become.

As the house began to take shape, something inside me shifted as well. The relentless pressure of grief was still heavy on my chest, but I could feel the weight of trauma lifting ever so slightly with each moment of progress, with each brushstroke of paint. The home was becoming a sanctuary not only because it was safe but because I was starting to reclaim the fragments of myself that had been lost.

The bamboo trees that Sue brought from across Melbourne grew taller and stronger with every passing day. Their shoots pushed through the earth, defying the weight of the soil and the harsh winds. They were a mirror of me, bent and weathered but growing all the same, finding my footing even when it felt like the world was stacked against me.

During the first year of my journey at the *School of Faith*, I was up and down, overwhelmed by a constant battle with shame and grief. I wasn't in a good way. Every day felt like a struggle, as I grappled with overwhelming emotions, suicidal thoughts, and an inability to cope with the physical and emotional pain that consumed me. I wasn't able to function properly, working, socialising, even simple tasks felt impossible.

The online class with the *School of Faith*, which I attended once a fortnight, became a lifeline, helping me navigate the stormy emotions that would threaten to swallow me whole. Still, the weight of it all was almost unbearable. Despite my best efforts, I couldn't shake the feeling of being overwhelmed, trapped in a constant cycle of loss and pain. My body was still riddled with the trauma of years of abuse, and every day it felt like I was fighting just to get through.

I was also struggling financially. The medicinal cannabis that I relied on for some relief from the pain was outrageously priced in Melbourne, and it wasn't something I could afford regularly. It felt like a cruel irony, I was trying to heal from the wounds of the past, only to be weighed down by the present. The lack of support, coupled with the mounting financial strain, made it feel like I was being buried alive.

At the start of 2022, I made an appointment to see a new doctor, transferring from my old GP in Southeast Gippsland to Melbourne. Dr. Sahar, an angel in human form, would become the first doctor who truly understood the depth of my pain. I remember walking into that first appointment with my older sister Sandra by my side for support. The weight of my struggles, both physical and emotional, felt unbearable as I shared with Dr. Sahar that I had been contemplating euthanasia. The period pain had become so chronic, it robbed me of any quality of life. I was housebound, unable to work, and the idea of death seemed like an easier alternative to the constant agony.

For the first time, I wasn't met with dismissal or told to just push through. Dr. Sahar sat with us, and we cried together. She didn't treat me like a case number or a symptom to fix. She truly saw me, understood my pain, and reassured me that while my suffering was immense, it didn't mean I had to end it all. There was a way through this, she said. It wasn't death; there was still hope.

Dr. Sahar's compassion and expertise gave me something I hadn't felt in a long time: the belief that I could find a way forward. She was the first doctor apart from the GP at *Jean Hailes Women's Clinic* I saw in 2019 who truly understood pelvic pain, and I was grateful for the comfort she gave me. It was a reminder that I wasn't alone in this journey.

Through it all, *1800 Respect* was an anchor for me. The support I received from the workers on the other end of the line was lifesaving, providing a steady presence in the storm of my emotions. At one point, during a particularly dark phone call, the pain became so overwhelming that the woman on the other end of the line supported me in calling an ambulance. The pain in my body and mind was so intense that I could barely breathe, and I knew I couldn't keep going like this.

I was taken to the *Northern Emergency Department*, where I was seen by doctors and given pain relief. A mental health nurse came to speak with me, and we discussed my suicidal thoughts. They referred me to the *Hope Team* in my local area, a suicide prevention team that would later become a vital support system during my darkest moments. It was mid-2022 when this all happened, and I felt like I had reached the lowest point in my journey. But it was in that moment of surrender, calling for help, accepting that I needed assistance, that I began to take a small step towards healing.

Despite everything, the process of reaching out, of accepting support, was a turning point. It reminded me that even in the darkest moments, there was help available, and I wasn't alone.

As I struggled to find my place in my family after leaving the marriage, a deep sense of loss and confusion overwhelmed me. I felt disconnected, out of place. The shame that clung to me made me feel dirty, unworthy of being around my nieces and nephews. It was as if I no longer belonged in the family I had once felt so close to. Their lives had moved on, and I couldn't reconcile myself with the person I had become after everything I had endured. I found myself feeling like an outsider in the family I had grown up in.

One day, it all became too much. I found myself back at the emergency department, this time at the *Royal Melbourne Hospital* with my dad by my side. The pain from my body and mind had reached a peak, and my family, too, was at their wit's end. They didn't know what to do, and neither did I. I was a mess, physically, emotionally, mentally. It was as if the trauma had seeped into every cell of my being, and I couldn't escape it. The fear of being trapped in this never-ending cycle of pain and confusion was overwhelming. My dad's presence was a comfort, but even he couldn't take the weight of it all away.

In my search for healing, I sought a counsellor, someone who could help me navigate the trauma, the pain, the shame that I couldn't escape. But no matter how many therapists I saw, I couldn't find anyone who truly understood what I had been through. I couldn't find anyone who grasped the complexity of trauma-informed care, the impact of family violence, childhood sexual abuse, and medical gaslighting had on my mind and body. No one seemed to truly understand how these experiences had rewired my brain, how they had made every moment feel like a battle. I was constantly triggered, each day a reminder of how much pain and confusion I carried. It felt like there was no one who could help me untangle the mess in my mind, no one who could truly understand the magnitude of what I was going through.

By the end of 2022, my body was still breaking down. The physical pain from endometriosis and adenomyosis, combined with the ongoing trauma, was relentless.

One day, it all became too much. I found myself back at the emergency department, this time at the *Royal Melbourne Hospital* with my dad by my side. The pain from my body and mind had reached a peak, and my family, too, was at their wit's end. They didn't know what to do, and neither did I. I was a mess, physically, emotionally, mentally. It was as if the trauma had seeped into every cell of my being, and I couldn't escape it. The fear of being trapped in this never-ending cycle of pain and confusion was overwhelming. My dad's presence was a comfort, but even he couldn't take the weight of it all away.

The doctors at the hospital gave me pain relief, but the emotional burden remained. There was no easy fix for what I was facing. The trauma, the years of abuse, and the toll it had taken on my body, were all still there, lingering like a shadow that followed me wherever I went. I didn't know how to keep going, but I knew I had to try. As exhausted as my body was, I knew I needed to keep writing, getting it out of me, but a wave would wash over me of pain and the writing had to take a pause. How was I ever going to finish this book, I thought to myself. Navigating dark waters of abuse and finding the learning is no easy feat.

I turned to God.

Reflection

Even in the darkest moments, when I could barely breathe, I realised that the act of rebuilding wasn't just about fixing the house. It was about reclaiming the parts of me that had been stolen, my dignity, my self-worth, my sense of belonging. Slowly, through the pain, the grief, and the work of writing my story, I began to reassemble a life that was no longer defined by the destruction that had come before. The bamboo trees, planted for privacy and protection, became more than a symbol of my external sanctuary; they represented the fortification of my own soul, the resilience that had been hard-earned but was mine to keep.

But the work was far from over. Each day was still a challenge, still a battle against memories that lingered, pain that wouldn't let go, and the temptation to hide away in the shadows.

Abuse and trauma profoundly affect the brain, reshaping neural pathways and altering our sense of self. When we experience prolonged stress or trauma, especially in abuse, our brain adapts for survival. The amygdala (the brain's fear centre) becomes overactive, making us hypervigilant and more prone to anxiety and emotional reactivity. Meanwhile, the prefrontal cortex, responsible for reasoning and impulse control, weakens, making it harder to regulate emotions, make decisions, and feel safe. The hippocampus, which processes memories, may shrink, leading to difficulties in distinguishing past trauma from present reality.

These neurological changes impact our identity by shaping how we see ourselves and the world. Abuse often instils deep feelings of shame, unworthiness, and self-doubt, leading to a fractured sense of self. We may internalise the abuser's narrative, believing we are weak, unlovable, or destined for suffering. Over time, these beliefs influence our behaviours, relationships, and life choices, often leading to self-sabotage, people-pleasing, or emotional numbness.

As I reflect on my journey, I find it interesting that the first year of my time at the *School of Faith* focused on something so fundamental, identity in Christ. I hadn't realised how deeply twisted my sense of self had become while I was in that marriage. The constant emotional and psychological abuse had eroded my foundation, leaving me with a warped sense of worth and purpose. I had become someone I didn't even recognise, shaped by the manipulation and control, lost in a cycle of shame and self-doubt.

The lessons I began to learn about my identity in Christ were like rays of light breaking through the darkness. For the first time, I understood that I wasn't defined by the abuse, by the brokenness, or by the lies I had been fed. My true worth wasn't tied to the approval of others or how much I could endure. It was rooted in something far deeper, my identity as a beloved child of God, someone deserving of love, respect, and dignity.

This revelation began to unravel the layers of shame that had built up over the years. It wasn't an overnight transformation, but each lesson in the School of Faith helped me shed the lies I had believed about myself and replace them with the truth of who I was in Christ. It gave me the courage to stand up again, to reclaim my space in this world, and to see that despite everything I had been through, I was still worthy of a life filled with peace, love, and purpose.

Even as the house came together, walls repainted, floors restored, the bamboo growing stronger each day, my body remained in ruins.

I had fought so hard to create a sanctuary, to build something safe, something sacred. But no matter how much I restored around me, I was still trapped in a body that refused to be healed.

I had rebuilt my home. Now, I had to find a way to rebuild myself.

20: A Reluctant Decision

I had rebuilt my home. Now, I had to find a way to rebuild myself. But how do you rebuild something that is still crumbling?

By late 2022, I had nothing left to give. The pain was no longer just unbearable, it was life-consuming. It felt like nothing could take away the ongoing agony inside my body.

I had done everything I could. I had rebuilt my home, surrounded myself with love, deepened my faith. But none of it had touched the agony inside my body. The contractions were relentless, the kind of pain that stole sleep, stole thought, stole sanity. It was as if an invisible force had its claws in me, tearing me apart from the inside out.

I had tried everything, medications, pelvic floor physiotherapy, alternative therapies, even prayer and fasting. Nothing worked. Nothing even touched the edges of my suffering. The menstrual pain I have suffered from all my life due was caused by the trauma I experienced, first from my grandfather and then from my husband.

According to science, trauma triggers physical pain through a complex interaction between the brain, nervous system, and body. When a person experiences trauma, whether emotional or physical, the body enters a state of heightened stress. The brain, particularly the amygdala, signals the release of stress hormones like cortisol and adrenaline, activating the autonomic nervous system.

Chronic activation of this stress response can lead to neuroinflammation, muscle tension, and changes in pain perception. The brain and spinal cord become more sensitive to pain signals (central sensitisation), while stress hormones keep muscles tight and reduce blood flow, contributing to tension headaches, back pain, and fibromyalgia. Trauma also disrupts the gut-brain axis, leading to conditions like irritable bowel syndrome (IBS).

Over time, if unresolved, trauma rewires neural pathways, making the body more reactive to pain and stress, even in the absence of an immediate threat. Healing from trauma through therapy, movement, and relaxation techniques can help rewire these pathways and reduce pain.

> *"Women's pain has often been dismissed as 'hysteria' or 'psychosomatic.' It's time we recognise women's pain as real and valid." - Dr. Jennifer Gunter, OB/GYN, author and advocate.*

I couldn't keep doing this. Something had to change. And that's when I knew.

The decision I had fought against for so long, the one I never wanted to make, was now staring me in the face.

A hysterectomy.

The word itself felt like a betrayal, like another thing my body was being forced to surrender.

Hysterectomy! The word felt like an execution. A finality I hadn't been ready for.

I had already lost so much, my body to my husband, my voice to doctors, my dignity to a system that refused to believe me. And now, I was losing this too. The space within me that had carried three babies who did not make it. The part of me that was meant to create life, was now the very thing killing me.

I wanted to scream. But what choice did I have?

I had built a sanctuary with the help of family and friends, yet my body was still a prison. I had reclaimed my life, yet the system still held me captive.

It was one thing to rebuild my home, to repaint the walls, to plant bamboo for protection. But what could I do with a body that kept breaking? With a physical system that thrived on my suffering! It seemed to me that doctors saw my pain as a mere inconvenience.

I had already lost so much. And now, it seemed, I was about to lose one more piece of myself.

By late 2022, I had reached a breaking point. The relentless pain from my endometriosis and adenomyosis had become a constant companion, robbing me of the ability to function even in the simplest of ways. No matter what treatments, medications, or doctor's visits I tried, the pain refused to ease. It felt like I was sinking deeper into a world of agony that no one could pull me out of.

I had been encouraged to apply for the *National Disability Insurance Scheme* (NDIS), but the process was daunting. It demanded energy, resources, money for appointments and reports and time, all things I could scarcely afford. Attending the required specialist appointments alone felt impossible, as the thought of sitting in a vehicle enduring the jolting pain was inconceivable. It seemed like the system was designed to make help inaccessible for those who needed it most.

With endometriosis and adenomyosis, it's expected that a woman will have a team of specialists to help manage the pain. While a hysterectomy can 'cure' adenomyosis, the decision to have one's uterus removed is not made lightly. The uterus is more than just an organ; it is a sacred space, the source of life itself. The thought of losing it felt like yet another loss in a life already marked by too many. Surgery might promise relief, but it came at the cost of something deeply personal and profound.

Yet, the financial and emotional toll of managing these conditions was unrelenting. The endless cycle of appointments with pelvic floor physiotherapists, pain specialists, psychologists, and gynaecologists drained me physically and financially. Each interaction reinforced the grim reality that women's pain was a profit centre. I was trapped in a system that exploited my suffering without offering true relief. This was not a life, but an existence defined by pain and the strain of surviving it.

Past encounters with pain specialists had left me jaded. In 2019, one specialist had simply apologised for my pain before charging $200 for a ten-minute consultation. Another time, a specialist watched me writhe on the floor in agony, only to present me with a bill for thousands of dollars to enter their program. It was clear that compassion was not a prerequisite for their care. Each appointment felt like another brick in the wall of despair, solidifying my belief that there was no way out.

I had already been violated in my marriage. I never expected to be violated again in a doctor's office.

The first gynaecologist inserted a cold, unyielding instrument that felt like knives ripping through me. My body recoiled in agony, but when I cried out, his voice was sharp with dismissal. 'Just relax,' he snapped, his tone flat, indifferent. The same words my husband used to say during sex. The same words that blamed me for my own pain.

The second was worse. His massive hand plunged deep into my pelvis, pushing and prodding as I wept. He didn't stop. He didn't slow down. My body tensed in agony, but to him, I was just another case, another inconvenience. He showed no care or acknowledgment of my pain, pressing on even as my tears fell. The physical and emotional trauma inflicted by these experiences has left me unable to trust gynaecologists again. They didn't just hurt my body; they compounded my fear, shame, and mistrust in ways I am still trying to recover from.

I walked out of their offices shattered, barely able to move. They didn't just hurt my body. They stole my trust completely.

It's not just an appointment with women's health; it is putting my body in the trust of another human being, praying they won't cause more harm. I am left dealing with the trauma after the harm done.

Many doctors and specialists seemed to me to lack a kind bedside manner. Perhaps due to burnout, time pressure, emotional detachment or a medical culture that prioritises efficiency and expertise over empathy.

My family did everything they could to support me, but even their love couldn't shield me from the toll the pain was taking. I was slipping further away, losing the ability to cope with the day-to-day. The strain was overwhelming, and it was clear to everyone that something had to change. After much deliberation, the decision was made. I would have a hysterectomy.

It wasn't a choice I wanted to make. Losing my uterus felt like losing another piece of myself, another thing my ex-husband and life circumstances had taken from me. My body had already been ravaged by years of childhood sexual abuse, medical gaslighting, and the grief of losing three babies. The thought of surrendering yet another part of myself was unbearable. But the pain was louder than my doubts, and I knew I couldn't go on without trying to reclaim my life.

The surgery was meant to bring relief, but instead, it led me into a nightmare I could never have imagined.

The hospital I attended supposedly had an 'endometriosis floor' but the treatment I experienced was torture.

Waking from surgery, I was met with excruciating pain and inadequate pain relief. The intensity of it was beyond anything I had endured before, leaving me feeling like a raw, exposed nerve. Instead of compassion, I was labelled 'non-compliant' for my inability to swallow pills and offered a psychiatrist instead of proper care.

They knew. The hospital had my history, years of abuse, trauma, pain so unbearable that I had considered euthanasia. They knew everything.

And yet, they did nothing.

No compassion. No patient-centred care. No recognition that my pain was real.

I woke up from surgery in excruciating pain. No IV pain relief. No gentle reassurances. Just white-hot agony, swallowing me whole.

Most nurses stood over me, cold and clinical. "Take a tablet," they said.

But I couldn't. My body was in shock, dry-heaving, trembling. I begged for relief. They offered me a psychiatrist instead of appropriate pain meds for my condition.

I wasn't a patient. I was a problem to be solved, a nuisance to be dismissed.

And all I could do was suffer.

A male surgeon who advertised himself as an "endometriosis specialist" called my parents early in the morning, panicked and asking them what to do. This was the man my family had paid over $15,000, and yet he seemed utterly unprepared to handle my case.

Even after discharge, I was denied adequate pain relief for the journey home, enduring every bump in the road with searing agony. The lack of care left me broken, both physically and emotionally.

The transport home was excruciating and exhausting. Every bump in the road sent waves of pain through my body, and I felt like I was being tortured.

The hospital advised my sister to withhold the medication I desperately needed. Leaving me to endure the journey home from hospital in unimaginable agony. I wanted to open the door and fall out, hoping that someone would run me over to end the torment. It was a moment of complete despair, where death seemed kinder than the life I was enduring.

But even in the darkest moments, glimmers of resilience and faith sustained me. Before my hysterectomy, I had found a sense of purpose in advocacy. My dad and I had joined the *Victorian Unharm Campaign*, fighting for the right to grow your own medicinal cannabis. For me, cannabis was not just a medicine; it was a lifeline. The cost of it in Melbourne was exorbitant, forcing me to ration the one thing that brought me relief. Through the campaign, I found a voice I didn't know I had, speaking out not just for myself but for all those who relied on cannabis to manage their pain and live with dignity.

Filming took place in my parents' backyard, surrounded by the calming presence of fruit trees and nature. The crew patiently waited as I navigated an attack of pain, supported by my parents and a dear friend, Sue. Those moments of advocacy became a beacon of strength, a reminder that I could still fight for something greater than myself.

Advocating for oneself becomes nearly impossible when overwhelmed by pain so intense it feels as though an entity is trying to tear its way out of your body, or like claws scratching relentlessly from within. These horrific hospital experiences left me feeling silenced and powerless, culminating in the despair that led to my overdose. It's exhausting to live in a system where the person in pain is blamed rather than supported. What will it take for Melbourne's healthcare to become heart-centred, person-centred, and not profit-driven?

In contrast, my time in Nimbin was a revelation. The entire town embraced a holistic approach, offering compassion and understanding in ways that Melbourne's healthcare system had failed to provide. Even during moments of public pain, such as when I had contractions, strangers in Nimbin showed genuine concern, asking how they could help. That sense of humanity, of being seen and cared for, highlighted just how much is missing from the sterile, dismissive environments I'd endured in traditional healthcare settings.

I wrote to the *Victorian Complaints Commissioner* (VCC) and to *Australian Health Practitioner Regulation Agency* (AHPRA) about my horrific experience following the hysterectomy. Despite detailing the medical negligence, gaslighting, and outright abuse I endured, not one person or organisation was held accountable for their actions, or their lack thereof. There was no acknowledgment from the surgeons, the hospital, or the system that failed me so profoundly. It left me questioning: What will it take to be heard? What will it take for women like me to be taken seriously? This lack of accountability is not just a personal injustice but a systemic failure, perpetuating the suffering of countless others. Women deserve better. We deserve to be believed, respected, and cared for with dignity.

Here is my letter to *VCC* dated February 2023:

Medical Negligence and Malpractice After Surgery.

On November 10, 2022, I underwent a laparoscopic hysterectomy, right salpingectomy, and cystoscopy at the hospital, co-located with (unnamed other) Hospital. The surgery was performed by Dr. Bleep (not his real name) from Bleep Specialist Centre. What followed was an experience of medical gaslighting, negligence, and malpractice that exacerbated my complex *Post Traumatic Stress Disorder* (PTSD), leaving me physically, emotionally, and psychologically scarred.

Hospital Experience

The Hospital with 'Endometriosis floor' claims to specialise in endometriosis care, yet my treatment was barbaric and retraumatising. There was no duty of care, no adequate pain management, and no understanding of my condition. Instead of being cared for, I was abused and left to suffer needlessly. The trauma began immediately after surgery and extended to the transport home, where I endured indescribable pain without relief. The entire experience was appalling and abusive, both for me and my family.

Gaslighting, Negligence, and Malpractice

Inadequate Pain Relief: Despite assurances, I woke up from surgery in severe pain with no IV pain relief. In contrast, my 2019 laparoscopy included a ketamine infusion, allowing for a much gentler recovery. This time, I was rudely jolted awake, shocked and traumatised by the intense pain.

Dismissive and Abusive Care: I was bullied and intimidated by nursing staff as I lay on the floor with uncontrollable contractions that felt like seizures. Instead of compassion, they blamed me for not being able to swallow tablets while I was dry heaving in agony.

Discrimination and Lack of Understanding:

As a person with a disability caused by chronic medical conditions, I was met with total disregard for my needs. My inability to swallow tablets was treated as a personal failing rather than a physical limitation.

Devalued and Dismissed: Assistant surgeon Dr. Bleep compared my experience to other patients, implying that something was wrong with me for not recovering like others. Her comments were demeaning and dismissive, further compounding my trauma.

Violation of Patient Rights: Dr. Bleep called my parents at 7 a.m., claiming I was screaming and refusing pain relief, a blatant lie. This startled my father and placed an unnecessary burden on my family to remove me from the hospital as quickly as possible. This was not care; it was abuse.

Medical Staff Involved

Surgeon: Dr bleep promised to provide pain relief and care but failed on every level. His actions and dismissive attitude post-surgery added to the trauma.

Anaesthetist: Dr. bleep assured me I would be looked after but did not follow through.

Assistant Surgeon: Dr. bleep gaslighted me by comparing my experience to others, diminishing the severity of my pain and recovery challenges.

Nursing Staff: While a few nurses apologised and acknowledged the harm done, the majority lacked understanding of endometriosis and failed to provide compassionate care.

Lasting Impact on Recovery The abusive treatment during my hospital stay has had a profound impact on my recovery and overall well-being:

Psychological Trauma: I now experience night terrors, panic attacks, and avoid sleep due to nightmares of being stood over by medical staff, powerless and retraumatized. These episodes have retriggered memories of family violence and years of medical gaslighting.

Anxiety: I struggle with severe anxiety about being a passenger in a car, a direct result of the trauma endured during the transport home without pain relief.

Physical Pain: Chronic pain continues to plague me, requiring daily pain relief to function and sleep.

Emotional Distress: My family, panicked and unsure how to help, has also been deeply affected. Their distress compounded my own, leaving us all scarred by the experience.

Barriers to Recovery: The lack of adequate post-surgical care and follow-up support has prolonged my healing, leaving me housebound and reliant on trauma-informed therapy.

Post-Operative Negligence Dr. bleep post-operative care further exemplified medical gaslighting and negligence. During a telehealth appointment on December 19, 2022, he dismissed my concerns, telling me to "Be positive and just move forward." He belittled my pain, labelled me 'non-compliant' based on nurses' reports, and showed no interest in addressing my ongoing struggles. His lack of accountability and dismissive behaviour added to the abuse I endured.

Demands for Accountability The harm caused by this experience cannot be overstated. My parents paid over $15,000 for this surgery, only to see me abused and neglected. I demand accountability from the hospital, the medical staff involved, and the broader healthcare system. My family deserves reimbursement, and I deserve compensation for the barbaric treatment I endured. The appalling behaviour of those entrusted with my care has left lasting scars, and I will not stop until justice is served.

A Call for Change This experience highlights the urgent need for systemic reform in women's healthcare, particularly in the treatment of endometriosis and chronic pain. Education, compassion, and accountability must become cornerstones of medical practice to prevent others from enduring the same harm. No one should have to suffer as I did, not physically, not emotionally, and not at the hands of those sworn to provide care.

Reflection and Moving Forward:

Reflecting on those days, I see the thread of faith woven through my journey. Even in the depths of despair, God's presence was there, pulling me back from the edge. When I couldn't bear the weight of it anymore and attempted to end my life, a message from Kim through the *School of Faith* arrived, piercing through the darkness. Her words, paired with the comforting presence of my cat, Kitty Cat, saved me in a moment when all seemed lost.

As I lay there, vomiting up the overdose in my body, I felt Kim's message reach into my soul and give me the strength to hold on. And then there was Kitty Cat, curling up next to me, her warmth grounding me in the here and now. Both were lifelines, pulling me back from the brink when everything else felt like it was crashing down.

As I move forward, the scars of the past remain, but they no longer define me. Each day of healing reminds me that my pain and experiences carry a deeper purpose. Through advocacy, faith, and resilience, I've discovered a wellspring of strength I never thought possible. My body has borne the weight of so much suffering, yet my spirit remains steadfast, fuelled by the belief that healing is within reach. Now, I hold onto the hope that my story can illuminate a path for others, a light breaking through the shadows for those who are still searching for their own strength and solace.

As Dr. Jennifer Gunter states, "Women's pain has often been dismissed as 'hysteria' or 'psychosomatic.' It's time we recognise women's pain as real and valid." This quote resonates deeply with my experience. The dismissal and invalidation of women's pain are not just medical oversights; they are forms of systemic harm that perpetuate suffering and silence. My journey has shown me that acknowledging and validating pain is the first step toward healing, both individually and collectively. Women deserve to be heard, believed, and treated with compassion and dignity. The time for change is long overdue.

By the time I reached the end of 2023, I had nothing left. The pain was unbearable, the system had failed me, and my body felt like a prison I couldn't escape. I had spent years crying out for someone to see, to hear, to understand. But the truth settled in, I would never find justice in the hands of a system that didn't care.

I wanted relief. I wanted peace. I wanted to be free from the weight of it all.

I had nothing left. The system had failed me. The doctors and Surgeons had broken me. My body felt like a prison I could never escape. I wanted relief. I wanted peace. I wanted to be free from the weight of it all.

So, in the silence of my room, I did the only thing I could do.

I called out to God. Not in eloquent words or structured prayers, just a raw, desperate cry from the depths of my soul.

And then, in the days that followed, something unexpected happened.

Help arrived. Not through the system. Not through medicine. But through love.

Through Kim. Through Bec. Through an invitation I never saw coming.

A baptism of cleansing.

A moment that would begin to strip the weight of shame and give me a chance to start again.

A baptism of cleansing. A moment that would begin to strip the weight of shame and give me a chance to start again.

21: Baptism of Cleansing

The morning air was quiet, but inside me, a storm churned.

The weight in my chest was suffocating, pressing down on me like an anchor I had carried for too long.

I woke up one Saturday, knowing, without knowing, that something was about to shift. A new beginning was coming, but would I have the strength to step into it?

Bec and Kim arrived like angels on assignment, gentle, unwavering, bringing peace into the space. I had been drowning for so long, but their presence reminded me that maybe, just maybe, I could still be saved. I met Kim through the *School of Faith* and Bec I met through Kim's connect group, which I attended maybe a handful of times.

They arrived with warmth and love, their presence filling my home with peace. That morning, the air felt different. The kind of quiet that comes before a storm, but this wasn't a storm of destruction.

It was a storm of release.

And I was ready.

> *"Shame dies when stories are told in safe places."*
> *- Ann Voskamp, Author of The Broken Way.*

Dear Kim and Bec,

Thank you for your love and for organizing the baptism of cleansing on Saturday, 21st October, a ritual that lifted the heavy cloak of shame weighing down my soul. That cloak had felt like carrying death on my shoulders. Shame can have an unbearable weight, a relentless grip on the spirit and it had me questioning if I even deserved to be alive.

It's hard to put into words what that day meant. My body felt as though it passed through a portal, leaving behind the slimy pit of shame and entering a place of light where I could see again, this time, with eyes of love and compassion for myself. As I write this, I recall it was only twelve months ago that God brought me back to a place of wanting to live.

Looking back, I see now that Kim's message to connect with me on October 18 wasn't just a coincidence.

It was God answering a cry I didn't even know how to pray.

Three days before the baptism, I had overdosed on morphine. I had reached the edge, exhausted beyond words.

I was so tired; I only wanted to sleep for a very long time, exhausted beyond words. I hadn't recovered physically or emotionally from my hysterectomy the previous November. The pain had been overwhelming, almost indescribable, and I wasn't sure if I had it in me to keep going.

But then Kim messaged. Checking in.

And because of that, I woke up.

Three days later, Bec and Kim arrived at my door.

Like angels in human form.

I knew I was safe with them, though even opening the door had been a struggle. My body was in severe spasms, with tics and contractions, but somehow, I managed to let them in. The day flowed like a gentle stream through green pastures. Even though I felt so messy and broken, I was beautifully held in that mess, allowing so much to be released from my body. That day was truly a miracle, a day of miraculous breakthroughs.

The water touched my skin, and for the first time in years, my body didn't recoil, it softened. The cold shock sent ripples through me, but instead of fear, there was release.

GRACE AMORE

Shame, grief, unspoken agony, years of it tangled my bones, my breath, my flesh began to unravel, carried away by the water.

I had spent so long fighting my own body, drowning in silence. But here, in this moment, the water whispered back, "You are free."

For so long, my body had been at war with me. Pain had defined my existence, dictated every moment of my life. But here, in this moment, the water spoke a different truth.

Not one of suffering. But of cleansing.

I had been suffocating under the weight of it all. But now, it was time to let go. Time to let go of the heavy cloak of shame I had carried for so long.

To let the past sink beneath the surface. And to rise again.

With Jesus Christ at the helm of my life, I found peace and clarity. Jesus, the one who gives me a reason to face each day, the light in my darkness. Through the love and kindness of hearts like Kim and Bec, I felt the presence of angels guiding me to where I am today.

It's interesting how God works. Kim, it was through your message, checking in to see how I was, that I woke up that Wednesday, 18th October. That simple act of care became a turning point. The year closed in a way I could never have anticipated. Ending the year with Kim and Bec's presence reminded me of the transformative power of connection and faith.

It was also through this season that I reconnected with my dear friend Gaynor, who highlighted how Rik Schnabel could help with writing my book. His experience in publishing his own books and coaching others inspired me to keep going.

This year brought many challenges, including ongoing pelvic pain, as the hysterectomy didn't seem to provide the relief I had hoped for. But it was also a year of renewal and new beginnings, with Kitty Cat joining Banjo and me. While life felt stormy at times, navigating these challenges with Jesus's guidance and the support of angels like you brought me closer to healing and hope. It was also the season when treatments started with Maryam, my Pelvic Floor Physiotherapist, Sharon, my Remedial massage therapist and Counsellor and Gaynor, my Osteopath and Coach.

1800 Respect

The *1800 Respect* worker explained something that finally made sense to me: when the body begins to feel safer, away from the perpetrator, it is perfectly normal for memories to flood back. She likened the brain to a house with many rooms. In the chaos of living with abuse, especially with a narcissistic partner, there is no time to pause, reflect, or process what has happened. Instead, each traumatic event gets shoved into a back room of the mind, locked away because survival demands it.

In a home filled with rages and unpredictable violence, the brain operates in survival mode, constantly scanning for danger. There's no time to think, "What just happened?" or "How do I handle this?" because the focus is on getting through the next moment safely. This relentless state of hypervigilance becomes a way of life.

The counsellor explained that in normal, everyday experiences, like having lunch, shopping, or taking a walk, the brain processes and releases these events naturally. But when an experience becomes traumatic, the brain doesn't have the luxury of processing it in the moment. Instead, it's stored away, like clutter in an overfilled room. Over time, that room gets so full that the memories begin to spill out, often as triggers, flashes of emotion, physical sensations, or vivid recollections that surface seemingly out of nowhere.

Living with a narcissist compound this. Narcissists thrive on control, keeping you off balance and ensuring you have no time or space to make sense of what's happening. They use manipulation, gaslighting, and emotional abuse to strip away your sense of self, leaving you questioning reality. In such an environment, every interaction can become a source of trauma, whether it's a sudden rage, a calculated comment to demean you, or an act of coercion.

What struck me most about the counsellor's explanation was how trauma doesn't just live in the mind; it lives in the body. Each unprocessed event leaves a residue that lingers in the nervous system, waiting for the safety and support needed to be released. It made sense why; after leaving my marriage, my body felt like a storm of emotions and sensations. Those 'rooms' in my brain were finally being opened, and years of suppressed pain and fear were demanding to be heard.

The *1800 Respect* worker continued to explain how everyday memories, like having lunch, going shopping, or taking a walk, are typically experienced and then released by the brain without much thought. These moments flow naturally, leaving no lasting imprint because they don't overwhelm the body or mind.

But traumatic experiences are different. When you're living in an environment of constant abuse, as I was in my marriage, there's no time to pause, reflect, or make sense of what's happening. Explosive rages and unpredictable violence keep you in a heightened state of survival, where your brain and body are focused solely on getting through the moment. There's no room to ask, "What just happened?" or "How do I handle this?"

Instead, these events are packed away in the back room of the brain, a place where unprocessed memories are stored. Over time, as more and more traumatic experiences are shoved into this mental storage, the room becomes overcrowded.

Eventually, the memories begin to spill out, demanding attention in the form of triggers. These triggers are the body's way of saying, "Something needs to be addressed. Please don't ignore this."

The counsellor explained that unresolved trauma doesn't disappear; it waits in the body, stored as sensations, emotions, and memories, until it's given the chance to be released. This usually happens when we're more ready to face them. This made so much sense to me. In my marriage, there was never time to process what I was experiencing. I was too busy trying to survive the next outburst or controlling the fallout from my husband's rages. There was no opportunity to pause, reflect, and ask, "What do I do with this pain?"

Hearing this explanation helped me understand why, after leaving the marriage, so many memories started flooding back. It wasn't that they had come out of nowhere, they had always been there, waiting for the moment my body felt safe enough to let them surface.

Maryam – Pelvic Floor Physiotherapist

Through the healing of painful experiences, I've learned how trauma is stored in the body and how essential the right treatments are for recovery. Maryam, my pelvic floor physiotherapist, has been an absolute Godsend. When my older sister Sandra discovered the *Modern Physiotherapy Clinic* in Moonee Ponds in September 2023, it felt like the angels were singing. I booked my first appointment for 1st October 2023, and the tagline on their website, "An experience like no other," couldn't have been more accurate.

Before finding Maryam, I had endured a number of painful and disheartening experiences with other pelvic floor physiotherapists. Many lacked the compassion and understanding necessary to work with trauma, especially the kind stemming from sexual violence. But Maryam was different. Her kindness and gentleness created a space where I finally felt safe. She brought a unique heart-centred approach to her work, acknowledging the layers of trauma stored in my body and addressing them with both skill and empathy.

Her treatments were transformative, but I couldn't shake the guilt I felt about the cost. My parents were paying for the appointments, and while I was endlessly grateful for their support, I struggled with the fact that I couldn't afford the treatments myself. Being on the disability pension made it impossible to cover the expenses, and my repeated applications to the NDIS were met with rejection.

The NDIS didn't recognise women's health conditions like endometriosis or pelvic trauma as qualifying disabilities. It was infuriating and disheartening, knowing that conditions so debilitating they had cost me my job were dismissed so easily. Despite having a thick stack of medical reports from specialists, my applications were still denied. The message was clear: women's health issues weren't taken seriously enough, even when they left women like me on the brink of collapse.

Maryam encouraged me to keep trying with the NDIS as my severe pain was hugely affecting my mobility and my ability to perform my daily tasks including personal care, reminding me of my worth and the importance of advocating for my health. Her unwavering support helped me see that these treatments were not a luxury, they were a necessity. Every session with Maryam brought profound relief and healing, validating my pain and allowing my body to finally begin letting go of the trauma it had carried for years.

Each appointment with Maryam brought a little more light into the darkness of my pain. While the guilt about the financial strain lingered, the transformative power of her work made me realise how vital it was to prioritise my healing. Maryam's care was a lifeline, a beacon of hope that reminded me I was worthy of compassion and healing, even in a system that so often disregards women's health.

When I first met Maryam, I was at my wit's end, a mess of twitching, spasming, and overwhelming pain. My body jolted uncontrollably, with spasms shooting up my legs and into my groin, leaving me unable to think clearly. Walking into that appointment, I felt both desperate and cautious, unsure if this would be another failed attempt at finding relief. But Maryam's presence immediately brought a sense of safety.

She saw me, not just the symptoms, but me. She didn't demand explanations or force me to recount the painful history that had brought me to her table. Instead, she validated my pain and gently invited me to lie down, creating a space where I could simply be. It's hard to put into words what happened in that moment, but when her eyes met mine, it was as though they spoke directly to my soul: "It's okay. I see you." Even as my body continued to jolt and twitch, I felt the tiniest glimmer of relief, knowing I was in the care of someone who truly understood.

Then Maryam brought over a machine called *Tecar Therapy*, and this was where everything began to change. After years of period pain being dismissed or ignored, this treatment felt like a gift from heaven. The device worked gently, placing a plate under my back and gliding a heated applicator across my pelvic region. The warmth penetrated deep into my body, calming the relentless spasms that had left me exhausted and broken.

For the first time in what felt like forever, my body whispered, "It's okay. You are safe. I've got you." The spasms eased, and the pain that had once felt insurmountable quieted into a soft hum, a whisper of acceptance and healing. There was no judgment, no pressure, just permission to exist exactly as I was in that moment.

Maryam explained that the *Tecar Therapy* machine wasn't something that came easily to her clinic. She had to push hard to acquire it, facing numerous obstacles along the way.

Her determination to fight for this machine speaks volumes about her dedication to her patients and her understanding of the urgent need for better care in women's health. Maryam's advocacy wasn't just about bringing in a piece of equipment; it was about creating a lifeline for people like me, whose pain had been dismissed or minimised for far too long.

It struck me deeply how much effort it took for her to secure something so essential. The very idea that a machine capable of bringing such relief had to be fought for made me think about the broader issue of how women's health is often undervalued. It's as if our suffering is expected to be endured, our pain normalised or ignored.

That machine, with its soothing heat and therapeutic effects, has been nothing short of miraculous for me. But what made it even more powerful was knowing the story behind it, knowing that someone cared enough to fight for my healing before I even stepped into her clinic.

Maryam also taught me about the fascia, which completely shifted my understanding of how trauma manifests in the body. The fascia is a thin casing of connective tissue that surrounds and holds every organ, blood vessel, bone, nerve fibre, and muscle in place. I had never considered it before, but Maryam explained that fascia is more than just a structural framework, it's alive, full of nerves, and nearly as sensitive as the skin. It responds to everything we go through, tightening under stress and trauma as a form of protection.

What struck me most was learning how deeply fascia is tied to our emotions. When the body endures prolonged trauma, like the painfully sadistic sexual violence I suffered in my marriage, the fascia tightens and holds onto those experiences. It doesn't just forget or let go; instead, it stores the pain, fear, and stress until we feel safe enough to begin releasing it.

Maryam helped me understand why my body had reached the state it was in after my marriage. It wasn't simply a matter of physical pain, it was years of stored trauma manifesting in spasms, tension, and exhaustion. My body had been doing everything it could to protect me, even as I endured unimaginable violations of my safety and welfare.

Learning about the fascia felt like unlocking a secret language my body had been trying to speak all along. Maryam's gentle approach, her ability to work with this intricate tissue, gave me hope that my body could heal. Each treatment felt like peeling back a layer of pain, revealing not just the scars but also the resilience hidden beneath.

Sharon – Remedial Massage Therapist, Reflexology, Counsellor and Craniosacral Therapy.

Sharon is another Godsend who has profoundly changed my life through her work. Her heart is truly at the centre of all she does, and I'll forever be grateful to my sister Sandra for researching and finding yet another practitioner who genuinely cares.

Sharon's trauma-informed approach, particularly her understanding of sexual trauma, has made all the difference in my healing journey.

From the very first session, I knew Sharon's work was exceptional. She meets my body exactly where it's at, creating a safe and nurturing space to release the layers of pain stored deep within. Her intuition and skill go beyond just physical care; she understands how trauma is carried in the body, especially the kind of trauma that comes from sexual violence.

During our treatments, there have been moments when triggers surfaced, memories buried so deeply that I thought I had locked them away forever. These memories, often tied to my husband's unwanted and cruel acts, would flood back like sharp, unrelenting waves. The pain was so intense it felt as though someone was cutting up my insides, leaving me frozen in terror, unable to move.

Sharon's brilliance lies in her ability to work with these triggers gently and compassionately. She doesn't force the body to move faster than it's ready, allowing me to process and release the trauma at my own pace. When I share what's happening in my body during a session, she listens without judgment, offering reassurance and guidance. This level of care has been a lifeline for me.

In her presence, I feel safe enough to confront the physical and emotional scars left by the marriage. The sessions are not just about alleviating pain; they're about giving my body a voice, a chance to express the anguish and terror it had to suppress for so many years. Sharon's work reminds me that healing is possible, even for wounds that feel too deep to reach.

Her ability to combine remedial massage with trauma-informed counselling creates a powerful space for transformation. I can now feel my body beginning to trust again, piece by piece, session by session. The impact of her care is not just physical but emotional and spiritual, helping me reclaim parts of myself I thought I had lost forever.

The way my husband treated me would often surface during my treatments, whether with Sharon, Maryam, or Gaynor, as each session worked to release the trauma stored deep within my body. Memories I had pushed deep down would flood back, triggered by the work she was doing to release the tension stored in my body. Sharon would guide me through these moments with patience and understanding, explaining what was happening inside me and why my body reacted the way it did.

The pain I experienced in the marriage was not just emotional; it was deeply physical. During those times, the agony would become so unbearable that I would leave my body entirely, disassociating to escape the terror. Afterward, I would return to myself feeling rattled, violated, and unsure how to process what had just happened, only to endure the same nightmare again and again.

The sexual trauma happened so frequently that I never had the chance to recover, to process, or even to seek help. My husband would control every aspect of my life, including my ability to reach out for support. He would monitor my phone calls, listen in, and inject his unwanted opinions, ensuring that I felt isolated and powerless.

Even when I managed to attend counselling, I was so gripped by terror and shame that I didn't know where to begin. It all felt too much. I was drowning in a sea of daily chaos where my body and mind were constantly on high alert, never knowing what would happen next or how I would be expected to endure it.

To him, I wasn't a person; I was an object, something he owned by virtue of being my husband. In his eyes, my body, my mind, and my life belonged to him. His needs came first, and if they weren't met, there were consequences. He was relentless, cruel, volatile, and violent. At times, he could appear kind and caring, but these were rare moments, offered as crumbs of kindness that only served to keep me confused and compliant.

I didn't realise it then, but my body was keeping score of every act of violence, every violation, just as Bessel van der Kolk describes in *The Body Keeps the Score*. Each experience of abuse left an imprint, stored in my muscles, my fascia, my very being. My body remembered what my mind tried so hard to forget.

Sharon's sessions became a lifeline, a space where I could begin to unpack the physical and emotional toll of those years. She taught me that the pain and tension in my body weren't just random, they were the echoes of the trauma I had endured. With each session, I started to feel the weight of those memories lessen, as though my body was slowly releasing what it had carried for far too long.

The way my body responded during treatments reminded me of what Bessel van der Kolk so powerfully describes that the body holds onto the trauma it has endured, long after the mind has tried to forget.

Family violence, childhood sexual abuse, and years of living in fear left their imprints on me, not just emotionally but physically, deep within my body.

In my marriage, I often felt as though I had gone from being human to becoming a rag doll, played with, mistreated, and discarded at will. My husband's aggression and cruelty were unleashed on me depending on his mood, treating me like a doll a child no longer cared about: tossed aside, limbs bent out of shape, eyes poked out, hair pulled, and ultimately left broken.

By the time I came out of the marriage, I saw myself as that discarded doll. I had started off new, full of hope, but by the end, I felt I had been stripped of my worth, my identity, and even my humanity.

This deep sense of brokenness surfaced during treatments, particularly in a session with Sharon when I felt my body tense up. A flashback overwhelmed me, the threat of an insistent intruder into my back passage came rushing back. The memory was so vivid, it took all my strength to speak up and let Sharon know what was happening. I asked her to move away from the triggered area and focus on my shoulders instead.

What made this moment transformative was Sharon's trauma-informed care. Her understanding of how trauma impacts the body gave me the safety I needed to work through that flashback. She didn't rush me or dismiss my experience; she listened and adjusted her approach with care and kindness. That sense of safety allowed me to begin unpacking the sexual trauma and its lasting impact on my body.

Having a space to voice what was happening in my body felt liberating. For so many years, I had been silenced, not just by my husband, but by the shame and fear that came with the abuse. Through Sharon's gentle guidance, I began to give voice to those parts of me that had been buried in silence. Each session became an opportunity to reclaim a piece of myself, to confront the pain and let it go, bit by bit.

The way trauma manifests in the body is profound. The tightening of muscles, the physical pain, the involuntary reactions, all of it is the body's way of saying, "This happened. This needs to be acknowledged." With Sharon's care, I started to understand that my body wasn't betraying me; it was trying to protect me, holding onto the memories until I was ready to face them.

Gaynor: Osteopath, Healer, Coach, and Dear Friend

Gaynor is another angel in human form, someone whose heart and work have profoundly impacted my healing journey. We first met in 2015 during Rik Schnabel's NLP course, and even then, I could see her incredible passion and wisdom. Now, as an osteopath with over 60 years of experience as a natural healer, she has become an absolute Godsend in my life.

What sets Gaynor apart is not just her expertise, but her immense generosity and the care she brings to her work. Despite living on opposite ends of Melbourne, she has gone out of her way to come to me for home treatments. This act of kindness alone speaks volumes about her heart. She has treated me gratis and gone above and beyond, offering her time and expertise without hesitation.

My body has responded to her treatments in ways I never imagined. Her approach is intuitive yet grounded in decades of knowledge, allowing her to meet my body's needs with precision and compassion. Gaynor's presence feels like stepping into a safe harbour; she creates an environment where healing can truly begin.

Her generosity isn't just in the physical care she provides; it's in the emotional and spiritual support she offers as well. Gaynor's belief in me and her encouragement to keep moving forward have been invaluable. Her treatments go beyond addressing physical pain; they nurture the whole person, helping me to reconnect with my body and my spirit.

I cannot express enough gratitude for the role Gaynor has played in my journey. She is a dear friend, a skilled practitioner, and a shining light in a world that often feels dark. Through her care, I've been reminded that healing is possible, not just for my body, but for the broken parts of my soul as well.

When I first met Gaynor in 2015, during Rik Schnabel's NLP course, we formed an immediate connection. We practiced our coaching skills on one another, and I admired her wisdom and warmth. However, during my marriage, it became increasingly difficult to maintain friendships or have anything that felt like my own. By 2017, I had slowly lost contact with Gaynor, as the isolation and control in my marriage consumed more of my life.

It wasn't until late 2022, after leaving my marriage, that I thought about Gaynor again. The realisation hit me like a revelation: I was free. Free to reconnect with friends, free to have conversations without fear of being monitored or criticised. I reached out to Gaynor, and it has been such a blessing to reconnect on so many levels.

Through her care and kindness, Gaynor has created a space of safety for my body, a sanctuary where I feel seen and nurtured. Her treatments cater to my body's needs, meeting me where I am with patience and understanding. It has been a profound gift to have someone who acknowledges how much my body has endured and treats it with the respect it deserves.

Even now, in January 2025, my body still carries the echoes of the past. There are triggers that surface during treatments, reminders of the thirteen years I spent in a relationship and marriage where my body's boundaries were repeatedly violated. It is taking time, time to rebuild trust with myself, time to teach my body that it is safe, time to believe that I am worthy of care and tender attention.

Gaynor's work has been pivotal in this process. Her care reminds me that healing is not just about escaping darkness but about stepping into light, where my body can finally rest and recover. She has helped me see that while the journey may be slow, it is moving forward, one gentle step at a time. With her support, I am learning to be patient with my body, allowing it the time it needs to release the trauma it has carried for so long.

With each session, my body has been able to release dark, buried memories, shadows of the sexual trauma I endured during my marriage. These memories, long hidden and locked away, have begun to surface and be drawn out into the light. The healing is nothing short of incredible. Gaynor's treatments are not just physical; they are emotional, psychological, and spiritual. Each session feels like being touched by an angel in human form, that's how I see her.

Gaynor holds space with a unique tenderness and strength, allowing the layers of trauma to come undone. She creates an environment where it's safe for the pain to be acknowledged, unpacked, and released, all while honouring the emotional weight these memories carry. She's not just treating the body; she's ministering to the soul, offering the compassion and understanding that are so essential to the healing process.

Her deep love for God's heart shines through in everything she does. Gaynor's kindness and compassion are gifts that ripple through her work, offering a tangible sense of God's love and grace. Her care has been transformative, working in harmony with Sharon's expertise in remedial massage therapy and Maryam's pelvic floor physiotherapy. Together, these incredible women have formed a trinity of healing in my life, addressing the physical, emotional, and spiritual wounds that had long been ignored or dismissed.

It's a reminder to me that healing isn't just about mending what's broken; it's about uncovering what was lost, my sense of worth, safety, and connection. Each session with Gaynor reinforces this truth: I am not defined by the darkness I've endured, but by the light I am stepping into.

3 Amazing Practitioners

My amazing remedial masseuse Sharon, pelvic floor physiotherapist Maryam from Modern Physiotherapy, and Gaynor with her incredible knowledge and skills as an osteopath, have all been instrumental in my healing journey. These three women, with their hands-on therapies and compassionate care, have gently guided my body toward a place of safety. Slowly, step by step, my body is beginning to trust me again after all we've endured together.

I am deeply grateful for each session with them. It feels like stepping into a portal of learning and healing, a sacred space where my body is comforted and reassured that we can move at the pace it needs in that moment. There is no pressure, no rush, just an invitation to listen and respond to what my body is ready to release.

Now that I am learning to truly listen to my body, I can feel how cultivating safety in my life is helping me in so many ways. It allows me to find the courage to write, to name the things that need to be voiced, and to give language to the pain and experiences that have shaped me. These sessions aren't just about physical healing; they are about reclaiming my connection to myself and my story.

Peter Quarry's Workshop: *How to Write a Psychological Memoir*

On a Saturday morning in May 2024, I attended a workshop called *How to Write a Psychological Memoir* by Peter Quarry. It was a transformative experience that illuminated areas of my story that desperately needed a voice. Peter's guidance gave me ideas for how to articulate the parts of my journey that had long been buried, waiting to be birthed into words.

Peter spoke about the significance of eras and events in a lifetime, encouraging us to identify the defining moments that have shaped us. This resonated deeply with me, particularly as I reflected on a pattern that had surfaced during my remedial massage sessions, the part of myself that is gullible and loses its voice.

This part of me emerges when I encounter someone dominant in personality, someone louder or forceful in their ways. Instead of standing firm in my beliefs and values, I find myself shrinking away, retreating to a corner within myself, denying my truth. It's as if I hand over my voice, allowing them to speak while I remain silent, afraid to risk my safety by voicing what's on my heart.

This theme has threaded through much of my life, starting in childhood and continuing into my marriage. When faced with conflict, my body reacts instinctively, my voice disappears, and I defer to the other person's narrative, even if it tramples over my own thoughts, beliefs, and values. Inside, another part of me is screaming, *"Make it stop! Tell them you're not interested. This isn't your truth!"* But outwardly, I stay quiet, paralysed by the fear of punishment or consequences for daring to speak up.

Since leaving my marriage, I've noticed this dynamic surfacing in new ways. There have been moments when others have been pushy with their belief systems, telling me how I should think, feel, or heal. They bombard me with unsolicited advice about my soul, my story, or what I *should* research or read. These interactions feel suffocating, there's no space for curiosity, only forceful opinions disguised as care.

In those moments, my body reacts as it always has. It freezes or flees the scene emotionally, waiting for my voice to emerge and make a stand. It's as though my body watches in horror as I remain silent, trapped in the old patterns of deference and self-abandonment.

Peter's workshop helped me begin to unravel this pattern, showing me how these unspoken parts of my story need to be voiced, not just for me, but for others who may feel similarly silenced. It reminded me that finding my voice, even in the face of dominance or judgment, is an essential part of my healing and growth. Writing has become the avenue through which I can reclaim my truth, offering both my body and my spirit a way to speak, to stand, and to be heard.

Rik Schnabel: The Brain Untrainer, Coach and Master NLP Trainer

Rik Schnabel is another angel in human form, someone whose dedication to his work changes lives. Words can't fully express the immense gratitude I feel for Rik and the way he has supported me through this journey. His knowledge, compassion, and understanding of trauma, family violence, childhood sexual abuse, and medical gaslighting have been transformative.

When I first encountered Rik in 2015 during his NLP training course, it was one of the few things I dared to do in my marriage without my husband's permission. That act of independence almost cost me my life. My husband's hatred for Rik and for the idea of me doing something without his control reached terrifying heights. I remember the rage, the threats, and the violence that followed when he found out I had enrolled in the course. He nearly killed me over it.

At the time, I couldn't fully absorb or appreciate what I was learning, as I was still trapped in the cycle of abuse. But reconnecting with Rik eight years later, in 2023, felt like completing a circle, like a door to healing and possibility had reopened.

Gaynor, my dear friend, was the one who suggested Rik when I mentioned my struggle with writing and publishing my memoir. She told me about his expertise, his bestselling books, and his ability to guide others through the publishing process. It was as if a light shone on me with revelation. After years of reaching out to writing and women's organisations, looking for someone who could help me tell my story about family violence, childhood sexual abuse, and medical gaslighting, I had found someone who truly understood.

The *HOPE suicide prevention team* had once given me a voucher for a four-day memoir-writing course at the *Council of Adult Education* (CAE), but physically and emotionally, I could only manage to attend two of the sessions. That had been a glimmer of support, but I still felt alone, drowning in the dark waters of trauma writing.

Reaching out to Rik in 2023 was like being thrown a life jacket. For the first time since starting my book in July 2020, during

Melbourne's lockdown, I felt I had someone who could help me navigate these overwhelming waters.

When we had our first appointment, I was desperate. I needed validation, guidance, and an anchor, something to hold onto so I wouldn't drown in the weight of revisiting my past. Rik provided all that and more. His knowledge and wisdom were, quite simply, a Godsend. Over the past year, he has been a steady presence, guiding me through the emotional turmoil of writing a book steeped in trauma. His coaching has been invaluable, not just for the structure of the book but for the healing process it has required.

What made working with Rik so unique was the way he created a space of safety, especially as a male practitioner. After enduring years of violence at the hands of my husband, I carry deep scars, both physical and emotional. My body has often reacted with tension and mistrust in the presence of men. But Rik's trauma-informed approach and understanding of family violence made all the difference.

Rik has a way of holding space that is both professional and profoundly empathetic. He understands the impact of childhood sexual abuse and how those experiences live in the body. He gets the insidious nature of medical gaslighting and the way it erodes trust in oneself. He knows how important it is for someone like me to feel truly seen, heard, and safe.

Through our work on *Zoom*, Rik has helped me traverse the darkest parts of my story. He's been a guide, a mentor, and a source of hope. His ability to combine practical advice with deep emotional insight has allowed me to bring my book to life in a way I never thought possible. For the first time, I feel like I have the tools, support, and courage to finish this project, a project that is so much more than a book. It's my story, my voice, and my path to freedom.

Rik's dedication to his work and his ability to change lives are extraordinary. Working with him has not only been a portal for my book but also a portal for my healing. He has given me hope, direction, and the belief that my story matters. For that, I am endlessly grateful.

Reflection:

It is because of this amazing team of people, angels in human form, that I have reached this point as I come to finishing this book. It is now January 2025, a new year, and my body has desperately needed to have a voice, a safe space to name and identify what happened in the brain and body growing up, and what led me into a marriage where I married someone who was kind and calm at first but eventually revealed his darkness in full force. I haven't come to this point alone; it has taken the support of family in the background, consistently helping me ask for help. My sisters and parents worked together to organise appointments for treatments, and my parents paid for them.

It's been hard because I felt like a loser, an adult unable to pay for myself. I was devastated that I had reached such a point, taken advantage of in so many ways in that marriage. Financially, he just took and kept taking, wanting to take even more when I didn't have anything left to give. My mum and dad's generosity in paying for treatments has helped me immensely, but I had hoped the NDIS would have funded treatments like Pelvic Floor Physiotherapy, Remedial Massage Therapy, and Osteopathy.

This flowing river of help came after my overdose. The baptism of cleansing with Kim and Bec opened up a river of flowing water that not only led me to these amazing angels in human form but also Tim's courses, "Hearing God's Voice Through Your Dreams" and "4 Keys to Hearing God's Voice." Alongside Rik's speaker training course, these gave me the courage to speak of my story in a way I had never done before.

GRACE AMORE

With all this help, I was able to take a risk last year and apply for a *Diploma of Justice* course, two days a week. It started in July 2024 and has become a pathway to break being housebound and scared of people. It has given my body confidence in stepping out into the world, even if the body is in pain at school. Some days, I sit on the floor, and that's okay. I give my body full permission to just be, even if it looks whacky to others. It's okay. Instead of berating my body for not doing all the things I want, I now give it love, telling it that it's safe to just be. It's a daily practice.

I haven't come to this point on my own. It feels like it has literally taken a village of people from all areas of life and expertise. My doctor, Sahar, is another angel in human form, an incredible human being. My local church, *Essendon Baptist*, is always there with open arms and love, even though I don't always attend. *Neuma Church* in Richmond, where I've been going on and off since I was a teenager, has been another space filled with love and open arms. My *School of Faith* family, precious friends, and my family have all played a role. I could go on and on with gratitude because it has not been easy coming out of hell.

As I reflect on the journey, I am reminded of Ann Voskamp's words: 'Shame dies when stories are told in safe places.'

By sharing my story, I hope to remind others that even in the depths of despair, healing is possible. We are not defined by the darkness we've endured but by the light we choose to step into.

The baptism washed over me, peeling back layers of shame, but my body still carried the history of it all.

I could feel it, even in the quiet after the cleansing, the deep knowing that my skin, my muscles, my bones held the memories of everything I had survived.

For so long, I had separated myself from my body, as if it was an enemy, as if it was something that had betrayed me.

But now, for the first time, I wondered, what would it mean to truly come home to my body?

To live in it, not as a prisoner, but as something sacred?

I had survived so much.

But could I learn to exist in my body, not just as something that endured, but as something that deserved care, safety, and belonging?

That journey, learning to live in a female body after a lifetime of violation, was just beginning.

"And I said to my body, softly, 'I want to be your friend.' It took a long breath and replied, 'I have been waiting my whole life for this.'" – Nayyirah Waheed.

But I am starting to see it differently now. My body is not just a vessel for suffering. It is a story, a history, a lineage. It carries the blood of my mother, who fought against a world that told her she didn't deserve an education. It carries the resilience of my father, who endured brutal beatings and backbreaking labour to create a better life.

This body, this existence, is not just a burden, it is a continuation of the strength that came before me. I have inherited pain. But I have also inherited survival. And that survival began long before I was born.

This is the first day I breathed deeply and didn't brace for impact.

Crossing the Threshold

There comes a moment in healing where something shifts, not in a loud, dramatic way, but like the whisper of wind moving through leaves. A moment where the body exhales in a way it never has before. Where the nervous system, long braced for attack, begins to loosen its grip. That moment came for me in the water.

It wasn't just a baptism of cleansing; it was a recalibration of everything. My body, for the first time in years, felt held instead of hijacked. Safe instead of silent. That morning, wrapped in the presence of God and the care of women who held space without needing answers, I crossed a threshold. And on the other side, I wasn't the same.

This wasn't the end of my healing, it was the beginning of embodiment.

Psalm 23 had carried me through the valley of the shadow of death. Now it was time to lie down in green pastures. To begin the restoration of my soul. Not just spiritually, but physically, cell by cell, breath by breath, through the sacred language of the body.

Healing for me didn't happen in one moment. It happened in hundreds of small decisions to stay present. To notice. To listen. To trust the body that had protected me, even when I felt it was betraying me. I had to rewire my thinking, reprogram my responses, and learn to feel safe in my own skin.

I began asking questions I'd never dared to ask: What would it mean to trust my body? What would it mean to speak without apology? What would it mean to no longer brace for impact?

I wasn't just recovering from abuse, I was recovering my voice, my agency, my connection with the Spirit who had never left me. The same Spirit who whispered, *"I will restore to you the years the locusts have eaten."*

As you move with me now into this next section, I'm no longer just telling my story. Now I'm sharing the truths that helped me survive.

The therapies that helped my body release. The tools that helped rewire my mind. The revelations that helped me choose life.

This is not separate from my story, it is the fruit of it.

Let this next part be a gentle invitation: To understand what trauma does. To listen to the language of your own body. To reclaim what was taken. And to remember, you were never meant to walk alone.

PART II

22: How Animals Absorb Trauma

Animals don't speak our language, but they understand pain. They listen without judgment. They bear witness to the things no one else sees. And sometimes, they take on the weight of what we cannot carry.

Animals absolutely feel pain. Studies have shown that mammals, birds, fish, and even some invertebrates have nervous systems capable of processing pain signals. Their reactions, such as limping, vocalising, or avoiding painful stimuli, are similar to how humans respond to pain.

As for feeling *your* pain, many animals, especially social and domesticated ones like dogs, cats, and horses, can sense human emotions. They pick up on subtle cues like body language, tone of voice, and even chemical changes in scent. Some studies suggest that dogs, for example, can recognise and even mirror human emotions, showing distress when their owner is upset. While they may not 'feel your pain' in the same way humans experience empathy, they can certainly respond to and be affected by it.

Grief comes in waves, and sometimes it takes different forms.

In my darkest times my cats, Matisse and Frida, were there, absorbing my pain, but when they were gone, the weight of loss became unbearable again. Matisse and Frida were born in 2004.

In the end, Matisse died in my arms, his body trembling in the car as we rushed his broken body to the vet. Another loss. Another grief. Another soul taken too soon.

To this day, I don't know the truth about how Matisse died. The husband told a story, but like so many of his stories, it didn't make sense. All I know is that he startled Matisse, so much that my sweet boy fell. In my gut I know he killed Matisse, as the husband was into startling me and our fur babies.

When Matisse passed away after the second miscarriage 2012, I fell again into a pit of grief and when Frida passed away with a massive tumour in her gut in 2019, she passed away shortly after Buddy was adopted. Frida knew. She always knew. She curled against my stomach night after night, pressing into the place where my pain lived.

She absorbed it all, my grief, my unease, the silent screams locked inside me. I swear she took my sickness into herself. The cancer. She carried the poison of that house, the weight of the dungeon, the darkness, the abuse. And in the end, it was too much. She bore it all until her own body couldn't take it anymore.

Animals may not speak, but they listen.

They feel. They take in the energy of a home, the undercurrents of fear, the unspoken cries.

Frida curled into my pain, taking it as her own.

But some burdens are too heavy, even for the most loyal of hearts.

And in the end, the weight of that house, that life, that suffering, It took her too.

23: Note to Younger Self: The Child

My sweet girl, I see you.

I see how you hold your breath, how you make yourself small, hoping, praying, that if you disappear, he won't find you.

I see the way you curl into yourself at night, the way you carry a silence that no child should ever have to bear.

I see the way you carry the weight of secrets that should never have been yours to hold.

I know you wonder if anyone sees you.

If anyone will come.

If anyone will ever stop this.

I need you to know, what happened to you was never your fault.

Not then. Not now. Not ever.

You don't have to be quiet anymore. You don't have to carry the shame that was never yours to bear.

One day, your voice will break the silence.

Not because you have to.

But because you are free.

And when you speak, the chains will shatter, not just for you, but for others too.

Your words will be a light in the darkness.

And you will never, ever be silenced again.

And when you do, your words will set others free, too.

One day, you will look back and see that the girl who was silenced now has the loudest, clearest, most powerful voice. You will build a life that is yours.

And now, you are free.

Free to belong to yourself.

Free to walk in God's love.

Free to live, not just survive.

A note to self in the marriage

I see you.

I see how hard you tried to hold onto the love, the hope, the dream.

I see the way you treasured those small, fleeting moments of peace, How you clung to them, praying they would last.

I see how much you wanted this to be real.

But I also see the pain that came after, the moments when this safety disappeared. And I want you to know, you deserved so much better. You deserve a peace that lasts, not just fleeting moments in between storms.

You deserved love that did not hurt.

Peace that did not come with conditions.

A life that was yours, not one you had to survive.

Poems:

This is the journey of emerging from captivity, learning to fly again, even with wounded wings. *I wrote this poem at the end of 2023 Inspired by doing Life Beyond Limits 'Speaker's training' with Rik Schnabel:*

Learning to Fly

She flew out of the cage……

She flew out of the cage into the open air, feeling the fresh sea air on her face.

Her feathers wilty, some needing urgent attention, but she could still fly out of that cage.

Not like a soaring eagle, more like a handicap soar, but it didn't matter, she was free

and safe enough to start healing from years of living in a prison of hells.

Jesus was there breathing new life into my wings.

Fly little bird, my love is the wind beneath your wings.

Time for nurturing the soul, mind and body, building up your spirit into new heights.

I love you little bird. I will never leave you nor forsake you.

The Garden after the marriage

The Garden was left unattended. It was neglected and dismissed.

The weeds outgrew the flowers that once were a delight.

Now the weeds were so many, she didn't know where to start.

Medical Gaslighting: Goodbye Uterus I love you.

It's all in your head.

My uterus says otherwise!

But your period pain is not valid.

Just take a Panadol, boohoo for you,

Every female gets their period.

What's so special about you?

Go have a baby and the pain will go away!

Sent off for another ultrasound.

Again, I'm sorry, 'There is nothing in the ultra-sound, all clear'.

You are fine, nothing wrong here. Ultra-sound doesn't show anything. Goodbye.

Scratches head, 'hmm, what to do?'

Pain grows and grows.

What to do, where to go?

Lost in the throes of life,

Period pain became strife.

Pain cut like a knife. Stab, stab, stab.

The pain was insane.

Who do I wake up in the mundane.

There is so much disdain, for female pelvic pain.

From bruised to blessed

The journey from pain to healing is not linear. It is filled with moments of grief, anger, and ultimately, renewal.

Her heart bruised; her soul beaten up. What was she to do, to get to the other side of the shit. She was in pain from the stain. Existing in the mundane, a state of no man's land, a muddy mire. She needed a new spiritual fire. The family grieve; they grieve what was lost. And that shows they care because she gave her pearls to swine, where she was continually undermined. The devil she dined.

But he appeared kind and of sound mind. But before she knew it, she was in a bind. Bound up and bind to darkness that came dressed up as a wolf in sheep's clothing with all the loathing of himself and others.

The swine would anger with wrath so strong that it would blow her hair back, as the breath of the swine filled up her breathing space. Now on their 2nd fight, something just isn't right. Before she knew it, 13 hurricane years had taken her breath and left her winded. Like a king hit to the gut winded for 13 years. She did not know what took hold of her soul. She was in a black hole. Help, help, Get me out of here. Then her sister friend hears her cry. She looked into her eyes take me to the stream to wash away all shame because I can't live with this anymore. And with conviction her friend said, 'Yes'. With the blame of the swine. I had to wash the old wine off, to wash away the stain of old skin wine. No more the devil she shall dine.

Closing Reflections

Poesia di fine anno as told by Mum. (End of year poem told by Mum for the new year ahead). Love you Mum and your parables, poems and singing.

This is told in Sicilian dialect: The Web version in Italian:(Chatgpt)

L'anno vecchio se ne va e mai piu ritornera. Io li o, datto una valigia di lezione fatti male e le of datto porta via questa e tutta roba mia.

Mum's version:

La poesia che hai citato è "Anno vecchio e anno nuovo." Ecco il testo originale: "L'anno vecchio se ne va e mai più ritornerà. Io gli ho dato una valigia di capricci e impertinenze, di lezioni fatte male, di bugie, disubbidienze, e gli ho detto: 'Porta via, questa è tutta roba mia'. Anno nuovo, avanti avanti! Ti fan festa tutti quanti.

"Anno vecchio e anno nuovo"

Tu la gioia e la salute porta ai cari genitori, ai parenti ed agli amici, rendi lieti tutti i Cuore. D'esser buono ti prometto, anno nuovo, benedetto." Questa poesia rappresenta un addio all'anno passato, carico di errori e mancanze, e un benvenuto all'anno nuovo, con la promessa di migliorare e portare gioia e salute a sé stessi e agli altri.

The poem is by Arpalice Cuman Pertile. It reflects on the transition from the old year to the new, symbolising personal growth and the shedding of past mistakes.

Here's a translation of the poem: English translation: (Chatgpt 1/11/2024)

"The old year departs and will never return. I gave it a suitcase filled with whims and impertinences, poorly done lessons, lies, and disobediences, and I said to it: "Take this away; it's all my stuff. New year, come forward, come forward! Everyone celebrates you. Bring joy and health to dear parents, to relatives and friends, make all hearts happy. I promise to be good, blessed new year."

This poem is often recited during New Year's celebrations in Italy, emphasizing the hope and renewal that come with the start of a new year.

The Silence – The Aftermath of Sensory Recalibration After the Storm

As I sit here, finishing this book, it's the silence that stands out. But not in the way most people think. After four years of clawing my way out of that mayhem, it's the silence that's the loudest.

It echoes in my body. My shoulders aren't drawn up in constant tension anymore. I have nails now, where once there were only stubs, chewed down from restless uncertainty. The never knowing. The unrelenting cycle of unpredictability that turned my nervous system into a sentry, stationed in a watchtower. Where is he? What's his tone like today? Is his expression neutral or simmering with something unspoken? How much has he been drinking? Has he had a good day? What's he been brooding over this time?

Even in the so-called silence of that dungeon-home, the lions lay awake, prowling. The tension lived in my pelvis, locked in the unknown, bracing for what lay hidden in the shadows. That house, broken down, neglected, screamed of what it held inside. Dark corners, broken hinges, curtains drawn tight, blocking out the last traces of light. The oppression was never quiet. It roared. It hung thick in the air, vibrating in my skull, filling every breath, every thought. My frontal lobe, my hippocampus, my amygdala, whirring, circling, replaying. A conveyor belt of memories, each one a threat to my survival, a reminder that danger had no schedule.

The wolf in sheep's clothing never truly slept. Even in sleep, he invaded my nights, teeth grinding, arms flinching, the weight of his presence pressing into the mattress. The stench of alcohol, of stale smoke, saturating the air. The silence of that dungeon was a poisonous gas, suffocating me in endless, unspoken demands.

That silence was never stillness. It was an illusion of rest, a deception that demanded I remain alert, always bracing, always ready.

But now, now the body can rest. The body is no longer in the dungeon.

24: Faith, Angels and God

"Trauma passed down through generations doesn't dissolve on its own. Healing is the gift we give to ourselves and those who come after us, breaking cycles and building paths of compassion, not repetition." - Gabor Mate

Psalm 34:18 "The Lord is close to the broken-hearted and saves those who are crushed in spirit."

A Spiritual Reflection

Even in the darkest nights of my marriage, the light of my family's love flickered in the distance. But beyond even that, there was one presence that never left me, a small but steady flame. But there were moments when that light felt too far away, when the weight of isolation and pain became unbearable. And in those moments, when no one could see my suffering, there was still one presence that never left me. It was the small quiet voice of God's love. He was there in the whispers of when I thought I had none left.

"As long as we feel safely held in the hearts and minds of the people who love us, we will climb mountains and cross deserts and stay up all night to finish projects." - λ Bessel A. van der Kolk, The Body Keeps the Score: Brain, Mind, and Body in the Healing of Trauma

He was there in the unseen hands that guided me when I was lost. And he was there in the quiet, persistent voice that told me: there is more for you than this. You were made for more than suffering. Even when I didn't know how to save myself, the light of hope was flickering with the whisper of clarity, 'Breathe.'

In moments of deep pain and brokenness, it can feel as though no one understands the depth of your suffering. Yet, Psalm 34:18 offers a profound truth:

> *"The Lord is close to the broken-hearted and saves those who are crushed in spirit." – Psalm 34:18*

This verse is a reminder that even in the darkest moments, God draws near to those who feel shattered. Healing from family violence is a journey, often messy and difficult, but God's presence is constant. As the body begins to release the stored pain, and the mind learns to find safety again, survivors can find peace in knowing that they are not alone. The Lord is a refuge, a source of comfort, and a healer for both the crushed spirit and the weary body.

Crying, screaming inside to God

When I was in the brink of madness, crying every day in the shower, in bed, on the way to work, twisted in a web of confusion, the husband's voice piercing my insides like razor sharp blades, cutting my insides up with his relentless bullying. I would breakdown when he wasn't looking, weeping, crying out to God, "This can't be normal for a marriage to have so much stress in it. Is this normal?"

As the beast lay next to me in the marital bed that was more so a bed of debauchery where the safety was ripped away and eaten by the angry wolves that devoured souls till there was nothing left to devour, but carcass.

What do I do God? You tell me I am worthy, but I live with a husband that tells me, I am unworthy, that he knows me better than I know myself and that if I just do as he says than everything will be okay. He calls me 'whore', he calls me 'slut' and I in turn repeat those names over my being. The names are not said in jest, they are spoken like venom, like a poison that drips into my spirit, taking life, precious life that sparks up when treated with respect.

One morning after I had seen my death in 2020, I had taken *Endone* and other pain meds. In the shower the water I cried, wept in desperation, then out of the shower, the weeping turned into anger, and I punched the bathroom wall. I wasn't one for punching and this action showed me I was in deep shit and needed to get out. But how. How does one get out of a situation so sticky, so muddy, so drenched in shit, it's a muddy mire of gloom and doom with a way through. What the fuck does someone do in that situation?

The one being I know is God, through the shit of life, the experiences that have questioned my sanity and reason for being alive, I turn to God. After the crying, screaming, swearing, its God I turn to because as I have experienced humans are not God. That's why God is God. As I have come to learn, that God is the creator, he wasn't created, hence the wonder of God, the mystery of God.

I don't marvel at man or woman; I marvel at God.

There are things that have happened in my life and seen in others that I can't deny that a being much greater than what I can imagine works in our heart space. Tapping into the love space, the heart space is like opening up dried up channels of water into rivers of living water.

After all the craziness of this world, I know I am here for one being, and that being is God.

How many times was suicide beckoning me, calling me but something in me wasn't a hundred percent about it, there was always a part of me that said think about the first person that will find your body. What will that do to them?

Pain. What is it?

Pain is a strange thing. It can break you. Or it can carve out something new inside you, A space where compassion grows.

A space where faith deepens. A space where healing begins.

I have known suffering so deep it felt like it would swallow me whole.

But I have also known the kind of redemption that only comes from God, the kind that turns ashes into beauty.

> *"Trauma passed down through generations doesn't dissolve on its own. Healing is the gift we give to ourselves and those who come after us, breaking cycles and building paths of compassion, not repetition." - Gabor Mate*

And wounds into testimonies

While faith was my anchor, I also needed tangible steps to get out. Here's what I wish I had known then.

As I began to heal, I realised I needed to understand what had happened to me, not just spiritually, but physically and psychologically. That's when I started researching trauma and its effects on the brain and body.

If you are reading this and you feel trapped, if the weight of shame, trauma, or pain still clings to your body, know this: You are not alone. There is more for you. Even when you can't see the way out, even when the darkness whispers that you won't make it, there is a light that never stops shining. You were made for more than suffering. And if God could bring me through, He can bring you through too.

25: Escape and Freedom

Whether you're a woman or a man, if you've escaped and found freedom, what helped you get out?

Healing doesn't happen in isolation. We need each other.

There were moments I truly believed I wouldn't survive. But I did. And if you're reading this, it means you've survived something too.

Maybe you're not free yet. Maybe you're still quietly, secretly, building your escape plan. If you are free, ask yourself:

What helped you break away?

What gave you the strength to go?

What was the moment you said, "Enough. I am worth more than this!"

These stories matter. They need to be told.

Because when we share them, we shine a light for those still searching for the exit.

Let's start that conversation.

Let's create a space where survivors can speak their truth and know, without a doubt, they are not alone.

Visit: **https://www.graceamore.com/** No one should have to find the way out on their own. And if you're not ready to speak yet, that's okay. Just know this:

You are not alone.

There *is* a way forward.

And when the time comes, your voice will matter. Your story will be heard.

Before You Continue

You've now walked through the story with me, through violence, loss, awakening, and finally freedom.

But healing wasn't just a one-time decision. It was a process that asked everything of me: mind, body, spirit. It took learning to trust my gut. It took understanding what trauma does to the nervous system. It took prayer, sound healing, breath, and the grace of God guiding me through every step.

In the chapters ahead, I want to offer what helped me most, not as a therapist or professional, but as a woman who survived. These tools, ideas, and insights gave me language for what I was feeling when I didn't know how to speak. I hope they do the same for you.

PART III - RESOURCES

26: Act When You Sense Danger

The moment you sense that something is wrong, the first whisper of intuition telling you that you are not safe, is the moment a seed of awareness is planted.

At first, it may be a faint warning, easy to ignore or rationalise away. Maybe you tell yourself: "It's not that bad."

"Maybe I'm overreacting."

"They didn't mean it."

But that first instinct, the voice deep inside you that says, "This person is not good for me", is the voice of wisdom. It is the part of you that knows or sees danger before your mind fully understands it. Listen to it. Trust your gut. Trust your intuition.

What to Do When You Realise You're in Danger

Acknowledge the Warning Sign

That gut feeling, that sense of unease, is your body's way of protecting you. Do not dismiss it. Recognising the first red flag is the beginning of your escape.

Do Not Try to Justify Their Behaviour

Abusers thrive on making you doubt yourself. They manipulate, gaslight, and twist reality until you second-guess your instincts. If something feels wrong, it is wrong. Period.

Find a Safe Person to Talk To

The moment you sense that your safety is at risk, reach out. Whether it's a trusted friend, family member, counsellor, or crisis support line, speak up. The longer you stay silent, the harder it becomes to leave.

Make a Plan, Even If You're Not Ready to Leave

Sometimes, leaving immediately isn't possible. But you can start planting the seeds of your exit.

Keep a small emergency bag packed if needed.

Save money in a hidden account if you can.

Document incidents in a private, secure place.

Slowly rebuild a support system, even if your abuser has isolated you.

Believe That You Deserve Safety

This may be the hardest part. Abuse conditions you to believe you are trapped, that you are powerless, that this is your fate. That is a lie. You are not trapped. You are not powerless. You are worthy of safety and peace.

The Seed of Freedom Will Grow

That first instinct, that first whisper telling you to get out, is a seed. Even if you ignore it, even if you push it away, it remains inside you, waiting.

The more you listen to it, the more it grows.

The more you nourish it, with truth, with courage, with the quiet act of acknowledging your worth, the stronger it becomes.

One day, that seed will take root.

One day, it will be impossible to ignore.

And when that day comes, you will walk away.

And when you do, you will not just survive. You will rise.

I felt broken, but I wasn't crazy. My body and brain had been responding exactly as they were designed to in the face of chronic danger. Understanding this was the key to reclaiming my power.

Even if you feel too exhausted, too lost, too afraid to take action today, just know this: You are not alone. And when the time is right, when you feel that whisper become a roar, you will know what to do. You will get out. And you will rise.

27: The Effects of Prayer on the Brain and Body

Prayer on the brain and body calms the nervous system.

Activates the Parasympathetic Nervous System: Prayer promotes relaxation by engaging the parasympathetic nervous system, also known as the "rest and digest" system. This helps lower heart rate, reduce blood pressure, and calm the body.

Prayer Reduces Stress Hormones

Regular prayer can decrease cortisol levels, the hormone responsible for stress, creating a sense of peace and well-being.

Prayer Strengthens Emotional Regulation

Prayer Reduces Amygdala Activity: Prayer has been shown to reduce overactivity in the amygdala, the brain's fear and stress centre, which helps individuals manage anxiety and emotional responses more effectively.

Prayer Enhances Prefrontal Cortex Function: Prayer engages the prefrontal cortex, the area responsible for decision-making, self-control, and focus. This helps with emotional regulation and logical thinking during stressful situations.

Prayer Promotes Healing and Resilience

Prayer and Neuroplasticity and Positive Change: Prayer can strengthen neural pathways associated with positive emotions, gratitude, and compassion. Over time, this rewires the brain to be more resilient in the face of adversity. If you think of the power of affirmations, this will make even more sense to you.

Prayer Improved Immune Function: Studies suggest that spiritual practices, including prayer, may boost the immune system by reducing chronic inflammation and promoting overall health (Koenig, 2012).

Prayer Deepens the Sense of Connection

Prayer Increases Oxytocin Levels: Prayer and meditation foster feelings of love, compassion, and bonding, partly due to increased oxytocin levels, the "love hormone." This creates a greater sense of connection with God and others.

Prayer Reduces Feelings of Isolation: Prayer offers comfort and a sense of being heard, which can reduce feelings of loneliness, especially in difficult times.

Prayer Provides Mental Clarity and Focus

Prayer Enhances Mindfulness: Prayer often involves focusing attention on God, scripture, or a specific intention. This mindfulness element helps quiet mental distractions and brings clarity.

Prayer Fosters Gratitude and Hope: Prayer helps shift focus from problems to solutions, fostering gratitude, hope, and a sense of purpose, which are essential for mental health.

Biblical Perspective

Prayer is not just a physiological practice; it is deeply spiritual. In Philippians 4:6-7, it says: "Do not be anxious about anything, but in every situation, by prayer and petition, with thanksgiving, present your requests to God. And the peace of God, which transcends all understanding, will guard your hearts and your minds in Christ Jesus."

This peace surpasses human understanding because it aligns the mind and body with God's presence, offering a sense of security and calm that nothing else can provide.

Example of How Prayer Can Heal

Imagine a survivor of family violence sitting quietly, speaking their fears to God. In that moment:

The body relaxes, with a slowing heart rate and deeper breathing.

The brain shifts from fear (amygdala) to rational reflection and connection (prefrontal cortex).

Over time, this practice reduces the hypervigilance caused by trauma and fosters emotional resilience.

I've experienced firsthand how prayer shifts the body from panic to peace. There were moments I felt like I couldn't breathe, but when I called out to God, my heart slowed, my mind cleared, and I felt His presence carrying me through.

References:

Koenig, H. G. (2012). Religion, spirituality, and health: The research and clinical implications. *ISRN Psychiatry, 2012*, Article ID 278730.

Newberg, A., & Waldman, M. R. (2009). *How God changes your brain: Breakthrough findings from a leading neuroscientist.* Ballantine Books.

28: Coercion and Sexual Control

Sex in my marriage was everywhere, and it was the beast in the husband. There was never just one place. It was always somewhere unsafe; sex cinemas, strip clubs, private rooms, domestic homes where women bathed while men sat, emotionless, watching them. Every time, I felt trapped. I lost track of how many panic attacks I had. And the worst part? He enjoyed it. Not just the place. Not just the women. But me – my discomfort, my fear, my desperate need to escape. That's what really got him off.

I'm not sure how to even put into words, the sexual perversion, darkness experienced in my time with the husband.

Coercion doesn't always look like violence. It can be the husband who financially controls you so you can't leave. The partner who uses threats, humiliation, or manipulation to force you into sex. The fear that saying 'no' will mean losing everything, your home, your children, your sense of safety. It's all coercion. And it's all wrong.

Understanding Your Rights: Legal Protection Against Sexual Coercion in Victoria

Abuse is not just a personal struggle; it's also a justice issue. Many survivors don't realise that coercion itself is a crime under Victorian law. Here's what you need to know.

Sexual Coercion & the Victorian Law:

Sexual Coercion in Victoria, the Crimes Act 1958 addresses sexual coercion through its definitions of consent and related offences. Specifically, Section 36AA outlines circumstances where a person does not consent to an act, including situations where the individual submits to coercion or intimidation (AustLII)

Additionally, Section 40 defines the offence of sexual assault, which occurs when a person intentionally touches another sexually without consent, and without a reasonable belief that consent was given. (AustLII) These provisions collectively criminalise acts of sexual coercion in Victoria. CRIMES ACT 1958 - SECT 36AA

Circumstances in which a person does not consent (1) Circumstances in which a person does not consent to an act include, but are not limited to, the following,

(a) the person does not say or do anything to indicate consent to the act;

(b) the person submits to the act because of force, a fear of force, harm of any type or a fear of harm of any type, whether to that person or someone else or to an animal, regardless of,

(i) when the force, harm or conduct giving rise to the fear occurs; and

(ii) whether it is, or is a result of, a single incident or is part of an ongoing pattern;

Examples:

Each of the following is a type of harm that can be done to a person as described in this paragraph,

(a) economic or financial harm;

(b) reputational harm;

(c) harm to the person's family, cultural or community relationships;

(d) harm to the person's employment;

(e) family violence involving psychological abuse or harm to mental health;

(f) sexual harassment.

(c) the person submits to the act because of coercion or intimidation,

(i) regardless of when the coercion or intimidation occurs; and

(ii) whether it is, or is a result of, a single incident or is part of an ongoing pattern;

(d) the person submits to the act because the person is unlawfully detained;

(e) the person submits to the act because the person is overborne by the abuse of a relationship of authority or trust;

(f) the person is asleep or unconscious;

(g) the person is so affected by alcohol or another drug as to be incapable of consenting to the act;

(h) the person is so affected by alcohol or another drug as to be incapable of withdrawing consent to the act;

Reference: Victorian current Acts. 2024. Crimes Act 1958- Sect 36AA.

https://www5.austlii.edu.au/au/legis/vic/consol_act/ca195882/s36aa.html.

In Victoria, the Crimes Act 1958 addresses sexual coercion through its definitions of consent and specific sexual offences. The Act stipulates that a person does not consent to an act if they submit due to coercion or intimidation, regardless of when the coercion occurs or whether it is part of a single incident or an ongoing pattern.

Additionally, the Act outlines that a person does not consent if they submit because of force, fear of force, harm, or fear of harm of any type, whether to themselves, someone else, or an animal. This includes various forms of harm, such as economic, reputational, or psychological abuse.

These provisions are part of Victoria's affirmative consent model, which requires active and voluntary agreement to sexual activity. The Justice Legislation Amendment (Sexual Offences and Other Matters) Act 2022 introduced these reforms to strengthen protections against sexual offences, including those involving coercion.

For detailed information, refer to sections 36 and 36AA of the Crimes Act 1958.

Consent Was Never Mine to Give

For a long time, I didn't realise I had a right to say no. I thought being married meant I had an obligation, that my body was no longer my own. I didn't know then what I know now: what I endured was not consent, it was coercion. I was taught that marriage was about love, commitment, and sacrifice. I believed that being a wife meant putting my husband first, even when it cost me my dignity, my peace, and my body. I believed that being 'good' meant giving in, keeping the peace, not making a fuss. But what I didn't understand was that true consent is never given out of fear, pressure, or obligation.

1. Consent is Freely Given, Reversible, Informed, Enthusiastic, and Specific

I now understand that real consent follows the F.R.I.E.S. model:

☑ Freely Given – Not pressured, not manipulated, not forced.

☑ Reversible – Can be withdrawn at any time, even in marriage.

☑ Informed – Based on full knowledge, not deception or coercion.

☑ Enthusiastic – A genuine *yes*, not an obligated one.

☑ Specific – Agreeing to one thing doesn't mean agreeing to everything.

But in my marriage, none of these applied.

My consent wasn't freely given, it was expected.

My 'no' didn't matter, he would whine, sulk, guilt-trip, or rage until I gave in.

I wasn't informed, he made decisions about my body without my knowledge.

I wasn't enthusiastic, I disassociated, I endured, I disappeared into myself.

I wasn't allowed to say no, because my body wasn't considered my own.

For years, I carried the weight of believing that because I didn't fight back, because I gave in, it must have been consent. I told myself, "Maybe I just wasn't strong enough. Maybe if I'd tried harder to say no, it wouldn't have happened."

But here's the truth: submission is not consent. Fear is not consent. Silence is not consent.

2. Coerced vs. Real Consent

One of the biggest lies I believed was that coercion was just part of marriage.

I remember the exhaustion, how I dreaded nighttime because I knew what was expected. If I wasn't in the mood, it was a problem. If I said no, it would turn into a fight. If I resisted, he'd accuse me of being cold, distant, or of 'not loving him.' If I tried to explain my pain, he dismissed it.

Looking back, I see now how my 'yes' was never really mine to give. It was taken. And when consent is not freely given, it is not consent at all.

Real Consent Sounds Like:

"I really want to do this."

"Yes, this feels right for me."

"I am choosing this because I want to, not because I have to."

Coerced Consent Sounds Like:

"If you loved me, you would..." *(Guilt and manipulation.)*

"You're my wife, it's your duty." *(Entitlement.)*

"Fine, I guess I'll just suffer." *(Emotional blackmail.)*

"You already did this before, so what's the problem now?" *(Past consent does not mean present consent.)*

Silence, freezing, or shutting down. *(A trauma response is not consent.)*

For years, I thought I was weak for not fighting harder. But the truth is, I was surviving. My body knew what my mind wasn't ready to accept: that saying "no" was dangerous. So, I shut down.

3. How Power Dynamics Affected My Consent

One of the hardest things to explain to people who have never been in an abusive marriage is how power takes away choice. I wasn't just saying 'yes' to avoid an argument, I was saying 'yes' because my survival depended on it.

Financial Control: I was financially dependent. Saying no came with the risk of being punished, emotionally or otherwise.

Religious Manipulation: "The Bible says you have to submit," he told me. But Jesus never asked anyone to submit to abuse.

Emotional Abuse: If I resisted, I was met with rage, coldness, or cruelty. So, I learned that my needs didn't matter.

Health Issues & Pain: When sex was painful, he didn't care. When I cried, he rolled over and went to sleep.

I was living in a system designed to keep me powerless. And when one person holds all the power, consent is impossible.

4. Marriage Does NOT Mean Automatic Consent

One of the most dangerous myths I believed was that being married meant I had to give my body to him, no matter what.

It wasn't until years later that I learned marital rape is a crime in Australia and many other countries. But I didn't know that then. I had been taught that 'withholding sex' was unfair, that men 'had needs,' that being a wife meant obliging.

Coerced vs. Real Consent

Often, people assume "She didn't say no" means "She said yes." But silence, hesitation, fear, or obligation are not consent. Here's the difference:

☑ **Real Consent:**

"I really want to do this."

"Yes, I feel comfortable with this."

"I am choosing this freely, without pressure."

🚫 **Coerced Consent (Not Consent):**

"If you loved me, you would do this." (*Emotional manipulation*)

"I did this for you, so you should do this for me." (*Obligation/guilt-tripping*)

"But we're married, it's your duty." (*Implying a right to your body*)

"You already did it before, so why not now?" (*Past consent doesn't mean future consent*)

Freezing or going silent due to fear. (*A trauma response, fear is not consent!*)

Reference: Anderson, I. (2007). *What is Consent? A Psychological Perspective on the Grey Areas.* Journal of Sexual Aggression, 13(1), 13-23.

But God never designed marriage to be a place of coercion.

🚫 Marriage does NOT mean:

You owe your spouse sex.

You cannot say no.

Your body belongs to someone else.

Marriage Does NOT Equal Automatic Consent

One of the most dangerous myths about consent is that marriage means permanent consent. This is false. Being married does not give anyone ownership over your body.

In fact, many legal systems now recognise marital rape as a crime:

Australia: Marital rape has been illegal in all states since 1991.

United States: Marital rape is illegal in all 50 states (though some still have loopholes).

United Kingdom: The House of Lords ruled in 1991 that marital rape is a crime.

4. Marriage Does NOT Mean Automatic Consent

I knew marital rape was a crime.

I knew, in my body and in my spirit, that consent mattered, even in marriage.

But in my marriage, that truth was constantly distorted.

He twisted it until I doubted myself.

He made it seem like saying no meant I was punishing him. That my boundaries were the real problem. That being a 'good wife' meant giving in, even when everything in me said no.

Over time, I was made to feel that my body wasn't really mine anymore. That I was selfish for needing space. That love meant giving in. That marriage meant surrendering myself, completely.

He twisted scripture, misused therapy language, and even played on my empathy to justify his behaviour and make me question myself.

But the truth never stopped being true:

Consent is never automatic, not in marriage, not ever.

What happened wasn't love. It was violation, dressed up as duty.

My husband cried, guilted, manipulated, humiliated and pestered me until I gave in. He made me feel like it was my responsibility to meet his needs, and when I didn't, I was punished, through coldness, resentment, drunken rages, humiliate me in front of others about how sex deprived he was along with more emotional pressure. He was relentless and wouldn't let things go.

I didn't feel safe enough to say no, so I avoided saying no. And because I never said the word 'no' outright, I didn't recognise it as rape.

It wasn't until years later, after I had left the marriage and was on the phone with *1800 Respect*, that I heard the words that shook me: "You were raped in your marriage."

That moment hit me like a wave. My body had known all along, but my mind had been too conditioned, too confused, too manipulated to see it for what it was. I wasn't safe to refuse, and when there is no true choice, there is no consent.

☑ **Marriage should be:**

A place where autonomy is honoured.

A relationship built on mutual love and respect.

A commitment, not ownership.

How Power Dynamics Affect Consent

When there is an imbalance of power, consent is compromised because the person with less power may not feel like they can safely say no. This happens in:

Financial Dependence: "I pay the bills, so you should do this for me."

Fear-Based Control: "If you don't, I'll get angry." *(When fear replaces choice, it's not consent.)*

Religious Manipulation: "God says you have to submit." *(Twisting scripture to remove bodily autonomy is abuse.)*

Guilt & Obligation: "I'm your husband/wife, this is my right." *(No one is entitled to your body.)*

Substance Use: If someone is intoxicated, they cannot consent.

Reference: Stark, E. (2007). *Coercive Control: How Men Entrap Women in Personal Life.* Oxford University Press.

I was treated like property, not a person.

For anyone reading this who has been told they 'owe' their spouse their body: You do not. You never did. You never will.

Final Thoughts: Naming the Truth

For years, I knew what was happening to me was wrong, but I struggled to fully name it. I didn't think I could call it rape because he made it seem like he was the one suffering.

He would cry, telling me I was killing him by not having as much sex as he wanted. He claimed he was dying from "blue balls," making it sound like his body was in crisis, as if my body existed to relieve his pain. When I resisted, he would sulk, guilt-trip, and get angry. And when he was drunk, that anger turned into something even darker, he would take it out on me.

One of the things that still makes me cringe to this day is what he called a "sucker punch." We had watched the movie Sucker Punch, and for whatever sick reason, he decided he wanted to recreate that violence during sex. So, he did, punching me in the back of the head.

Then he wanted me to do it to him. I didn't want to. But somehow, I still did. I still did.

Even though it went against every grain of my being as it made me sick to re-enact something that caused death in the movie we had just watched. I made sure not to punch hard or cause pain or death. This was twisted, and I did it for my own safety, had I not, who knows what he could have done to me.

Even now, the thought of it makes me sick. Because that wasn't love. That wasn't sex. That was power, control, and violence disguised as intimacy.

I knew it was bad. I knew I felt sick inside. But I didn't feel safe enough to say no.

But the truth is, I was raped in my marriage.

I didn't want to say it. I didn't want to believe it. But the moment I finally let those words sit; I felt the weight of my silence break.

I share this now because I know I am not alone. Because there are others, maybe even you, who have been told that what happened to you wasn't abuse, that you should have fought harder, that if you stayed, you must have wanted it.

None of that is true.

What happened to me was not my fault.

What happened to you was not your fault.

And if there is one thing, I want you to take away from this, it's this:

- 🚫 Silence is not consent.
- 🚫 Fear is not consent.
- 🚫 Marriage is not consent.

🚫 Intimate partner relationships are not consent.

You do not owe anyone your body. Not your husband. Not your partner. Not anyone.

And if no one has told you yet: You deserve real love, real safety, and real choice.

The *Power and Control Wheel*

The key categories of the *Power and Control Wheel*, such as coercion, intimidation, emotional abuse, isolation, minimising/blaming, using children, economic abuse, and threats.

The *Power and Control Wheel* illustrates the ways abusers maintain dominance over their victims. In my own experience, I faced multiple forms of coercion, sexual, emotional, financial, and legal, each reinforcing the cycle of abuse. Understanding this framework helped me see how deeply embedded these patterns were in my marriage and why escaping them was so difficult."

The *Power and Control Wheel*, developed by the *Domestic Abuse Intervention Programs* (DAIP), outlines the tactics abusers use to dominate their partners. It includes forms of coercion such as emotional abuse, financial control, intimidation, and sexual violence. You can view the full wheel at: https://www.theduluthmodel.org/?s=power+and+control+wheel .

When I first came across the *Power and Control Wheel*, I recognised so many of the patterns I had endured. It was a stark reminder that abuse is not just about physical violence, it's about control in every aspect of life.

Many survivors, like me, struggle to prove coercion because the abuse is psychological, emotional, sexual and gradual. The system often focuses on physical violence while ignoring these insidious forms of control. This wheel makes it clear that abuse is not just about bruises, it's about domination in all aspects of life.

When I first came across the *Power and Control Wheel*, I recognised so many of the patterns I had endured. It was a stark reminder that abuse is not just about physical violence, it's about control in every aspect of life.

I had already known about the *Power and Control Wheel* through my work in the community sector. I had seen how it applied to survivors seeking support, how it helped professionals identify patterns of abuse that weren't always visible. But recognising it in my own life was something entirely different. I wasn't just reading about coercion; I was living it. Seeing the tactics laid out so clearly made me realise that the abuse I had suffered wasn't just isolated incidents, but part of a larger system of control.

The *Power and Control Wheel* in My Marriage

Abuse is not just about physical violence; it is a system of control that infiltrates every part of a survivor's life. The following sections outline how power and control were exerted in my marriage, making it nearly impossible to recognise the full extent of the abuse while I was still in it.

Medical Gaslighting:

By the Medical System: Dismissing my pain as 'all in my head' and pushing antidepressants on me instead of addressing the root cause.

Doctors trying to convince me that my symptoms weren't serious or that I was 'overreacting.'

Preventing me from accessing proper medical care by sending me off to endless ultrasounds that were useless, never informing me that a women's clinic ultrasound existed, one that could have actually detected my condition earlier.

Making me doubt my own health concerns, leading me to question whether the pain was real.

By My Ex-husband:

Using my medical struggles to keep me dependent, only being 'supportive' when it benefited him.

Reinforcing the idea that doctors knew best, even when I felt dismissed and unheard.

Minimising my pain, making me feel like I was weak or imagining things.

Becoming enraged when I had period pain, as if my suffering was an inconvenience to him. Instead of offering support, he saw it as an obstacle to sex. Over time, I became afraid of my own period because I knew it would trigger his anger.

Making me feel guilty for something I couldn't control, treating my body's natural functions as a personal offence against him.

1. Sexual Coercion and Marital Rape

Pressuring, guilt-tripping, or manipulating me into sex when I didn't want to.

Using my body as if it belonged to him, with no regard for my consent.

Ignoring my pain, discomfort, or trauma, making sex an obligation instead of an act of love.

Punishing me emotionally when I didn't comply, nagging, incessant pestering or the silent treatment, anger, or threats.

Becoming furious when my period disrupted sex, making me feel like I had failed or was depriving him of something he was entitled to. Instead of respecting my pain, he would become enraged, if we were out at festivals and my period came, at first, he would become angry than later come back with a pain relief he would source out like Special K to help with the pain.

2. Spiritual Manipulation

Twisting scripture to justify his actions and silence me. Like telling me I had to submit to him as his wife, but the bible doesn't say for a husband to do what he wants to his wife. The relationship is meant to be about respect and honouring one another, not domination.

Mocking my faith when I needed comfort, by publicly humiliating me in front of friends.

Using my faith in Jesus Christ to reinforce control and twist my beliefs around to dismiss what I find comfort and solace in. The husband would make ridiculous statements suggesting that he is God, that is powerful, seeking constant admiration.

3. Financial Control

Controlled the money, as soon as money came in he had decided where it was going to be spent on.

Encouraging financial decisions that benefited him while leaving me vulnerable.

Making me feel guilty for spending money, even on basic needs like health.

Using his connections in finance and banking to manipulate me into prioritising his home loan over mine. He presented it as the 'smart' decision, and if I questioned it, he would call me stupid or dismiss my concerns.

Rolling his eyes, making frustrated noises, or acting impatient whenever I needed time to understand financial discussions, especially at banks. His intolerance made me feel incompetent, reinforcing the idea that I wasn't capable of handling money. He would tell me that I was stupid and that he knew best.

Checking to make sure I had paid into his home loan, ensuring that I didn't put any extra money toward my own. This financial surveillance kept me in a position where I was constantly second-guessing myself, afraid of doing something 'wrong.'

4. Sexual Coercion and Marital Rape

Pressuring, guilt-tripping, or manipulating me into sex when I didn't want to.

Using my body as if it belonged to him, with no regard for my consent.

Ignoring my pain, discomfort, or trauma, making sex an obligation instead of an act of love.

Punishing me emotionally when I didn't comply, silent treatment, anger, or making me feel unworthy.

Taking me to seedy sex places around Melbourne that I had no interest in going to, then blaming me for being uncomfortable and not doing sexual acts that he wanted.

5. Emotional and Psychological Abuse

Constantly shifting blame onto me, making me feel responsible for his actions.

Gaslighting me into doubting my own memory and reality.

Using intimidation, humiliation, or mockery to erode my self-worth.

Keeping me isolated from support, ensuring I had no outside perspective to challenge his control.

Butting into my phone conversations, interjecting with his ongoing opinions about everything.

No privacy.

Tickling can equally be psychological and physical abuse.

There was a night I drove to his place in the dating phase where after our dinner, he decided to start tickling me. It started off fun but when he wouldn't let up and I found it hard to breathe from the overwhelming sensation of been tickled harder and harder in places in my body where I couldn't protect because he had me like spaghetti. Entwined in his long arms of tickling madness. It was hard to speak let alone say stop. All the while thinking what is this behaviour, what has gotten into him and why isn't he stopping. He is making me sick. When asked why he wouldn't stop tickling me, he blamed his mum because that's what she did to him as a kid.

It didn't really matter how I responded, bringing up the fact that he is now an adult and tickling like that is painful causing my body to get sick, feel unwell from. It was as though whatever I said went out into the wind and he didn't hear it. He kept on that's what happened to him and so he does it to others.

Pixie was also subjected to the tickling abuse from the start of their friendship. He continued to do it to her daughters, when they screamed "stop" and he didn't. Pixie stepping in and sternly said, "Stop! NO means NO! – they have told you to stop, so STOP." He wasn't stopping until Pixie intervened further with slapping him on the arm, to bring him to attention. To stop terrorising her young girls.

6. Legal Manipulation

Making me feel like I had no power or rights when it came to protecting myself.

Disputing the date of separation during the divorce, deliberately trying to drag out the process and complicate things unnecessarily. He knew that prolonging it would make it harder for me emotionally and financially. I paid for the divorce; he did not offer to pay half.

Openly stating that it was important for men 'not to leave bruises' because women could use them as evidence to go to the police. This showed his awareness of the system and how to work around it to avoid consequences.

GRACE AMORE

Expressing a deep hatred of authority, especially police. He resented any system that could hold him accountable and dismissed law enforcement as something to be manipulated rather than respected.

29: Recognise Coercion For What It Is

The *MARAM* (*Multi-Agency Risk Assessment and Management*) Framework and Sexual Coercion is a framework legislated under the *Family Violence Protection Act* 2008 (Victoria). In Australia, each state and Territory have their own framework.

MARAM was initiated by the Victorian Government in response to the 2016 Royal Commission into Family Violence and introduced in 2018. It legally requires professionals across multiple sectors, including health, education, and community services, to assess and manage family violence risk.

When I first gathered the courage to tell someone about what was happening in my marriage, I didn't go to the police or a family violence service, I went to a psychologist, a sex therapist. I thought maybe I was the problem, that something was wrong with me for not wanting to give in to my husband's demands. I told her I was being pressured to do things I didn't want to do sexually. I felt trapped and that saying no would only lead to more pressure. I didn't feel safe and needed guidance.

I was isolated. I didn't have family around me at the time. I didn't have the language to call it coercion yet. I only knew that I felt trapped. She could have been my saving grace, but she wasn't.

She put up her hand to my face and said, "Stop. That's not how counselling works. We need to build rapport first." I saw black after that.

I had built up so much courage to finally tell someone, someone who I thought was trained to understand what I was saying. I needed to be heard. I needed the space to say:

"My husband is forcing me to do acts and be in sex spaces that give my body panic. The panic is so intense, it feels like a sacrificial offering, his way of giving me up to get what he wants. And when I panic, he blames me. He says I am causing him suffering. That I am giving away my power to childhood sexual abuse with my grandfather. I need to reclaim my power and be free. I just need to do what he wants, and everything will be okay. That if I don't, I am denying his needs. That I am his 'wife' and I need to submit."

I needed to get the ball of twine in my gut out and have someone help me name what this was, what I was experiencing, just two years into my marriage.

It was early days. Just after our first miscarriage in November 2009. Just after our road trip in 2010 across Australia. After coming back to Melbourne in 2011 to settle.

We moved into his house in Cranbourne, far from everything familiar. I was lost on the other side of the city, away from family, in a foreign land, married to someone who was starting to show a side of himself I hadn't seen before.

Day by day, little things were leaving me questioning my sanity.

"Am I imagining this?"

"Why does he believe I need to submit, just because I am his wife?"

"What makes this person I am married to feel like he possesses me somehow?"

"Why does he have such a problem with my family?"

Before we married, he didn't or at least, that's what I thought. But his words changed after the vows. The first warning sign came in small, seemingly harmless comments, "You're married to me now, not your family." I didn't realise at the time that this would shape the years to come. Because he didn't just have a problem with my family. He had a problem with the love in my life. He had a problem with the people I loved.

He didn't like that I was close to my family and friends. He'd punish me for it. When he cracked it, I was the one who paid the price.

The System That Could Have Helped, Didn't

At the time, there was no formal system like *MARAM* in place to ensure professionals recognised and responded to family violence. My experience highlighted that some psychologists were devoid of understanding about family violence and not sensory acute to the signs.

Even in 2011, coercion was abuse. My experience should have been taken seriously.

Today, under Victoria's *MARAM* Framework, this psychologist would have had a legal obligation to respond differently.

MARAM is designed to help professionals recognise and respond to family violence. If it had been in place back then, and if she had followed its principles, she should have:

- ☑ Identified that what I was describing wasn't a 'communication issue' but coercion, control, and violence.
- ☑ Asked further questions to assess the extent of the abuse and its impact on my safety.
- ☑ Made a referral to the right services, such as a family violence support worker, who could help me understand my rights.
- ☑ Helped me develop a safety plan instead of making me feel like I needed to earn the right to be heard.

But none of that happened. I left her office shut down. The door to getting help closed just as quickly as I had opened it. And that is what happens to so many women, they reach out for help, but the help doesn't reach back.

What Can Women Do?

At the time, I didn't know that psychologists, doctors, and even social workers are now meant to follow *MARAM*.

I didn't know that when I described coercion, it should have been taken seriously.

If you ever feel dismissed by a professional, you can ask:

"Are you following the *MARAM* framework?"

This question alone can remind them of their legal responsibility to assess and manage risk properly.

MARAM was created so that no woman is left alone to figure out if what she's experiencing is abuse.

But a framework only works when it's actually used.

If my psychologist had been trained properly, or had simply followed the principles that exist today, it could have changed my trajectory.

Maybe I would have left sooner. Maybe I wouldn't have spent years thinking something was wrong with me. Because he wasn't always like that.

We Need Professionals to Know the Signs

We need them to understand that:

✓ Pressure is not consent.

✓ Coercion is violence.

✓ Women shouldn't have to beg to be heard.

Because when we reach out, the system should reach back. And of course this goes for anyone reaching out for help. They need to be seen, heard and validated.

30: Impact of Violence on Brain and Body

The perception of threat of family violence creates a pervasive sense of danger in the home. Imagine a scenario where a partner slams a door or raises their voice. The moment this happens, the brain's amygdala, the alarm centre, detects a threat. It sends a distress signal to the hypothalamus, which activates the body's fight, flight, or freeze response (Van der Kolk, 2014).

In this moment, the body doesn't distinguish between physical and emotional threats. A loud voice or the sound of breaking glass can trigger the same survival response as being physically struck.

The Body Reacts

Once the hypothalamus signals danger, the sympathetic nervous system (SNS) takes control:

Heart rate increases to prepare for potential action.

Breathing becomes rapid and shallow, optimising oxygen intake.

Adrenaline and cortisol flood the system, suppressing non-essential functions like digestion and immune response.

Muscles tighten, including those in the jaw, shoulders, and abdomen, often creating tension patterns stored in the body's fascia (Schleip et al., 2012).

Example: A survivor of family violence may develop chronic neck or shoulder pain. Over time, the fascia, connective tissue that surrounds muscles, becomes stiff, reflecting the body's chronic state of tension and readiness to respond to threats.

The Brain Processes the Threat

While the body reacts instinctively, the brain works to process the situation:

The amygdala remains hyperactive, keeping the individual on high alert.

The prefrontal cortex, responsible for logical thinking and decision-making, is temporarily suppressed, making it difficult to plan or respond calmly.

The hippocampus, which stores memories, becomes impaired. In cases of repeated trauma, this leads to fragmented or incomplete memories of the abuse (Van der Kolk, 2014).

The Freeze Response

If escape or confrontation feels impossible, the body may enter a freeze state:

This response is characterised by dissociation, where the survivor feels detached from their body or surroundings (Porges, 2011).

Physical immobility may occur, as if 'frozen' in place.

Example: A child witnessing violence may curl up and feel 'invisible,' their body instinctively trying to minimise the threat by becoming still and unnoticeable.

Long-Term Effects

Chronic exposure to family violence keeps the body and brain in survival mode. This can lead to:

Fascia dysfunction: The connective tissue stiffens, limiting movement and creating pain that persists even after the threat is gone (Schleip et al., 2012).

Amygdala hyperactivity: The brain becomes overly sensitive to perceived danger, causing hypervigilance even in safe situations.

Cortisol dysregulation: Prolonged stress can weaken the immune system, disrupt digestion, and lead to fatigue.

Memory and emotional challenges: Impairments in the hippocampus make it harder to regulate emotions or recall events clearly.

The Role of Fascia

Fascia, the body's connective tissue, plays a critical role in storing trauma. Abuse survivors often report physical pain in areas like the neck, back, or pelvis, regions where tension accumulates during stress. Over time, unresolved trauma in the fascia can lead to chronic conditions such as fibromyalgia or pelvic floor dysfunction (Schleip et al., 2012).

Example: Survivors of domestic violence may experience pelvic pain due to trauma stored in the pelvic floor fascia, compounded by years of physical and emotional abuse.

Healing and Recovery

Recovery from family violence involves both body and mind.

Restoring safety: The body must relearn that it is no longer in danger. Practices like somatic therapy, yoga, therapies like neuro linguistic programming (NLP) or mindfulness help regulate the nervous system.

Releasing trauma from fascia: Techniques such as myofascial release or trauma-informed bodywork can help release tension stored in the connective tissue (Schleip et al., 2012).

Therapeutic interventions: Therapy approaches like *Eye Movement Desensitization and Reprocessing* (EMDR) or trauma-focused *Cognitive Behavioural Therapy* (CBT) help survivors process their experiences (Shapiro, 2017).

Reconnecting with the body: Somatic therapies encourage survivors to notice and address physical sensations, fostering a sense of safety and empowerment (Van der Kolk, 2014).

By understanding the step-by-step effects of family violence on the brain and body, we can see that trauma is not just a mental experience, it is deeply physical. Healing requires a holistic approach that addresses both the mind and the body, empowering survivors to reclaim their lives.

For years, I carried trauma in my body without realising it. My pelvis ached, my shoulders tensed at the slightest noise, and my nervous system lived in a state of constant anticipation. Doctors dismissed my pain. I knew deep down something was not right. But learning how trauma reshapes the brain and body changed everything. It wasn't 'just stress.' It was survival. And knowing this helped me finally begin to heal.

References

Porges, S. W. (2011). *The polyvagal theory: Neurophysiological foundations of emotions, attachment, communication, and self-regulation*. W.W. Norton & Company.

Schleip, R., Jäger, H., & Klingler, W. (2012). What is fascia? A review of different definitions and terminology. *Journal of Bodywork and Movement Therapies, 16*(4), 496-502.

Shapiro, F. (2017). *Eye movement desensitization and reprocessing (EMDR) therapy: Basic principles, protocols, and procedures*. Guilford Publications.

Van der Kolk, B. (2014). *The body keeps the score: Brain, mind, and body in the healing of trauma*. Penguin Books.

Childhood sexual abuse – Understanding what happens to the brain.

Understanding what happens to the brain during childhood sexual abuse can help make sense of the long-lasting effects you may be experiencing. When someone is molested or abused, especially as a child, it can significantly impact brain development and functioning. Here's an overview of what likely occurred:

1. Activation of the Stress Response (Fight, Flight, Freeze and Fawn). During the abuse, your brain likely entered survival mode, activating the amygdala, the part of the brain responsible for detecting threats.

As a child, you may have experienced:

Fight: Feelings of anger or attempts to resist.

Flight: Wanting to run or escape.

Freeze: Feeling paralysed or dissociated, as if you were 'numb' or watching the events from outside your body.

Fawn: This is a trauma response where a person prioritises people-pleasing and conflict avoidance to feel safe, often at the expense of their own needs and boundaries. It's driven by the amygdala's survival instinct to appease perceived threats.

This intense activation floods the brain with stress hormones like cortisol and adrenaline, designed to protect you in emergencies but harmful when prolonged.

2. Dissociation and the brain's defence mechanism

Many children dissociate during abuse as a way to cope with the overwhelming trauma. This means the brain disconnects from the present moment to protect itself.

The prefrontal cortex, responsible for reasoning and self-control, often 'shuts down,' while the brain's emotional and instinctive centres (like the amygdala) take over.

This can result in:

A Feeling of "leaving your body."

A fragmented or incomplete memories of events.

Difficulty distinguishing reality from memory.

3. Altered brain development

Childhood trauma can affect the developing brain in significant ways:

Hippocampus: Responsible for memory and learning, this part of the brain may shrink under chronic stress, which can lead to fragmented or suppressed memories or abuse.

Amygdala: Often becomes overactive, making you more sensitive to fear, hypervigilance, and triggers.

Prefrontal cortex: May become underdeveloped leading to difficulties with decision making, impulse control, and emotional regulation.

4. Emotional and Behavioural Impact

During and after the abuse, the brain's imbalance can create:

A sense of shame or guilt, even though the abuse was not your fault.

Difficulty trusting others due to the activation of fear and hypervigilance.

Feelings of worthlessness or 'dirtiness' due to the brain's misinterpretation of the abuse.

5. Long-term effects on the Nervous system

The trauma likely caused your nervous system to remain in a state of hyperarousal (always on high alert) or hypo arousal (feeling shut down or numb).

This dysregulation can lead to:

Chronic anxiety, panic or stress

Depression or low energy

A sense of being 'stuck' emotionally or physically.

6. Memory and Trauma

The abuse likely affected your ability to process. Traumatic memories are often stored differently than regular ones:

Rather than being processed logically by the hippocampus, traumatic memories are stored in the amygdala, often in fragmented, sensory forms (smells, sights, sounds)

This can explain why certain triggers, like smells or objects, can bring back powerful feelings without a clear narrative.

7. Impacts on identity of relationships

Abuse during formative years may have disrupted your sense of self and boundaries.

The brain learns relational patterns early on, and abuse may have taught you to associate closeness with harm, creating confusion around trust, love and safety.

Healing and rewiring your brain

The brain is resilient and capable of healing through neuroplasticity – its ability to rewire itself. Here are ways to begin healing the effects of trauma:

Therapy such as Neuro Linguistic Programming (NLP), somatic therapy, can help process fragmented memories and regulate the nervous system.

Stillness practices: Meditation, Prayer, deep breathing can calm the overactive amygdala and strengthen the prefrontal cortex.

Bodywork practices like yoga or trauma-informed bodywork can reconnect you to your body and help release stored trauma. Shaking the body. Listening to the body and moving to how it needs to move, stretch, dance, swaying etc.

Journalling: writing about your experiences can help organise and process memories stored in the emotional brain.

Safe relationships: Building trusting relationships with safe people can retrain you brain to associate closeness with safety and connection.

Understanding how your brain was affected can validate your experiences and give you insight into your behaviours and feelings today. Healing is possible, and by working with professionals and engaging in practices that promote recovery, you can reclaim your sense of self and power.

Understanding the profound impact of childhood sexual abuse (CSA) on brain development and function is crucial. Here's an overview of the effects, supported by research:

1. Activation of the Stress Response (Fight, Flight, Freeze and Fawn)

During abuse, the brain's amygdala, responsible for detecting threats, activates the body's stress response. This leads to the release of stress hormones like cortisol and adrenaline. Prolonged exposure to these hormones can be harmful.

2. Dissociation and the Brain's Defence Mechanism

Many children dissociate during abuse to cope with overwhelming trauma. This involves the prefrontal cortex, responsible for reasoning and self-control, 'shutting down,' while the brain's emotional centres take over. This can result in fragmented or incomplete memories of events.

3. Altered Brain Development

Childhood trauma can significantly affect brain development:

Hippocampus: Responsible for memory and learning, it may shrink under chronic stress, leading to fragmented or suppressed memories.

Amygdala: Often becomes overactive, increasing sensitivity to fear and hypervigilance.

Prefrontal Cortex: May become underdeveloped, leading to difficulties with decision-making and emotional regulation.

4. Emotional and Behavioural Impact

The brain's imbalance can create:

A sense of shame or guilt, even though the abuse was not the victim's fault.

Difficulty trusting others due to heightened fear and hypervigilance.

Feelings of worthlessness or 'dirtiness' due to the brain's misinterpretation of the abuse.

5. Long-term Effects on the Nervous System

Trauma can cause the nervous system to remain in a state of hyperarousal (always on high alert) or hypo arousal (feeling shut down or numb). This dysregulation can lead to chronic anxiety, depression, and a sense of being 'stuck' emotionally or physically.

6. Memory and Trauma

Traumatic memories are often stored differently than regular ones:

Rather than being processed logically by the hippocampus, traumatic memories are stored in the amygdala, often in fragmented, sensory forms (smells, sights, sounds). This can explain why certain triggers can bring back powerful feelings without a clear narrative.

7. Impacts on Identity and Relationships

Abuse during formative years may disrupt one's sense of self and boundaries. The brain learns relational patterns early on, and abuse may teach one to associate closeness with harm, creating confusion around trust, love, and safety.

Healing and Rewiring the Brain

The brain is resilient and capable of healing through neuroplasticity, its ability to rewire itself. Engaging in practices that promote recovery can help reclaim one's sense of self and power.

Understanding how the brain is affected by childhood sexual abuse (CSA) can validate experiences and provide insight into behaviours and feelings today. Healing is possible, and by working with professionals and engaging in practices that promote recovery, one can reclaim their sense of self and power.

Reflection:

"The fundamental issue in resolving trauma is to restore the proper balance between the rational brain and the emotional brain ... the amygdala, or emotional brain, and the prefrontal cortex, or rational brain, must work together to help trauma survivors feel safe." - Bessel Van der Kolk.

Leave the children alone.

No matter how much trauma rewires us, healing is always possible. The brain can change, the body can recover, and survivors can reclaim their lives."

References

Bremner, J. D. (2006). Traumatic stress: Effects on the brain. *Dialogues in Clinical Neuroscience, 8*(4), 445–461. https://doi.org/10.31887/DCNS.2006.8.4/jbremner

Cozolino, L. (2014). *The neuroscience of human relationships: Attachment and the developing social brain* (2nd ed.). W.W. Norton & Company.

Felitti, V. J., Anda, R. F., Nordenberg, D., Williamson, D. F., Spitz, A. M., Edwards, V., Koss, M. P., & Marks, J. S. (1998). Relationship of childhood abuse and household dysfunction to many of the leading causes of death in adults: The adverse childhood experiences (ACE) study. *American Journal of Preventive Medicine, 14*(4), 245–258. https://doi.org/10.1016/S0749-3797(98)00017-8

Kolk, B. van der. (2015). *The body keeps the score: Brain, mind, and body in the healing of trauma*. Penguin Books.

Ogden, P., Minton, K., & Pain, C. (2006). *Trauma and the body: A sensorimotor approach to psychotherapy*. W.W. Norton & Company.

Perry, B. D., & Szalavitz, M. (2017). *The boy who was raised as a dog: And other stories from a child psychiatrist's notebook: What traumatized children can teach us about loss, love, and healing*. Basic Books.

PsychCentral. (n.d.). The roles neuroplasticity and EMDR play in healing from childhood trauma. Retrieved January 2025, from https://psychcentral.com/ptsd/the-roles-neuroplasticity-and-emdr-play-in-healing-from-childhood-trauma

Verywell Mind. (n.d.). How childhood abuse changes the brain. Retrieved January 2025, from

https://www.verywellmind.com/childhood-abuse-changes-the-brain-2330401

31: Saving Grace: My Recovery and Healing

Final Reflection – A Testimony of Where I Am Now

I once lived in survival mode, bracing for the next wave of chaos. My body remembered what my mind couldn't process, and silence used to terrify me. But now, now, silence holds me like a prayer. It is no longer a punishment. It's a presence. A peace. A place I come home to.

I still have healing to do. I still have triggers, tears, and questions that I bring before God. But I also have joy. I have breath. I have wisdom. I have boundaries. I have laughter in my home, even if it's just me and the cats. I can say no without guilt. I can eat a meal slowly. I can go to sleep without fear.

I've written this book as a way to honour the girl who stayed too long, the woman who nearly died, and the survivor who decided to live. This book is not a product of my strength alone, it's a record of God's mercy, grace, and provision.

What I see now is blessing. I see the way God walked me out of abuse. I see how He helped me reclaim my voice, my body, and my future. I see how every broken piece has been gathered, named, and held. I see growth in the very places I thought would stay barren.

I'm not finished. None of us are. But I'm free. I'm held. And I'm whole in ways I never imagined I could be.

If my story has touched something in you, if you see yourself in these pages, then hold on.

Healing is not a single event, it is a journey of reclaiming myself, body, mind, and spirit. Each step, each choice, each practice has helped me move from deep pain, physical, emotional, and mental, to a place of empowerment, healing, and rediscovery. This chapter is a testament to everything that has brought me here.

Listening to My Body: Honouring Its Needs

Learning to recognise and respect my body's signals.

Getting a voucher from the Salvation Army for the Melbourne Breakroom, where I smashed things and let out deep-seated rage.

The importance of rest, nourishment, and movement.

Healing through *pelvic floor physiotherapy*, *remedial massage therapy*, and *osteopathy treatment*.

The *Body for Life* program, starting with body weight, then gradually building strength through weights.

Eating *live foods* for nourishment and vitality.

Medical Medium's (Anthony William) 3:6:9 Medical Cleanse, detoxifying my body, resetting my system, and supporting deep healing.

The *Daniel Fast*, a deep spiritual and physical cleanse.

Spiritual Renewal: Reconnecting with God

My relationship with God as the anchor of my healing.

Daily prayer, Bible reading, singing, and journaling as a way of listening to God.

School of Faith, learning to hear God through dreams and the *Four Keys to Hearing God's Voice*.

Baptism of cleansing with Bec and Kim, a powerful act of renewal.

Practicing *gratitude*, giving thanks for what I have, even in the struggle.

Church families and the strength of a faith-based community.

The Power of Naming: Writing as a Path to Healing

Writing this book as a way of getting trauma out of my body.

Naming the pain, the abuse, and the struggle, reclaiming my voice.

Coaching with Rik Schnabel for *trauma recovery and writing* to shape my story and share my truth and publish this book.

CASA (Centre Against Sexual Assault) counselling, 16 sessions that provided deep emotional support.

Reading extensively about *trauma, the brain, and the body*.

Understanding *narcissism and people-pleasing* as part of my healing.

Education, Support and Community: Finding Strength in Learning

Emily Kim – Somatic healing work.

Studying *Diploma of Justice*, attending school twice a week to be part of a community.

The *Love Out Loud* course, learning deep self-awareness and conscious leadership.

The Institute of New Paradigm Intimacy, Somatic integration, healing relational wounds and redefining connection with my body.

Drama classes as a way to rebuild confidence and self-expression.

Rik's, Life Beyond Limits speaker training/NLP and Master NLP, learning the power of communication and personal growth within a community of encouragers.

Movement, Expression, Creation and Nature: Healing Through the Body

Daily yoga as a practice of grounding and self-care.

Expressive art therapy, painting, drawing, and movement/dance to release emotion.

Nature walking, being in the bush, near streams, connecting with creation.

Gardening, growing vegetables and flowers, nurturing life as I learned to nurture myself.

Attending church and drama classes for connection and personal development.

Mosaics, rebuilding and piecing myself back together, one fragment at a time.

The Love and Comfort of My Fur Babies

Banjo, Tilly, and Kitty Cat, my loyal companions who have been with me through it all.

The unconditional love and comfort they have given me during my hardest days.

Banjo's playful and calming presence.

Tilly, who was with me for a short but deeply meaningful time.

Kitty Cat's steady companionship, always close when I need comfort.

Seeking Support: The Strength to Ask for Help

Reaching out to *1800 Respect* when I needed it.

Accepting support from *family, friends, and professionals*.

Understanding that healing is not a solo journey, it takes a village.

Conclusion: Final Words to the Reader

To the one who has walked through darkness, who has felt unseen, unheard, and broken, you are not alone.

Healing is not a straight path. Some days, you will feel like you are rising; other days, you may feel like you are drowning again. But no matter how deep the waters get, there is a way out.

Your pain does not define you. Your past does not own you. You are worthy of safety, peace, and love, not just from others, but from yourself.

If you take anything from my story, let it be this: You are stronger than you know.

You are more loved than you realise.

And you are never beyond redemption.

Keep going. Keep rising. Because the life waiting for you on the other side of this storm is worth it.

With love and hope,

Grace

What Others Say About Grace

"I have been struggling with my self-image for a while until I met Grace. With her incredible coaching skills, I have been able to unleash the powerful businesswoman I always had inside allowing me to land the promotion I wanted - Thank you, Grace" - **Mary Coz, Victoria Australia.**

"Grace Amore is the very definition of resilience, strength, and triumph. To say she has overcome trauma is an understatement, she has risen from the depths of unimaginable pain, transforming her past into a beacon of hope for others. Surviving sexual abuse and a marriage from hell, she has not only reclaimed her life but has become a guiding light for those seeking their own freedom. Grace is more than an inspiration, she is living proof that healing is possible, a true angel who empowers women to break free and step into their own power." - **Rik Schnabel, Life Beyond Limits NSW Australia.**

"Grace has a steady and calm presence, and I feel immediately at ease when I am with her. She has coached me through an overwhelming emotion I was experiencing that I was allowing to take over, and she coached me to continue in my faith, to continue trusting in Jesus. I used to feel fear in certain situations, but now I feel capable to face my fears and not let any hurdle stop me from achieving my goals. Thanks Grace!"- **Anna Ware, NSW Australia.**

"I am amazed and privileged that my dear friend Grace has included one of our sessions in her book. Our journey together has been extraordinary. I would come to our sessions ready to treat her, yet never fully knowing what would unfold. However, as one of Rik Schnabel's core teachings suggests, establishing rapport is key. Grace had a way of slowing me down, whether through prayer or simply pausing to breathe. She helped me shift from the chaos of daily life into a space of healing. In truth, our sessions were always mutual. Grace helped me as much as I helped her. With a background in osteopathy, chiropractic care, natural therapies, kinesiology, and coaching, I have worked with many people over the years. But my time with Grace was different. Our sessions were never just about physical treatment; they were spiritual and emotionally healing. We shared deep conversations, which mirrored my own past struggles. I saw in her a strength that was both heartbreaking and inspiring. I remember seeing a vision of her journey, she walked brightly down a path, unaware that brick walls were rising behind her, cutting off her way back. I, too, had been in such a place. She had once lived in safety and trust, seeking happiness and fulfillment, only to find herself trapped in a nightmare of abuse, loneliness, and suffering. Her story is a testament to resilience, faith, and survival.

Her journey back to herself was neither easy nor straightforward. Did COVID-19 save her? Or was it divine intervention? Perhaps both. But without question, it was also her own courage, persistence, and deep faith in God that brought her through. Her life is a miracle, and her book is an inspiration. As someone who has spent a lifetime in natural therapies, I deeply resonate with her words about healing, the body's wisdom, and the all-too-common experience of having one's suffering dismissed or misunderstood by others.

Grace, thank you for being you. You have blessed me beyond words, and I know your book will bless countless others. With love and gratitude". - **Gaynor O'Connor, Victoria, Australia**

Book Grace as a Speaker

Book Grace Amore as your next Keynote Speaker – A Voice of Strength, Resilience, and Transformation

Are you looking for a keynote speaker who will captivate, inspire, and empower your audience? **Grace Amore** is a force of resilience, a woman who has turned pain into power and adversity into triumph. Her journey from surviving deep trauma, including sexual abuse and an unthinkably toxic marriage, to reclaiming her freedom is nothing short of extraordinary.

Grace doesn't just share her story, she ignites transformation. With raw authenticity, deep wisdom, and an undeniable passion for helping others, she speaks directly to the hearts of those who feel lost, broken, or stuck. Her message is one of **hope, courage, and breaking free from the chains of the past**, proof that no matter how dark the storm, the sun can rise again.

Whether you're hosting a **conference, empowerment event, corporate seminar, or healing retreat**, Grace will leave your audience inspired, motivated, and ready to reclaim their own strength. **Don't miss the opportunity to bring this powerhouse of resilience to your stage.**

Book Grace Amore today and give your audience the gift of transformation. Visit: https://www.graceamore.com/.

Domestic and Family Violence Services

I felt that it might be helpful to list a comprehensive, up-to-date directory of family violence–related support services available for people in need and for family and friends of someone in need. This list is divided into services available in Victoria and those available nationwide across Australia. Please note that if anyone is in immediate danger, they should call triple zero (000) immediately.

Victoria – Family Violence Support Services

Crisis & Immediate Support

Crisis Housing Australia
A registered charity dedicated to supporting victims of domestic violence and individuals experiencing homelessness by providing immediate rental relief and working toward long-term housing solutions.
https://www.crisishousingaustralia.org.au/

Crisis Housing Australia
A registered charity to support victims of domestic violence and individuals experiencing homelessness by providing immediate rental relief and long-term housing solutions.
info@crisishousingaustralia.com.
https://www.crisishousingaustralia.org.au/

Safe Steps Family Violence Response Centre.

A 24/7 crisis support service providing confidential help, safety planning, and referrals.

Phone: 1800 015 188. https://safesteps.org.au/

The Orange Door

Offers assistance for those experiencing family violence and extra support for the wellbeing of children and families. https://www.orangedoor.vic.gov.au/

Sexual Assault Crisis Line

A 24/7 telephone counselling service for people who have experienced sexual assault.

Phone: 1800 806 292. https://www.sacl.com.au/

Specialist Services for Specific Groups

Men's Referral Service

Provides free, confidential support for men who use family violence to help them change their behaviour. Phone: 1300 766 491. https://ntv.org.au/

Victims of Crime Helpline

Offers information and support for adult male victims of family violence and other violent crimes.

Phone: 1800 819 817 (or text 0427 767 891; available 8am–11pm).

Kids Helpline

A confidential counselling service available 24/7 for young people aged 5–25.

Phone: 1800 55 1800. https://kidshelpline.com.au/

Rainbow Door

Specialist support for LGBTIQ+ people and their friends/families experiencing family violence.

Phone: 1800 729 367 or text 0480 017 246 (10am–5pm). https://www.rainbowdoor.org.au/

InTouch – Multicultural Centre Against Family Violence

Provides culturally safe support for migrant and refugee women.

Phone: 1800 755 988 (available 9am–5pm, Mon–Fri). https://intouch.org.au/

Seniors Rights Victoria

Offers free, confidential support for older Victorians experiencing abuse.

Phone: 1300 368 821 (available 10am–5pm, Mon–Fri). https://seniorsrights.org.au/

MensLine Australia

Provides 24/7 telephone and online counselling support for men with emotional health and relationship concerns.

Phone: 1300 78 99 78 https://mensline.org.au/

Services for Aboriginal and Torres Strait Islander Communities

Victorian Aboriginal Child Care Agency (VACCA)

Statewide support service for Aboriginal children and families. Phone: (03) 9287 8800 (available 9am–5pm, Mon–Fri). https://www.vacca.org/

Djirra

Offers telephone counselling for Aboriginal people who have experienced family violence.

Phone: 1800 105 303 (available 9am–5pm, Mon–Fri). https://djirra.org.au/

13 Yarn

A 24/7 telephone crisis line for Aboriginal people and families needing to "have a yarn" about their wellbeing. Phone: 13 92 76. https://www.13yarn.org.au/

Child Protection & Family Services

Report concerns for children at risk: During business hours, contact your local division (e.g., North, South, East, West intake numbers available on the Child Protection website). AH: 13 12 78

Family Relationship Advice Line

For assistance with family issues and separation support. Phone: 1800 050 321

Hours: Mon–Fri, 8am–8pm; Sat, 10am–4pm

Australia-Wide (National) Support Services - Crisis & Counselling Services

1800 Respect

The national domestic, family, and sexual violence counselling, information, and support service available 24/7. Phone: 1800 737 732 (or text 0458 737 732). https://1800 Respect.org.au/

Lifeline Australia

Provides 24/7 crisis support and suicide prevention services. Phone: 13 11 14

https://www.lifeline.org.au/

Ask Izzy

A free, anonymous online directory to find local support services including housing, healthcare, counselling, and legal advice.

https://askizzy.org.au/

Life Beyond Limits

Support for people who need psychological and trauma relief. Phone: 03 8669 1121 (Mon-Fri. 9am-5pm).

rik.schnabel@lifebeyondlimits.com.au.
https://lifebeyondlimits.com.au/help

WIRE - Women's support and Information

A centre for gender and economic equity. We are proud intersectional feminists, committed to creating a fair society for all women and gender diverse people.

Phone: 1300 134 130
https://www.wire.org.au/

ADDITIONAL SUPPORT SERVICES

Family Relationship Advice Line

Phone: 1800 050 321 (also available nationally)

National Debt Helpline

Phone: 1800 007 007 (open Mon–Fri)

National Legal Aid & Community Legal Centres

For free or low-cost legal advice, contact your local Community Legal Centre

Phone: 1800 737 732 (24/7 Crisis Line)

https://nationallegalaid.org.au/

Family Violence Law

Visit familyviolencelaw.gov.au for guidance on legal rights and assistance.

People With Disability Australia and *Qlife*

Offer additional support and counselling services tailored to people with disabilities and the LGBTIQ+ community respectively. Phone: 1800 184 527 (3pm to midnight/7 days a week)

Important Reminders: If you or someone you know is in immediate danger, call 000 immediately.

This directory is intended for immediate crisis support and ongoing assistance. Service hours may vary, so please check the relevant websites for the most current information.

The above details are current as of early 2025 and are subject to change; please verify via the official service websites.

These resources represent a broad cross-section of support services, ranging from 24/7 crisis lines, specialised support for diverse communities, legal aid, and counselling services, to help individuals, families, and friends navigate the challenges of family violence.

For further details and any service updates, please refer to the official websites provided.

Acknowledgements

While firstly, I would like to acknowledge my best friend Jesus Christ and to all my supernatural midwives that have helped me birth this book.

My darling babies that I lost in my marriage, Violet, James and Christy. My fur babies; Frida, Matisse and Buddy, followed by Tilly out of the marriage.

My parents that I dearly love, I love you mum and dad thank you for your persistent care and love to help me get better and rise above the ashes. To my amazing sisters, Angela and Sandra and their families. Without family I wouldn't be here writing the story. I would have died in Melbourne lockdown 2020 and been another statistic. This I know without a doubt as I was near death coming out of the marriage, a skeleton myself.

My Aunty Aurora and her son John and sister Carmel, thank you. My Aunty Arora, my hairdresser who gave me a new haircut out of the marriage, encouraging me with hope while submitting my online divorce while cutting my hair.

Thanks to Carmel's friend Natalie that told me about doing an online single divorce, so I didn't have to have any contact with the husband. Forever grateful for that online divorce, it helped keep me safer.

To my cousin, you know who you are. We made it out alive as kids, surviving a grandfather who violated our little bodies. It's a testament to our resilience. It's striking how we both developed endometriosis as a result of that childhood abuse. I know we weren't the only ones he abused. We are all survivors of a self-entitled, nasty grandfather who took advantage of innocent souls.

Thank you to both sides of the family.

Jo the healer with her three amazing dogs and Jackson that reminded me of Buddy. The three of you were part of the treatments of helping me get through the first bout of lock down. Animals are healers.

With Gratitude to *1800 Respect* that have been there around the clock since coming out of the marriage. Incredibly grateful to all the *1800 Respect* workers, for your care, wisdom and holding space for some of the messiest times in my life. You have been a lifeline in helping me in navigating the dark waters of coming out of an abusive marriage and helping me to process, unpack and make sense out of madness.

Thank you to *CASA – Centre Against Sexual Assault*: Aisha you were the first advocate that worked with me at the start of 2021 whilst I was at the Peninsula at Rye on my own during lockdown. Isolated and suicidal you carried and held me by phone sessions with your sisterhood of love. I was sad to know that funding only gives women 13 sessions and 16 for emergency, which you gave me 16 sessions of a lifeline fresh out of an abusive marriage. A sister journey of helping me self-regulate whilst going through the divorce. Forever grateful. We need more funding as 13 sessions is not enough, the impact of the abuse from the marriage alone was devastating and just as I had started to feel safe, our sessions ended, and I had to look elsewhere for support.

The *Hope Team* in Broadmeadows (The suicide team)– what an incredible team. So very grateful for your support after coming out of emergency and funding the writer's course from the CAE – sadly only attended 2 classes out of 4 as I was very unwell at the time but desperately needing to get the book out, and this was the first formal class I did with getting help in writing my story. Thank you.

Thank you, Gaynor, for your big heart of kindness, with giving so much I don't even know how to put it into words, what you have given. Your generosity of time, of driving to the other side of Melbourne and giving of your treatments for gratis. So very grateful for the light therapy device that has been a god sent. I am so grateful that God prompted me to make contact out of that marriage, my shame was so heavy in the marriage I found it hard to reach out. Your heart and love are truly a blessing to this world, my body is eternally grateful for your 'miracle hands' that have brought a realignment on so many levels from physical, to spiritual and emotional.

Your love for what you do – Osteopathy, Healer and natural therapies has been a God sent. I am so grateful for your prompting me to reconnect with Rik Schnabel, to help with coaching in navigating the stormy waters of coming out of an abusive marriage with his expertise writing and publishing books.

Rik has been instrumental in helping me write my book and keep myself safe whilst writing about traumatic events. Being a part of Rik's Program 'Publish your own book' has been life changing. Through you I was able to contact Rik late 2023 and what a blessing it has been. It has made all the difference in having the support in writing through the deep oceans of this book. I needed a way to get through to the other side of the story. Truly a miracle.

Thank you, Sue for your big heart of kindness, compassion and good will gave me a light in Melbourne's peak lockdown after I saw my death, you were a light in that dark pit of death in that marriage. Thank you, God, for your conviction in God's love that heard my cry for help, driving me to get help in Nimbin, *The Hemp Embassy*, June 14, 2020, that helped me get off pharmaceuticals and onto plant-based medicine, Cannabis. I had the biggest wake up call to my life. I was in a marriage, a skeleton of myself and you were a rock, a life jacket when I was near death. You helped me wake up to madness of the abuse in my marriage, holding space as I screamed out in pain while staying at Teretre cabins Nimbin. Thank you to all those times you dropped off food after work, you were an angel in the darkness. I may not have got anything out of the marriage as far as a settlement, but I got something so much more valuable than money, I received a sisterhood bonded in God's love.

Thank you, Pixie, for your colourfully big heart with a bounty of kindness, giving me refuge in your safe place the 'Hippie Palace' caravan, a true gem of a haven. Especially during Melbourne's lockdown fresh out of that crazy marriage when I was an absolute mess of a mess, how many tears were cried, so many. You gave me sanctuary and so much more during the craziness of 2020 lockdown. In all that darkness we were shrouded in light from the heavens above on earth. You alerted me that the husband was a narcissist, that was a massive wake-up call in November 2020 Lockdown. Now I had a name for his abusive behaviour from doing that survey, lo and behold most of that list in that survey affirmed those unhealthy behaviours he displayed in the marriage aligned with narcissistic traits. To the 13 shooting stars that lit up the night sky that night around the campfire. Thank you, Pixie, as it was a truly an incredible night sky of new beginnings. Our sisterhood is a gift out of that crazy marriage.

Thank you, Narelle for holding me up at work when I was at my lowest. Holding space for me at work, as I crumbled with pain and tears in that kitchen room you held space for my messy emotional state. Your heart held space for my broken heart in that time, allowing me to just be, without judgement. Incredible grateful.

Thank you, Judith for your honesty and boldness in calling out what you see with love. So very grateful we met 2014 during our *Bachelor of Community Mental Health & Alcohol and other drugs*. It was the last course I was allowed to do in the marriage. What a blessing you are. Your love and open mind and your family. Thank you to your son Jeremy for introducing me to INPI -Institute of new paradigm intimacy 2020: Victoria her work with learning to listen to the body helped me to regulate my nervous system and help me come back to my body. How amazing it was that night in November 2020 when on your back porch that Jeremy gently held a safe space for my body to breakdown fresh out of that painful marriage. That was a light in the dark. Hope for a way forward in coming back to my body. Thank you that I was able to enrol at the start of 2021 undertaking 6 months of intensive learning to listen to my body by learning how to self-regulate and work through trauma responses. Jeremy, you have an innate ability to hold space, you held space for my body at a time when I was a triggering mess especially around males, but there I was with permission to just be, from a male, that was huge coming out of that marriage. Massive.

Thank you, Emily; meeting you through the *Institute of New Paradigm Intimacy* in 2021 was a God sent, thank you for helping me get back to my body through your somatic healing work with love, how grateful I am for your trauma informed wisdom in helping me listen to my feminine during the toughest times of lockdown when I was alone at the Peninsula. Your kindness and wisdom helped me through some very deep waters, like the night I got the email, and you carried me through that messiness. Your generosity and love were paramount in helping me to listen to my body again.

Thank you for working with me one on one over the three-month period in helping me through the aftermath of the marriage. I was a mess, and you held space that helped me navigate that madness and all those emotions that needing expression and validation. Your gentle way of working and understanding trauma informed care was pivotal in giving my body a safe space to move through dark waters.

Dear Kim and Bec, thank you for your love and for organizing the baptism of cleansing for that Saturday 21st October, a ritual that washed away the cloak of shame that had been weighing my soul down. That cloak was so heavy, it felt like carrying death on my shoulders. Shame can have an unbearable weight on the soul and it had me questioning if I even deserved to be alive. It's hard to put into words what that day meant. My body felt as though it passed through a portal, leaving behind the slimy pit of shame and entering a place of light where I could see again, this time, with eyes of love and compassion for myself. As I write this, I recall that it was only twelve months ago that God brought me back to a place of wanting to live.

Just three days before, I had overdosed on morphine. I was so tired; I only wanted to sleep for a very long time, exhausted beyond words. I hadn't recovered physically or emotionally from my hysterectomy the previous November. The pain had been overwhelming, almost indescribable, and I wasn't sure if I had it in me to keep going. That overdose was on a Wednesday, and three days later, on Saturday, Bec and Kim arrived, like angels in human form. That's how it felt, like an angelic presence had entered my home. I knew I was safe with them, though it was hard to even open the door. My body was in severe spasms, with tics and contractions, but somehow, I managed to let them in.

The day flowed like a gentle stream through green pastures. Even though I felt so messy and broken, I was beautifully held in that mess, allowing so much to be released from my body. That day was truly a miracle, a day of miraculous breakthroughs. With Jesus Christ at the helm of my life, I found peace and clarity. Jesus, the one who gives me a reason to face each day, the light in my darkness. Through the love and kindness of hearts like Kim and Bec, I felt the presence of angels guiding me to where I am today. Interesting how God works, it was through your message Kim of seeing how I was, checking in, that I woke up that Wednesday 18th October.

GRACE AMORE

Thank you, Rik Schnabel and the team at *Life Beyond Limits* for your kindness of heart, compassion and wealth of experience in the work you do. You have been a pillar of strength in helping me to write and publish my first book. Thank you for your instruction, inspiration and helping me to find my voice and stay on track with my 'Why' of undertaking the task of writing a memoir about heavy topics. The care and conviction in your work has been a tremendous light in the dark of navigating stormy waters of traumatic memories. Grateful to you and your family in supporting the work you do.

Thank you, Rik for the Speakers course, late 2023, in helping me find my voice in speaking up about family violence. What an incredible group of people in that course, so very grateful, it was a light in the dark. The first time speaking up, was like going through a portal into hope. An absolute God sent.

To the amazing NLP group that Rik held early 2024 to October which went over 35 weeks with amazing souls, Mary, Peter, Paula, Elysse, Bryce, Ian and Alex. Very grateful to all of you and the safety in the group which has been an incredible part of the healing journey in writing this book.

Thank you too for Masters NLP and everyone in the training, it is helping me write the book, to come to completion, finally.

To *The School of Faith* family, thank you for your prayers and loving support giving me permission to be with all the mess I was working through. Thank you, Julie, for introducing me to Tim's course in '4 keys to hearing God's voice' and 'Hearing God through your dreams', these courses have been safe spaces to go deeper into relationship with God, life changing.

Thank you to *Essendon Baptist Church*, my home church, Pastor Jo, Pastor Adam, Rachael and Ann and the whole church where God's gentle love lives and shines. So very grateful.

Turning Point Church in Cranbourne that carried me during that crazy marriage. Thank you, Pastor Norma, for your calls to check in and say hi, it was a light in the dark while living with the husband. Thank you for taking me in as a volunteer after my 2nd miscarriage 2012, you gave me hope in the darkness of living in that marriage.

With Gratitude to Dr Kilani in the last couple of years in my marriage, for allowing me to fall apart after work. I was barely holding it together, while trying to survive that crazy marriage, living in Cranbourne where I was isolated away from family. I spent so much time crying in your office, thank you for believing that period pain is real and terribly debilitating. Being believed is half the battle. Thank you for your patience and compassion.

Thank you to Dr Sahar, what a God find. Incredible human being, an angel in human form. How relieved I am that people like yourself work in the health care system. I'll never forget the first appointment 2021 at *Moonee Ponds Super Clinic* with my sister, telling you I had had enough of the pain and was seeking euthanasia for period pain. I had had enough, and your kind words and compassion carried me through the wilderness of the aftermath of coming out of domestic abuse, sexual trauma with excruciating chronic pelvic pain. Forever grateful to you.

To Maryam my pelvic floor physio in Moonee Ponds, thank you for helping my body get better and feel safer in the world. You have been the first Pelvic floor physiotherapist that has understood Endometriosis/women's health. Absolute God sent. The day my older sister discovered you was like finding gold. You truly are a wonderfully gifted practitioner that cares with a heart of compassion. Your heart is a blessing, thank you for having the first equipment in Victoria that helps with endometriosis, thank you for pushing government to have treatment that actually makes a difference in healthcare.

Thank you to Sharon my Remedial Therapist, thank you for your healing hands and encouragement in helping me to find my voice and feel safety in my body. A God sent. Your encouragement and support of working with my body with all the triggers and sexual trauma, you have had a profound impact on my life. I am so grateful that my sister found you. Thank you for giving me a safe space to release sexual trauma during treatments and move through the pain that the body was speaking. A true blessing. You helped me give a name to the unspoken pain in your god sent treatments.

Cathy the angel who I met in the street, saving me from walking onto the Nepean Hwy after being treated badly from the Dr at *Rosebud Clinic* next door to Rosebud emergency because I wasn't able to wear a mask. I couldn't breathe and was hyperventilating and he was making me take the appointment in the car park where people were coming and going.

To Joy, (ex-husband's mum) I love you and miss your hugs. Always in my heart. I am sorry for all the pain you experienced in your life.

Thank you to Joanna, the Chief Executive Drama Queen of *Dare Drama*, and my fellow *Dare Drama* members for helping me break out of my shell, supporting my recovery and healing from family violence, and bringing joy and fun back into my body and life.

Thank you to the *Justice Team,* and my fellow classmates in helping me reclaim my life back.

To Mary and Anna, thank you both for generously offering your time, insight, and care in reading over my manuscript. Your thoughtful feedback, encouragement, and attention to detail helped shape this book into something ready to be shared with the world. I'm deeply grateful for your support in preparing it for publication.

I acknowledge the Traditional Custodians of the land on which I was born and now stand. I pay my deepest respects to their

Elders, past and present, and to the generations of First Nations people who have cared for this land for thousands of years.

I also acknowledge all who have come before us, the brave men and women who fought, struggled, and sacrificed so that we may have the freedoms we hold today. I honour those who spoke up, who risked everything, who paved the way, so that I, too, can speak up and have a voice.

May we never take for granted the courage and strength of those before us, and may we continue their legacy by standing for truth, justice, and freedom for all.

An overall big thank you to everyone that has helped me along the way to get through the wilderness of life and back to my body.

Thank you.

About The Author

Grace Amore is an author, survivor, overcomer and advocate for women who have endured domestic violence, coercive control, medical gaslighting, and childhood abuse. Her story is one of faith, resilience, and ultimate freedom, sharing the raw and painful realities of escaping an abusive marriage and the spiritual transformation that followed.

Through her personal experiences, she highlights the hidden forms of abuse, the ones that leave no visible bruises but deeply wound the soul. Her book is more than a memoir; it is a testament to the power of truth, faith, and healing.

But this story is not just about one person, it is about all of us. It is about men and women coming together to heal, to affect change, and to help the next generation rise up. It is about reclaiming her life and helping others in reclaiming their lives. We are meant to start from our ceiling, not the floor, ensuring that those who come after us are not burdened by the same cycles of pain and silence.

Grace is passionate about empowering others to recognise and break free from generational abuse. She writes with a deep conviction that no one should suffer in silence and that healing is possible for those who seek it.

She has completed her Diploma of Justice, Masters NLP, equipping herself with the knowledge and skills to further advocate for survivors and push for systemic change. She lives in Victoria in God's Sanctuary where she continues to write, speak, and advocate for family violence awareness and justice reform. When she's not writing, she finds peace in nature, prayer, and her love for animals, including her two beloved cats, Banjo and Kitty Cat.

Say 'Hello!'

If you would like to reach out to Grace Amore and say 'hello' or to seek her help, you can visit Grace at https://www.graceamore.com/.

Selected Bibliography

- Anderson, Chris. *TED Talks: The Official TED Guide to Public Speaking*. HarperCollins. 2017.
- Arabi, Shahida. *Becoming the Narcissist's Nightmare*. Audible Studios. 2016.
- Babcock, Linda & Laschever, Sara. *Women Don't Ask: Negotiation and the Gender Divide*. Princeton University Press. 2021.
- Batty, Rosie & Corbett, Bryce. *A Mother's Story Rosie Batty*. Harper Collins. 2015.
- Blue Knot: Empowering Recovery from complex trauma. https://blueknot.org.au/survivors/sharing-your-story/
- Breen, Candance, Nadine. *After the Darkness: A survivor's true story of childhood incest, rape, abuse, domestic violence, and her ability to overcome the negative impact these events had on her life*. Awakened Path Books, LLC. 2018.
- Brewster, Annie, MD. *The Healing Power of Storytelling: Using personal narratives to navigate illness, trauma and loss*. North Atlantic. 2022.
- Brodsky-Chenfeld, Dan. Above all Else.
- Broken to Brillant. *Broken to Brillant: Breaking Free to Be You After Domestic Violence, Stories of Strength and Success*. Broken to Brillant. 2016
- Brown, Brene. *Men, Women and Worthiness: The Experience of Shame and Being Enough*. Sounds True. 2012.
- Brown, Brene. *The Gifts of Imperfection: Let Go of Who You Think You're Supposed to Be and Embrace Who You Are*. Hazelden Publishing. 2022.

- Brown, Brene. *Braving the Wilderness: The Quest for True Belonging and the Courage to Stand Alone.* Ebury Publishing. 2017.
- Brown, Jeff. *Love it Forward.* Enrealment Press. 2014.
- Brown, Jeff. *Grounded Spirituality.* Enrealment Press. 2019.
- Brown, Melanie & Gannon, Louise. *Brutally Honest.* Quadrille. 2018.
- Childre, Doc & Martin, Howard & Beech, Donna. *The Heart Math Solution: Revolutionary Program for Engaging the Power of the Heart's Intelligence.* Harper Collins Publishers. 1999.
- Dana, Deb. *Polyvagal Exercises for Safety and Connection: 50 client-centred Practices.* Norton Agency Titles. 2020.
- Easteal, Patricia & McOrmond-Plummer, Louis. *Real Rape, Real Pain: Help for women sexually assaulted by male partner.* Hybrid Publishers. 2006.
- Estes, Clarissa Pinkola. *Women Who Run with the Wolves: Myths and Stories of the Wild Woman Archetype.* Random House Publishing Group. 1995.
- Evans, Melanie Tonia. *You can Thrive after Narcissistic Abuse: The #1 System for Recovering from Toxic Relationships.* Watkins Media. 2018.
- Dispenza, Joe Dr. *Breaking the Habit of Being Yourself: How to lose your mind and create a new one.* Hay House Pty, Ltd. 2012.
- Durvasula, Ramani, PHD. *Should I Stay or Should I Go?: Surviving a Relationship with a Narcissist.* Post Hill Press. 2015.

- Evans, Melanie, Tonia. *You can Thrive after Narcissistic Abuse: The #1 System for Recovering from Toxic Relationships.* Watkins Publishing. 2018.
- Frankl, E. Viktor. *Man's Search for Meaning.* Ebury Digital; New e. edition. 2013.
- Frost, Jack. *Experiencing the father's embrace.* Destiny Image, Publishers, Inc. 2002.
- Fisher, Janina, PhD. *Transforming the Living legacy of Trauma: A Workbook for Survivors and Therapists.* PESI Publishing & Media. 2021.
- Ford, Clementine. *Fight like a Girl.* Allen & Unwin. 2016.
- Gibbs, Jesse, Rene. *Girl Hidden: A memoir.* Jesse Rene Gibbs, 2022
- Gilbert, Elizabeth. *Eat Pray Love: One Woman's Search for Everything.* Bloomsbury Publishing. 2007.
- Golberg, Natalie. *The Art of Writing Memoir: Finding the Past in the Present.* Writer's Audio Shop. 2010.
- Gregory, Suan. *The Daniel Fast: Feed your soul, strengthen your spirit, renew your body.* Carol Stream, Ill. : Tyndale House Publishers, c2010.
- Heer, Dain Dr. Embodiment. *The Manual You Should Have Been Given When You Were Born.* Access Consciousness Publishing Company. 2016.
- Heer, Dain Dr. *Being You Changing the World.* Access Consciousness Publishing Company. 2016.
- Herman, Judith Lewis MD. *Trauma and Recovery: The Aftermath of Violence – From Domestic Abuse to Political Terror.* Basic Books. 2015.
- Hills, Jess. *See what you made me do: Power, control and domestic violence.* Shwartz Publishing Pty, Limited. 2019.

- Hoover, Colleen. *It ends with us*. Atria Books. 2016
- Jamieson, A B. *Prepare to be Tortured: The Price You Will Pay for Marrying a Narcissist*. Independently Published. 2015.
- Johnson, Bill. *Strengthen yourself in the Lord: How to release the hidden power of God in your life.* Destiny Image Publishers, INC. 2015.
- Johnson, Bill. *Face to Face with God*. Charisma Media. 2007
- Johnson, Will. *Awakening The Body: The Path of Somatic Surrender*. Sounds True. 2013.
- Joseph, Gabriel, R. *Limbic system: Amygdala, Hypothalamus, Septal Nuclei, Cingulate, Hippocampus: Emotion, memory, Language, Evolution, Love, Attachment, Sexuality, Violence, Fear, Aggression, Dreams, Hallucinations, Amnesia.* Cosmology Science Publishers (Cambridge). 2012.
- Joseph, Stephen, PH.D. *What doesn't kill us: The new psychology of posttraumatic growth.* Basic Books. 2012.
- Lesser, Elizabeth. *Broken Open: How difficult times can help us grow*. Ebury Digital. 2010.
- Liardon, Roberts. *God's Generals: The Revivalists, Volume 3*. Whitaker House. 2008.
- Mackenzie, Jackson. *Psychopath free (expanded edition): Recovering from emotionally abusive relationships with narcissists, sociopaths, and other toxic people*. Penguin Random House. 2015
- Malchhiodi, Cathy A. *Trauma and Expressive Arts Therapy: Brain, Body, & Imagination in the Healing Process*. The Guilford Press. 2020
- McCourt, Frank. *Angela's Ashes*. Scribner. 1996
- McGowan, Rose. *Brave*. Harper Collins Publisher Limited. 2018.

- McKenna, Martin. *The Boy Who Talked to Dogs*. Sky Horse Publishing. 2015.
- Miro, Elena. *Narcissist Survivor: 2 Books in 1 – My Toxic husband & Free Yourself from abusive to Healthy Relationships.* Independently Published. 2021.
- Morgan, Hannah. *Nowhere to Hide: Trapped, Abused and Sold for Sex.* HarperCollins Publishers. 2021.
- Morningstar, Dana. *The Narcissist's Playbook: How to Identify, Disarm, and Protect Yourself from Narcissists, Sociopaths, Psychopaths, and other Types of Manipulative and Abusive People.* Morningstar Media. 2019.
- Myss, Caroline. *Transforming Trauma: The Path to Hope and Healing.* HarperCollins Publishers. 2021.
- Nadine, Breen Candace. After the Darkness: *A Survivor's True Story of Childhood, Incest, Rape, Abuse, Domestic Violence, and Her Ability to Overcome Negative Impact These Events Had on Her Life.* Independently Published. 2018.
- New International Version. *The Woman's Study Bible: receiving God's truth for balance, hope and transformation.* Thomas Nelson 2018.
- Nordby, Jacob. *Blessed are the Weird: A Manifesto for Creatives.* Manifesto Publishing House, Incorporated. 2016.
- Omartian, Stormie. *Lead me, Holy Spirit: Longing to Hear the Voice of God*. Harvest House Publishers. 2012.
- Orloff, Judith. *Becoming an Intuitive Healer – A professional Health Development Course for Health Practitioners*. Sounds True; Unabridged edition. 2007.
- Polizzi, Nick & Shojai, Pedram. *Trauma: Healing your past to find freedom now*. Hay House Inc. 2021

- Pullman, Audrey Dr. *Cool Breathing: Your Path to Self-Empowerment*. CreateSpace Independent Publishing Platform. 2107.

- Quarry, Peter. *If I were you: A psychologist puts himself on the couch*. Hardie Grant Media 2022.

- Riley, Kaitlyn. *Domestic Violence Memoirs: A Collection of True Stories of Domestic Abuse*. Independently Published. 2019.

- Romano, Lisa A. *The Road Back to Me: Healing and Recovery from Co-Dependency, Addiction, Enabling, and Low Self-Esteem*. Lisa A. Romano. 2012.

- Saad, Gad. *The Parasitic Mind: How Infectious Ideas are Killing Common Sense*. Skyhorse Publishing. 2020.

- Sarkis, Stephanie PhD. *Gaslighting: How to recognise manipulative and emotionally abusive people and break free*. De Capo Press. 2018.

- Scavella, Koni. *SOAR- Think Bigger, Move Faster, Rise Higher: The 4- Step Instant Freedom Formula To Unlink Your Past From Your Potential and Live an Unlimited Life....On Earth as I Did in Heaven*. Independently Published. 2017.

- Schnabel, Rik. *The Secrets to creating a life beyond limits*. Brolga Publishing Pty, Ltd. 2012.

- Scott, Jeremy. *Women who dared to break all the rules*. One World Publications. 2020.

- Shapiro, Dani. Still writing: *The perils and pleasures of a creative life*. Grove Press / Atlantic Monthly Press. 2014.

- Silk, Danny. *Keep Your Love On: Connection, Communication and Boundaries*. NEWTYPE Publishing. 2015.

- Silk, Danny. *Culture of Honor: Sustaining a supernatural environment*. Destiny Image Publishers, INC. 2009.

- Simpson, Rick. *Pheonix Tears: The Rick Simpson Story – One man's battle to prove cancer is curable*. Simpson RamaDur. 2016.

- Smith, Marion Roach. *The Memoir Project: A Thoroughly Non-Standardized Text for Writing and Life*. Grand Central Publishing. 2104.

- Stamp, Nikki, Dr. *Scrubbed: A Heart Surgeon's Extraordinary memoir of Life, Death and Everything in Between*. Allen & Unwin. 2022.

- Strayed, Cheryl. *Wild: From Lost to Found on the Pacific Crest Trail*. Random House Publisher. 2012.

- Sunfellow, David. *The Purpose of Life as Revealed from Near Death Experiences from Around the World*. Independently Published. 2019.

- Steiner, Leslie Morgan. *Crazy Love*. St. Martin's Griffin; First Edition. 2010.

- Tame, Grace. *The Ninth Life of a Diamond Miner: A Memoir*. Pan MacMillan Australia Pty, Limited. 2022.

- Thomashauer, Regena. *Pussy: A Reclamation*. Hay House Australia Pty, Ltd. 2016.

- Tsabary, Shefali Dr. A Radical Awakening: Turn Pain into Power, Embrace your Truth, Live Free. Harper One. 2021

- Tutu, Desmond & MPHO. *THE BOOK OF FORGIVING -The fourfold path for healing ourselves and our world*. William Collins 2015.

- Vallaton, Kris. *Spirit Wars: Winning the Invisible Battle Against Sin and Enemy*. Baker Publishing Group. 2012.

- Vallatton, Kris & Johnson, Bill. *The Supernatural ways of Royalty: Discovering your rights and privileges of being a son or daughter of God*. Destiny Image Publishers, INC. 2017.

- Van Der Kolk, Bessel. *The Body Keeps the Score: Mind, brain and body in the transformation of trauma*. Penguin Books Random House. 2014.
- Virkler, Mark Dr. & Kayembe, Charity Virkler. *Hearing God Through Your Dreams: Understanding the Language God Speaks at Night*. Destiny Image Incorporated. 2016.
- Virkler, Mark & Virkler, Charity, Kayembe. *Hearing God through your dreams: Understanding the language God speaks at night*. Destiny Image Publishers. 2016.
- Warren, Rick. *The Purpose Driven Life: What on Earth am I Here For?* Zondervan. 2012.
- Watson, Jessica. *True Spirit- The Girl who Took on The World*. Hachette Australia. 2011.
- Westover, Tara. *Educated: A Memoir*. Random House. 2018
- White, Amy. Gaslighting Recovery Workbook: How to Recognise Manipulation, Overcome Narcissistic Abuse, let go, and Heal from Toxic Relationships. Kindle Edition. 2020.
- Wood, Stephanie. *Fake: A startling true story in the world of liars, cheats, narcissists, fantasists and phonies*. Penguin Random House Australia. 2019
- X, Katherine & Smethurst, Sue. *Behind closed doors: Four children by her father. Thirty years of horrific sexual abuse*. Simon & Schuster Australia. 2015.
- Zukav, Gary. *The Seat of The Soul*. Simon & Schuster. 2014.
- Forward: Source:
  1. Gender-related killings of women and girls (femicide/feminicide): Global estimates of female intimate partner/family-related homicides in 2022, UN Women, 2023. https://www.unwomen.org/en/digital-library/publications/2023/11/gender-related-killings-of-

women-and-girls-femicide-feminicide-global-estimates-2022- Accessed 15 October 2024

2. Child Trafficking and Human Slavery, World Vision, 2024. https://www.worldvision.com.au/global-issues/work-we-do/child-slavery - Accessed 15 October 2024.

Closing Prayer

Heavenly Father, I pray for an awakening, within our hearts, minds, and spirits. May we rise by lifting others, walking in love and truth, and stepping boldly into the fullness of who You created us to be. Let this book be a vessel of hope, healing, breakthroughs and transformation, guiding every reader toward freedom, restoration, and the unwavering love of God.

As Coach Rik has encouraged me throughout this journey, may my pain be turned into purpose, and may my story serve as a light for those still searching for their way. Lord, I hold onto Your word in Proverbs 31:8 "Speak up for those who cannot speak for themselves." May this book be a voice for the silenced, a beacon for the broken, and a testimony to Your restorative power.

In Jesus' name, Amen.

www.ingramcontent.com/pod-product-compliance
Lightning Source LLC
Chambersburg PA
CBHW071951070526
44583CB00015B/1154